D1623818

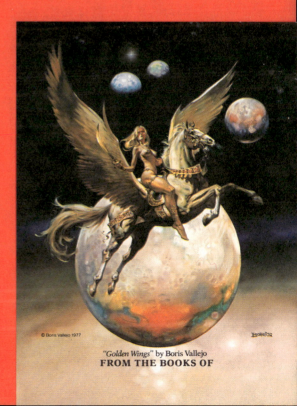

© Boris Vallejo 1977

"Golden Wings" by Boris Vallejo
FROM THE BOOKS OF

THE COMPLETE LHASA APSO

Colarlie's Pitti Sing, dam of two champions, at 12½ years. Pitti Sing was bred by Ruth Smith and owned by Patricia Chenoweth. She is a daughter of Ch. Taylor's Ming of Miradel and Miradel's Ming Fu Chia.

Ch. Crest-O-Lake Kin Go ROM is a son of Ch. Zijuh Tsam and Crest-O-Lake Tru So and is owned by Diane Dansereau.

THE COMPLETE

LHASA APSO

by Norman and Carolyn Herbel

First Edition—Third Printing

1981

HOWELL BOOK HOUSE INC.
230 Park Avenue
New York, N.Y. 10169

Lhasa Apso puppies at three weeks of age.

Library of Congress Cataloging in Publication Data

Herbel, Norman.
   The complete lhasa apso.

   Bibliography: p.304
   1. Lhasa apsos.   I. Herbel, Carolyn, joint author.
II. Title.
SF429.L5H47   636.7´6   78-21601
ISBN 0-87605-208-1

Dedication

This book is dedicated to the foundation breeders, now exiled from their country of origin, who have preserved and perpetuated the Lhasa Apso so that our beloved breed may live on in the Free World.

Ch. Kinderland's Mi Terra ROM is a daughter of BIS Ch. Kham of Norbulingka ROM and Kinderland's Buddha. She was bred by Ruth Fairfield and Ellen Lonigro and is owned by Carol Kuendel, Chok.

Sinbad of Abbotsford ROM, bred by Mr. and Mrs. James Roberts and owned by Robert and Nancy Damberg, is the sire of at least seven champions. He is the son of Can., Am. Ch. Teako of Abbotsford and Brackenbury Dochen.

Contents

Ch. Karma Tat-Ka-La, a son of Ch. Karma Chang Tru and Ch. Karma Torlu, was bred by Dorothy Cohen and is owned by Laura Shein. "Tati" is the foundation sire for Laura Shein's Shen-Pa Lhasa Apsos.

BIS Ch. Hamilton Torma with her last puppy, Ch. Americal's Torma Lu.

Carolyn Herbel

Norman Herbel

About the Authors:

Norman and Carolyn Herbel, native-born Kansans, have success-fully raised animals most of their lives.

A graduate of the University of Kansas, Norman Herbel was a coach and teacher, now retired. At the present time he is actively inbreeding registered Herefords with particular emphasis on a strain developed by the United States Range Stations.

Carolyn Herbel was an active 4-H participant raising prize-winning California rabbits and Shorthorn dairy cattle. She was also active in Junior Leadership activities.

While the Herbels were attending the University of Kansas they acquired their first registered dog, a German Shepherd they named "Tabu," a name that was to become celebrated in the years ahead as the Herbels' highly successful prefix.

Participation in an obedience class led eventually to competition in obedience trials. Tabu acquired her CD degree and won seven points, including a major, in conformation competition before being retired. By breeding Tabu and showing her, the Herbels resolved to become more deeply involved in dogs in the future.

English Setters were added to the program, and it was with a bitch of this breed, Ch. Devoncote's All The Way, that Carolyn won the first of many variety Groups.

The Herbels' daughter, Carmen wanted to be an active part of the family hobby. So a Cairn Terrier was added to the family, and Carmen successfully bred Cairns, producing several champions and finishing one before she was old enough to compete in junior showmanship!

Lhasa Apsos first attracted the Herbels' attention at the Heart of America show in Kansas City, and they later elected to concentrate on Lhasas, much to the benefit of the entire breed.

Norman and Carolyn Herbel have both held important positions in the American Lhasa Apso Club. Norman is a past-President and Board member. He also served as the ALAC Futurity Chairman and devel-oped and edited the magazine-style *The Lhasa Bulletin,* ALAC's official publication.

Carolyn, a professional handler, served several years as ALAC Secretary and has been on the Board of Directors for many years.

The impressive, continuous success of the Tabu Lhasas is a matter of record. Combining a natural ability with animals and an understanding and appreciation of the special entity that is a Lhasa Apso, the Herbels have owned and bred many of the finest ever seen in competition. Their most far-reaching contribution to the breed, *The Complete Lhasa Apso,* provides a valuable reference for all who are drawn to the Lhasa's distinctive charm. It is a book written for lovers of the breed by a lover of the breed *in* the breed.

What makes the Lhasa special, and the expertise the Herbels have gathered over the years are in the pages to follow. Read, enjoy and learn.

Multiple Group winner Ch. Tabu's King of Hearts ROM is the sire of at least 20 champions. King is owned by Stephen Campbell, Rimar, and bred by Carolyn Herbel.

Foreword

FOR SOME YEARS I had bred and raised several different dog breeds, but in a rather casual manner. In 1963 I encountered the Lhasa Apso for the first time and lost my heart to the breed. Soon thereafter KeKe's T'Chin T'Chin, who was to become my first champion, joined our family. In due course I also became seriously involved as a Lhasa breeder and exhibitor.

Several years later I met Carolyn and Norman Herbel. They were involved in German Shepherd Dogs at the time and were completely devoted to the scientific breeding of dogs. To their everlasting credit, they were also completely generous in sharing their knowledge. They, too, became enamored of the Lhasa. They made extensive inquiries throughout the country to learn about the breed from its earliest history in Tibet to its current status in the United States.

Carolyn, an experienced dog handler, showed my KeKe's T'Chin Ting T'Chin to her championship, finishing her at the Bucks County Kennel Club show in May 1967. On that very same day, the Herbels and I journeyed to Hershey, Pennsylvania to use a stud dog belonging to the late Paul Williams. In Mr. Williams' Cornwallis Kennel Norman found "Mr. Tibs", the now-famous top producer and Best in Show dog. We not only used this dog as a stud, but we purchased him that day as co-owners. Mr. Tibs became the catalyst for an even closer association with the Herbels in our continuing search for greater knowledge of the breed. Later, they purchased my interest in the dog and he is still with them. He remains the gorgeous, great dog he was and is very much loved by both Norman and Carolyn.

Out of all this work and in-depth breed involvement has now emerged an authoritative text on the Lhasa Apso, co-authored by the Herbels. THE COMPLETE LHASA APSO presents thorough, carefully considered information about the breed from the selection of a puppy to its care, training and exhibiting. Special chapters explain the Lhasa's unique temperament and present detailed instructions on the important matter of grooming. In addition, Norman and Carolyn go into the history of the breed extensively and give us complete lists of earlier and more recent champions and their lineage. Their enumeration of the fine breeders of Lhasas in the United States and abroad makes most interesting and informative reading.

The Lhasa Apso's popularity has grown tremendously during the last decade. Our numbers, both canine and human, have swelled by leaps and bounds in this relatively short period, so THE COMPLETE LHASA APSO comes at a time when breeders, fanciers, judges and anyone seeking information on the breed can use this book to the fullest possible extent. For those who love the breed—as I do—THE COMPLETE LHASA APSO is a MUST!

Keke Blumberg

(The authors and the publisher are deeply honored to have this Foreword by Keke Blumberg. Mrs. Blumberg is in the front rank of Lhasa Apso breeders in the world and is currently President of the American Lhasa Apso Club. As an AKC approved judge of Lhasas and a number of other breeds, Mrs. Blumberg is popular among exhibitors and her opinions are highly respected. She has been active in the breed since 1963 and has been closely identified with some of the breed's most outstanding winners and producers.)

Acknowledgements

WE WISH TO EXPRESS heartfelt appreciation to our good friend, Charles Steele, without whose help in organizing our research material this book would not have become a reality.

Our special thanks to Ann Crawford who very graciously shared the information compiled over the years by Mrs. Dorothy Cohen of Karma Lhasa Apsos.

We wish to thank Bobbie Lee for helping us research back issues of *Purebred Dogs—American Kennel Gazette* for statistical data and Lenore Rosselot for her verification work on Tibetan data.

Our sincere gratitude to Grace Licos, Dorothy Benitez, Georgia Palmer and Patricia Chenoweth for sharing their photographs of early dogs.

Our appreciation to André Cuny, Frances Sefton and Annie Schneider-Louter for their contribution of photographs and information concerning the Lhasa Apso in other countries.

We also wish to thank the many breeders, exhibitors and handlers who have shared their photographs in order to make this book truly THE COMPLETE LHASA APSO.

The Potala—the Dalai Lama's palace prior to the Chinese take-over and the building of modern Lhasa at the foot of the monastery.

1

Origin and History
of the Lhasa Apso

THE LHASA APSO comes from the mountains and high plateaus of Tibet, a country often called *The Roof of the World*. The history of the breed is as elusive and mystical as the history of the people with whom it originated. The geographical, political and cultural isolation of the Tibetan people has resulted in only scattered information regarding them reaching the rest of the world.

Tibet

Tibet lies in a remote section of south-central Asia contiguous to India, China, Siberia, Mongolia and Sinkiang. It is a country of high plateaus and mountainous terrain with severe winter weather. In the southern part of the Tibetan plateau the snowy Himalayas rise higher than any other mountain chain in the world. Mount Everest, rising 29,028 feet, is the most famous summit in the Himalayas. The Great Snowy Mountains on the eastern border reach heights of over 25,250 feet. On the north and northwest, the peaks of the Kunlun range rise almost as high. The average elevation of Tibet is 16,000 feet above sea level.

Lhasa, the principal and capital city, is about 12,000 feet above sea level. Its extremes of weather include violent winds with basically low temperatures in the winter and hot, dusty daytimes in the summer. Altitude acclimatization is necessary for the jet-age traveler flying into

Tibet. The overland traveler adjusts more easily because of the gradual increase in altitude. In 1976, when an American delegation visited Lhasa, the members were screened for their physical capacity to withstand the rigors of high elevation. Those who were permitted to go were supplied with oxygen masks and required to take rests along the way. Truly, Tibet is the *Roof of the World.*

The city of Lhasa is also the center of the Tibetan religion. The "Potala," palace of the Dalai Lama, rises over 700 feet above the city. The summer palace, the "Norbulingka," is also located in Lhasa. The Tibetans are intensely religious people following the beliefs of Tibetan Buddhism. The Dalai Lama was the spiritual and temporal leader of the country. The present Dalai Lama, the 14th, now lives in exile in India.

In 1904 the British extended their influence in Asia and signed a trade treaty with the Tibetans. Thus in the early and middle 1900s there were many English speaking visitors to Tibet who later wrote their observations. Other Europeans wrote of their visits, in their languages. However, Americans generally did not have much access to information regarding Tibet. Only scholars and adventurers were aware of the isolated, mysterious land.

No one knows how many people have lived in Tibet at any one time in history. The 20th Century figures vary from six million down to two million and now to 1.7 million under the current Chinese administration. This last figure reflects the 1976 number of pure Tibetans. An additional 300,000 Chinese now live in Tibet.

From 1959, when the 14th Dalai Lama fled from Tibet into India, until recent years the Chinese Communist Government banned foreign travel to Tibet. On rare occasions since 1975 foreign dignitaries, including Han Suyin, Neville Maxwell, James Schlesinger and Lowell Thomas, have been permitted limited stays in Tibet. Since the 1959 Chinese takeover of Tibet, over 100,000 Tibetans have sought refuge throughout the world.

Before Chinese control, one fifth of the population were monks or lamas who lived in monasteries supported principally by their land ownership incomes and private donations. Many of the monasteries had amassed great wealth in land. The balance of the population included poor farmers, nomads, small shopkeepers, traders, merchants and a few very wealthy landowners.

During the relatively short span of years between 1904 and 1959, the Lhasa Apso as we know it today became popular in other countries of the world. While there has been considerable conjecture as to the origin of the Lhasa Apso, there is not sufficient fact to warrant indulging in discussion of the various theories. All that is known is that it is a small, long-haired, companion dog of ancient origin from the country of Tibet.

The Tara Tulku, head of the Buddhist Tantric College in
Dalhousie, India.

L. Rosselot

In Tibet, a monk with a treasure
in his arms—a Lhasa Apso .
Courtesy of André Cuny

The Tibetan People

Since there is so little written history of Tibet available to the Western World we must develop an understanding of its people and through them the Lhasa Apso.

Tibetans, often called the "Hermit People," enjoyed the confinement of the natural barriers of altitude, climate and rugged terrain as protection against foreigners. They feared that outsiders would oppress them. Hence they rebuffed outside efforts to develop trade relationships.

Initially Tibetans were wary of strangers until they learned that neither their persons nor way of life were threatened. During the initial contact they were politely courteous. Once they found there was no danger to them they revealed their warm, friendly and happy side.

Difference of class and economic advantages apparent to visitors to Tibet seemed to cause little concern to the Tibetans because as part of their religion they believed in *Karma*. Karma is the concept of rebirth and that the good and evil one experiences in this life is determined by the good and evil deeds of prior life and that there will be later lives. The Karma concept did not, however, prevent an individual from trying to improve his present lot. Due to their religion Tibetans accepted their niche in the social and economic system even though the difference between top and bottom was very great.

Tibetans are physically strong, emotionally courageous, independent, merry, courteous, free from self-consciousness but not friendly to strangers.

The Tibetan and his Animals

Tibetans and their dogs shared a close affinity. The people loved animals. Their interest in their animals was revealed by the pantheon of their religion before Buddhism. It reflected the human psychology searching for a peaceful interrelationship between themselves, their animals and their god. The Buddhist pantheon also shows each guardian deity associated with a particular animal pictured as its master's messenger. That meant to the Tibetan that he should not only love but also protect animals.

The nomadic people lived by rather crude means. They were usually accompanied by a flock of sheep or small herd of cattle and it is here that the long-haired animals make their importance known. Because of severe cold weather there were many useful purposes served by long-haired animals; not only for the protection of the living animal but also for the domestic value of the hair they grew. The hair of the

20

Sarligues (long-haired cattle) was made into coarse cloth which served a useful purpose to man as well as protection for the living animal. The people of Tibet prided themselves on the value of a living animal's contributions rather than through the destruction of the life of that animal. It was not uncommon to see people rescuing animals from slaughter in order to preserve that life.

In the travels of the nomads, every animal had a useful purpose as well as a life value; however, little thought or planning was employed to improve the physical qualities of their animals. The traveling people took what life had to offer and felt little need to improve their lot.

The small land owners and tenant farmers were more stationary. Their humble dwellings housed both people on an upper level and the family's animals on a lower level. Their animals were a close, integral part of their lives. The small land owners and tenant farmers lived a rather simple but full life. They worked hard and enjoyed their relationship with nature.

Economically, the lower social classes were less capable of developing specific breeds of animals; therefore, it became somewhat of a luxury enjoyed by the nobles, and especially by the clergy. Because of their economic security the clergy not only had the resources but also the time to develop specific breeds of animals. Even some of those financially able to engage in planned breeding programs did not do so, however, since their primary interest was in the direction of spiritual and mental development, rather than physical improvement. This produced a variety of sizes and lack of uniformity in Tibetan animals. Usually humans and animals merely existed and contributed to the success of each other's existence in the harsh environment.

The homes and monasteries were guarded on the outside by large working dogs known primarily as mastiffs. Because of the Tibetans' extreme distrust there were smaller warning dogs found inside the dwelling. Therefore it is believed that the smaller dogs were developed more for the purpose of companionship and protection than for their religious significance.

The Lhasa Apso as we know it today is a product of the Tibetan way of life, for the people themselves have developed the breed in somewhat their own character image.

Mr. C. Suydam Cutting (center) with the Tibetan Commander-Chief Tsarong Shape and his wife. Tsarong Shape's wife, now Mrs. Mary Taring is the author of *Daughter of Tibet* published by Murray.

22

2

The Lhasa Apso Reaches
the West

To UNDERSTAND the circumstances under which the Lhasa Apso came to the United States it is necessary to have a general grasp of the breed's story in England.

First Lhasas in England

The year 1901 saw the Lhasa Apso come to England. In that year Miss Marjorie Wild acquired her first Lhasa Apso from the Honorable Mrs. McLaren Morrison who saw some of the breed in Darjeeling, India and brought some with her on her return to England. Thereafter, Miss Wild devoted seventy years to breeding and showing the breed until her death in 1971.

In 1902 a successful application for separate breed registry was granted by the English Kennel Club. The breed was then called Lhasa Terrier and was divided into 10-inch and 14-inch height classes.

Since Lhasas were shown in sufficient numbers, the Kennel Club (England) was able to issue Challenge Certificates from 1908 until World War I decimated the breed to such an extent that it lost the right to issue Challenge Certificates.

The comeback of the breed in England dates from the 1928 return of Lieutenant Colonel Eric and the Honorable Mrs. Bailey bringing five descendants, Taktru, Droma, Tsitru, Pema and Litsi, of their original foundation stock (Apso and Sangtru obtained in 1922 from Tsarong

Shapé and Demon, a leased bitch) and Lhasa, a gray and white male. These six dogs were exhibited in 1929 at the Ladies Kennel Association.

In 1930 Miss E. M. Hutchins returned to England from China bringing Hibou, a male owned by General and Mrs. Douglas Brownrigg (later Sir Douglas and Lady Brownrigg) and two of her own females, Lung Fu Ssu and Mei Mei, who died in quarantine. The following year the Brownriggs returned to England from China with Shu Ssa and her second litter, born in quarantine.

When the Brownriggs saw the Bailey dogs they commented on the marked difference between their own dogs and the Bailey dogs. The two different kinds were, however, shown together in 1933 at the Ladies Kennel Association show. Droma and Taktru, which the Baileys had brought from Tibet, were shown by their owner, Mrs. A. C. Dudley. Miss Hutchins showed Lung Fu Ssu and Tang while Mrs. Brownrigg showed Hibou and Yangtze.

In 1934 the English Tibetan Breeds Association ruled that the Chinese dogs owned by Miss Hutchins and Mrs. Brownrigg were not Apsos. The English Kennel Club General Committee decided in May of 1934 to allow showing of those dogs under, "Any other variety, Shih Tzus," and to allow Shih Tzus already registered as Lhasa Apsos to be reregistered as Shih Tzus. In September 1934 it was decided to adopt the name Shih Tzu for the breed. Application was granted by the English Kennel Club to change the title of the Apso and Lion Dog Club to Shih Tzu (Tibetan Lion Dog) Club. In 1935 that title was again changed to Shih Tzu Club.

The English Kennel Club approved the Lhasa Apso Standard in 1934. The English Standard was substantially copied in April, 1935 for use in the United States.

American Beginnings

It is against this background that the following dogs with the four Hutchins-Brownrigg dogs in their background (Lung Fu Ssu, Tang, Hibou and Yangtze) and denominated in England by Sepember, 1934 as Shih Tzus, were exported and came to the United States between 1937 and 1950:

   *Kota Tang AKC Reg 145260 in 1937
    Wuffy of the Mynd AKC Reg A330952 in 1939
   *Mai Ling of Boydon AKC Reg A653124 in 1943
   *Lindi Lu of Lhakang AKC Reg R64026 in 1943
   *Linyi of Lhakang AKC Reg R64027
    Yay Sih of Shebo AKC Reg 65904 EKC# 73537/49
    Fardale Fu Ssi AKC Reg R71400 in 1950 EKC# D18550
   *Imported to the USA through Canada

Ch. Fardale Fu Ssi owned by Dorothy Sabine de Gray is the grandam of Ch. Las Sa Gre's Manchado Dorado.

Ch. Chumpa of Furzyhurst was bred by Mrs. Hervey-Cecil and imported from England by Mrs. E. M. Simpson. He was owned by Mrs. Albertram McFadden of Lui Gi Lhasa Apsos.

(l) David Goldfarb in the April, 1977 *Lhasa Tales* states authoritatively that Kota Tang, Wuffy of the Mynd and Mai Ling of Boydon were descendants of the Shih Tzus, Hibou, Lung Fu Ssu, Tang and Yangtze.

(2) Will C. Mooney, author of *Your Shih Tzu,* Copyright 1973 by William W. Denlinger, page 79, gives Lhakang Kennels as the source of his exceptional Shih Tzu Dog, Elfann Chang Lo of Lhakang.

(3) The British Shih Tzu Club's brochure of June, 1956 lists the following as Shih Tzu kennels: Taishan, Boydon, Shebo, Lhakang, Shuanghsi, Hungjao and Antarctica. This same brochure states that Hibou, Shu-Ssa and Lung-Fu-Ssu became the foundation of present-day stock and the well known Taishan strain.

(4) Also note the English Kennel Club numbers for Yay Sih of Shebo and Fardale Fu Ssi.

(5) A letter from Mr. John A. Brownell, Assistant to the Executive Vice President of the American Kennel Club, to Mrs. Albertram McFadden dated December 12, 1955 states in part: " . . . it is a fact that 'Fardale Fu Ssi' is registered by the Kennel Club in England as a Shih Tzu and this bitch was one of these accepted for registration as foundation stock as a Lhasa Apso."

The American Kennel Club registered these imported dogs as Lhasa Apsos in accordance with a practice current at the time of their entry based on reasons which were then good and sufficient. That practice was terminated in 1950.

It is sufficient for present purposes to point out that those imported Shih Tzus registered as Lhasa Apsos are found in the pedigrees of many of the breed in this country. They form one bloodline of the American Lhasa Apso.

Further history of the Lhasa Apso in England between the mid-1930s and 1950 need not concern us since after World War II the number of registered dogs of that breed was so small that the breed lost its championship status and did not regain it until 1965. The line from the Baileys' original foundation stock of Apso, Sangtru and Demon became virtually extinct. Miss Wild's dogs died of disease shortly after the War.

Only the Ramblersholt Kennel of Mrs. Florence Dudman and the Furzyhurst Kennel of Miss Hervey-Cecil had any connection with the original Bailey foundation stock.

Ramblersholt Le Pon, male, and Ramblersholt Shahnaz, a female, were imported into this country and acquired by Mrs. Winifred Drake, of Drax Kennels in Florida. In the early 1960s she advertised stud service by Le Pon and puppies from a mating of those two English imports. One or both of them appear in a number of American Lhasa

Mrs. Cutting with a Lhasa Apso in her arms. Possibly this is the bitch, Tsing Tu, mentioned in Mr. Cutting's book *Fire Ox and Other Years*.

Mr. Fred Huyler pictured with the last two Lhasas received from Tibet by Hamilton Farm. Note the ideal head structure on these specimens.

Apso pedigrees. Ramblersholt Shahnaz not only became a champion but also received her American Lhasa Apso Club Register of Merit award. That forms a second bloodline of American Lhasa Apsos.

Similarly, Chumpa of Furzyhurst, a male, was imported into this country and acquired by Mrs. Albertram McFadden of Lui Gi Lhasa Apsos, in California. Chumpa became a champion and sired a number of champions. His grandson Ch. Lui Gi's Shigatzoo went from that kennel first to the San Saba Kennel in Texas and in 1966 to the Cho Sen Kennel in Kentucky. Unfortunately that third bloodline has not been so active now as it was a decade ago.

Since it is not clear from this distance, and without more information about English Lhasa Apso pedigrees during and shortly after World War II, we have assumed or conceded that the Ramblersholt and Furzyhurst Kennels' lines may not be identical. For that reason we have treated them as different bloodlines. In any event the imports from the Ramblersholt and Furzyhurst kennels have had a different history and impact upon American Lhasa Apso breeding.

The Cuttings

The fourth bloodline of the American Lhasa Apso came to this country as the result of the activities of Mr. and Mrs. C. Suydam Cutting and their associates in the Hamilton Farm Kennel.

Mr. Cutting was a world traveler. Following World War I he was a member of an expedition, with a brother of Theodore Roosevelt, that visited Tibet. As a result Mr. Cutting wanted to return to that country and did so about 1930. At that time he met and became friendly with the 13th Dalai Lama with whom he exchanged gifts.

During the decade between 1930 and 1940 the 13th Dalai Lama gave the Cuttings three Lhasa Apsos. Following the 13th Dalai Lama's death the Interim Regent sent a pair of golden Lhasa Apsos as a gift to the Cuttings. Finally in 1950 the 14th Dalai Lama sent a last pair of Lhasas. They were Le, a male, and Pehma, a female. Both became American champions. Le sired a number of puppies. Pehma never had a litter. They lived to an old age in retirement with Mrs. Dorothy Benitez who had worked at the Hamilton Farm Kennel.

The Cuttings' dogs were kenneled at Hamilton Farms, Gladstone, New Jersey, under the supervision of Fred Huyler and James Anderson. These men skillfully bred and showed the Hamilton Lhasas.

Through the efforts of the Cuttings and their associates the Lhasa Apso quickly gained a position on the American scene. In April, 1935 the American Kennel Club recognized the breed and approved the Lhasa Apso Standard. That Standard, which was essentially the same

The Cuttings' home at Hamilton Farm in Gladstone, New Jersey.

Mrs. Dorothy Benitez with Ch. Hamilton Kung and Mr. James Anderson chat at the Hamilton Farm Kennel benching at one of the Westminster Kennel Club shows during the late 1950s.

as the original English Standard, was in effect until revised in July 1978. The Lhasa was originally in the Terrier Group. It was transferred in 1959 to the Non-Sporting Group and has continued there ever since.

The Cuttings' interest in preserving the heritage of the Lhasa Apso prompted them to obtain breeding stock and to employ the excellent personnel previously mentioned to accomplish their goal. Shortly, results of rigorous selection and linebreeding developed a uniformity of type which became synonymous with the prefix, Hamilton, and formed the fourth basic blood line of the American Lhasa Apso

Hamilton Lhasa Apsos first recorded in the 1936 *AKC Stud Book* for March were: Hamilton Bidgy (bitch) imported (sandy and light slate) and Hamilton Tsaring (dog) imported (golden). Their offspring Hamilton Taski (dog) whelped 1/10/33 and Hamilton Drepung (dog) Hamilton Khampa (dog), Hamilton Lhun Po (dog), Hamilton Padmeh (dog), Hamilton Rimpochi (bitch) and Hamilton Sera (dog) all whelped 7/26/35 and Hamilton Sarong (dog) imported (sandy).

Las Sa Gre

The fifth bloodline of the American Lhasa Apso resulted from the use by Mrs. Dorothy Sabine de Gray of the Las Sa Gre Kennel at Encinitas, California, not only of her imported Shih Tzu bitch registered as a Lhasa Apso, Ch. Fardale Fu Ssi, but also of a bitch known as Las Sa Gre AKC Reg. No. 32151 of uncertain background.

Las Sa Gre's AKC registration states that she was bred by a Dr. Flowers but contains no other information. A pedigree of Numba Seix Boi R154187 (possibly in the handwriting of Mrs. de Gray) shows that Las Sa Gre was the daughter of one Sikkim Johnny and Chong Fey, who in turn also was the daughter of Sikkim Johnny and Haitsai not otherwise described. We have seen an allegation by Mrs. Albertram McFadden, purchaser of Numba Seix Boi from Mrs. de Gray, that Las Sa Gre's father was the "ST (for Shih Tzu) Ch. of Peking Kennel Club."

If that allegation were true Las Sa Gre would have been a Shih Tzu. Of course, if not true she would be a Lhasa Apso. In any event, against the background of no information in the AKC records we cannot be certain that such allegation was groundless. Under the circumstances we will from time to time in this book call attention to the presence of Las Sa Gre and her offspring in pedigrees without any representation by us whether Las Sa Gre was, or was not, a Shih Tzu.

Las Sa Gre's offspring combined with those of other lines have produced some of the most important Lhasa Apsos in the country in the last thirty years.

Chinese Imports

A sixth bloodline of the American Lhasa Apso came from Chinese imports. Shortly before World War II William Patch, a navy officer, bought two dogs from Holly Heath Kennels operated by Mrs. Harvey Hall of Shanghai, China. They were Ming Tai, a dog, and Tai Ho, a bitch and were littermates produced by Rags out of Peggy at that kennel. While in quarantine in Hawaii, Tai Ho whelped three puppies sired by her father, Rags.

Shanghai, another bitch also produced by Rags and Peggy, and Lhassa, a bitch out of Monk and Prim and born in China, were other imports from that country.

Canadian Influences

A further source of American bloodlines results from dogs imported from Canada. The first two were Dinkie, a bitch of raw silk color and Taikoo of Kokonor a black and white dog. Tarzan of Kokonor, a male whelped September 5, 1933, and Empress of Kokonor, a female whelped August 28, 1933, are typical. Bred by Miss M. Torrible of Canada and owned by Bruce Heathcote of Berkeley, California, they are unique only in that they were the first two Lhasa Apsos registered with the AKC after the Standard for the breed was approved in April, 1935. Their registration date was May 1, 1935. It is of course impossible to conjecture what the effect of such imports over the years have had or may have upon the breed in this country. This statement is made without any intention of denigrating the breeding programs in or the dogs imported from the Dominion of Canada.

This story of these seven basic American Lhasa Apso bloodlines, (1) Brownrigg Shih Tzus, (2) Ramblersholt-Drax imports, (3) Furzyhurst-Lui Gi imports, (4) Hamilton Farm Kennel imports, (5) Las Sa Gre dogs, (6) Chinese imports and (7) Canadian imports, although there may well have been more, sets the stage for the further story of the breed in this country from such beginnings.

The following list of imports derived from the extensive research in the American Kennel Club records by the late Mrs. Dorothy Cohen of Karma Kennel and included here with the gracious consent of Mrs. Ann Crawford of Walshana Kennels, repository of Mrs. Cohen's records, shows the variety of foreign sources of the present day Lhasa Apsos.

Imports from Tibet

Hamilton Tsaring (M), Lhasa Terrier, A-5-586, golden
Hamilton Bidgy (F), Lhasa Terrier, A-50587, sandy and light slate
Hamilton Sarong (M), Lhasa Terrier, A-50588, sandy
Tundu (M), Lhasa Terrier, A-57947, No color given, no parentage given, no whelping date given, no breeder given, recorded in April 1936 *AKC Stud Book,* owner: Arthur Vernay
Le (M) Lhasa Apso R-65501 11/48 sandy, breeder: the Dalai Lama, owner: Mr. and Mrs. C. S. Cutting
Pehma (F) Lhasa Apso R-65502 11/48 breeder: the Dalai Lama, owner: Mr. and Mrs. C. S. Cutting

Imports from England

Wuffy of the Mynd (F), Lhasa Terrier, A-330952, 5/2/38, fawn, white markings, breeder: Mrs. H. Eaden, England, owner: Mrs. H. Van Beuren
Yay Sih of Shebo (F), Lhasa Apso, R-65904(England), 6/3/49, fawn brindle, breeder: Mrs. A. Fowler, England, owner: James Madison Doyle
Fardale Fu Ssi (F), Lhasa Apso, R-71400(England), 11/26/48, red brown and white, breeder: R. Dale, England, owner: Dorothy Sabine de Gray

Imports from Canada

Dinkie (F), Lhasa Terrier, CKC 114902, 4/10/28, raw silk
Taikoo of Kokonor (M), Lhasa Terrier, CKC 114903, 7/19/30, black and white
Empress of Kokonor (F), Lhasa Terrier, 987979, 8/28/33, cream with a little black on ears
Tarzan of Kokonor (M), Lhasa Terrier, 987980, 9/5/33, white with black markings
Foochow (F), Lhasa Terrier, CKC 151655, 12/1/34, black and white
Kota Tang (F), Lhasa Terrier, A-145260, 9/27/34, biege, breeder: Madam A. C. Arline, England
Mai Ling of Boydon (F), Lhasa Terrier, A-654124, 8/1/39, black and white, English import
Lindi Lu of Lhakang (F), Lhasa Apso, R-64026, 9/13/46, sable and white
Linyi of Lhakang (F), Lhasa Apso, R-64027, 4/29/48, white and brown,

32

Shanghai (F), Lhasa Terrier, A-326454, 3/3/36, black and white, importer: Mr. Hubert, owner: Mrs. E. J. Barber

Lhassa (F), Lhasa Terrier, A-351865, 10/1/35, fawn and white, breeder: R. Lynn, China, owner: Mr. and Mrs. Cutting

Tai Ho (F), Lhasa Terrier, A-401000, 5/33, black and white, breeder: Annette S. Perkins, China

Ming Tai (M), Lhasa Terrier, A-401001, 12/23/34, black and tan

Apso (F), Lhasa Terrier, A-401002, 8/18/36, brown and white, bred in China and whelped in USA

Ding Hao (F), Lhasa Terrier, A-419657, 8/18/36, white and black, bred in China and whelped in USA/Bingo (M), Lhasa Apso, A-940597, 12/37, black and white; this dog appears in February 1946 *AKC Stud Book* with no parentage given, breeder: Denzil Clarke owner: Mr. and Mrs. Richard S. R. Hubert

Monk II (M), Lhasa Apso, A-940598, 10/10/37, tan and white, importer: Mr. Hubert, breeder: Ralph Lynn, owner: Mr. and Mrs. R. S. R. Hubert

Intermixture of Early Bloodlines

To make this background story complete it is also necessary to point out some of the intermixture of these bloodlines at the very beginning.

Two of the Chinese imports, Ming Tai and Tai Ho, produced Ch. Ming Lu, foundation bitch of Ming Kennel. Hamilton Dakmar was bred to her to produce Ch. Wu Tai. He was the father of Ch. Ming Tali II CD, foundation stud of Miradel Kennels. The bitch who was the latter's mother was a descendant of Mai Ling of Boydon, one of the English imports.

One of Mai Ling's sons, also mated to Ch. Ming Lu, produced Ch. Ming Changnopa, one of the foundation studs for Ming Kennels.

Ch. Yay Sih of Shebo, also an English import, was bred to Hamilton Sandur to produce Chika Rinpoche of the well-known kennel of that last name.

Ch. Fardale Fu Ssi, one of the last imported English Shih Tzu bitches registered as a Lhasa Apso, was owned by Mrs. Dorothy Sabine de Gray who also owned Las Sa Gre. Bred to Chiang Foo, Las Sa Gre's son, Ch. Fardale Fu Ssi produced Ch. Fu Al Tirito and Ch. Fu La Diablita. Bred to each other they produced the famous sires with the Las Sa Gre prefix, Manchado Dorado and Hijo D'Al Tiro. Ch.

Ch. Ming Changnopa, October 8, 1949, was the only Lhasa Apso to win a Terrier Group. He was by Pedro ex Ch. Ming Lu, bred and owned by Judge Frank T. Lloyd.

Fardale Fu Ssi and Chiang Foo also produced Ch. Fu La Simpatica, who appears in many pedigrees.

Hamilton Sigmi mated to Shanghai, one of the Chinese imports, produced Hamilton Kyi Chu. She in turn was the mother of Hamilton Yangchen, a dog who was the sire of the great producer, Ch. Hamilton Tatsienlu.

Hamilton Sigmi was also bred to Lhassa, another of the Chinese imports, to produce Hamilton Kala, Hamilton Dele and Hamilton Lang-Cha.

Somehow the English imports Kota Tang, Wuffy of the Mynd and Lindi Lu of Lhakang (except as the mother of that other import, Linyi of Lhakang) have not turned up in the pedigrees with which we are more familiar.

We have briefly mentioned a few of the early interrelationships to call attention to the fact that at the outset the different bloodlines were neither polarized nor kept separate. They were mixed. Some of the mixtures had good results and others did not. But, there was not the

34

unfruitful insulation between and isolation of the different bloodlines that began in the early 1950s and continues to a large extent even today.

Differences of choice and of opinion as to conformance to the Lhasa Apso Standard are understandable. Each of us has his own preference and is entitled to further it without denigrating the breeding and opinions of others. Judicious outcross or cross breeding regardless of its name is not a bad thing if it actually improves the breed. The extent, if any, of its use is again a matter of reasoned choice for each breeder.

Can. Ch. Tedi B'ar of Zaralinga, bred by Sheila Pike and owned by Nancy E. Bruce, Teb'ar.

Hamilton Kalon, a Ch. Hamilton Tatsienlu son.

3

Lhasa Apso
Breeding Kennels
in the United States

OUR STORY in this chapter is of the breeders and dogs who have significantly influenced the type and structure of the Lhasa Apso in the United States.

Hamilton Farms

Mr. and Mrs. C. Suydam Cutting were responsible for the introduction of the Lhasa Apso to this country. Originally they bred German Shepherds. The importation of Lhasa Apsos from Tibet in the 1930s and 1940s for their Hamilton Farm Kennel provided the nucleus for a substantial part of the Lhasa Apso population explosion in this country since 1950.

Mr. Fred Huyler, manager, and Mr. James Anderson, kennel man, ran the kennel. Mr. Huyler was later the first President of the American Lhasa Apso Club. Mr. Anderson had an exceptional eye for good dogs as well as a deep understanding of their breeding.

Under the management of Messrs Huyler and Anderson, Hamilton Farm Kennels bred a number of dogs which are in the pedigrees of most American Lhasa Apsos. Some of these Hamilton dogs are:

Mr. Fred Huyler and Ch. Hamilton Sandupa at the Twin Brooks KC (New Jersey) dog show.

Mr. James Anderson handling Ch. Hamilton Chang Tang at the Morris and Essex KC show, May 23, 1957.

Dorothy and Rudy Benitez with (left to right) Ch. Hamilton Achok, Ch. Hamilton Den Sa and Ch. Hamilton Kung in the grooming facility at Hamilton Farm.

Ch. Hamilton Tatsienlu	Hamilton Lachen
Ch. Hamilton Sandupa	Hamilton Tughar
Hamilton Kyi Chu	Hamilton Dobra
Hamilton Dakmar	BIS Ch. Hamilton Torma
Hamilton Nanning	Ch. Hamilton Samada
Hamilton Novo	Ch. Hamilton Chang Tang
Hamilton Yangchen	Hamilton Maroh
Hamilton Sandur	Ch. Hamilton Achok
Hamilton Muni	Hamilton Amdo
Hamilton Urga	Hamilton Yogi
Ch. Hamilton Den Sa	Hamilton Docheno
Hamilton Kalon	Ch. Hamilton Jimpa
Ch. Hamilton Kung	Ch. Hamilton Namsa ROM
Ch. Hamilton Katha	Ch. Hamilton Droma
Ch. Le	Hamilton Nakkin

The Cuttings were friends of the Baileys who brought the Lhasa Apso to England in 1928. They had visited Lhasa under the aegis of Colonel Bailey. In return when they visited the Baileys in England they gave them Hamilton Dewatas.

Mrs. Cutting died in 1961 and Mr. Cutting sold the Lhasa Apsos in the Hamilton Farm Kennel in 1962 to Mrs. Dorothy Cohen of Karma Kennels in Las Vegas, Nevada.

Karma

Mrs. Cohen was responsible for significant improvements in the Hamilton Farm type. She improved the quality and texture of the coat. She also improved the head and bite while retaining the merits of the Hamilton Farm stock. Her unrelenting efforts have earned her a respected position among Lhasa Apso breeders not only in this country but also in other parts of the world.

While numbers of champions bred is not alone significant it is some measure of a breeder's contribution when the quality of these champions is of a high caliber.

When Mrs. Cohen announced that, as of September 1974, Karma Kennels would no longer actively breed dogs she published a list of her 71 champions.

Some of the famous Karma-bred Lhasas that appear in many modern pedigrees are:

BIS Ch. Karma Frosty Knight O Everglo ROM

Group Winner Ch. Karma Rus-Tigu

Group Winner Ch. Karma Getson

Group Winner Ch. Karma Rus-Tilopa

Ch. Hamilton Tatsienlu at 16½ years of age.

Ch. Hamilton Samada, the full sister of BIS Ch. Hamilton Torma.

Ch. Hamilton Sandupa at over 10 years of age.

Ch. Hamilton Karma the foundation dam of Karma Kennel is the daughter of Hamilton Maroh and Hamilton Docheno.

Ch. Karma Getson is the son of Ch. Hamilton Kung and Ch. Hamilton Karma. Getson was owned and bred by Dorothy Cohen.

Group Winner Ch. Karma Gyapso	Group Winner Ch. Karma Tenzing
Group Winner Ch. Karma Rus-Ti	Group Winner Ch. Karma Lingtam
Group Winner Ch. Karma Skar-Cen	Am., Mex. Ch. Karma Sangpo
Ch. Karma Kanjur	Ch. Karma Kushog
Ch. Karma Mi Ser	Ch. Karma Kan Sa ROM
Ch. Karma Muffin of Norbulingka	Ch. Karma Ja Lu
Ch. Karma Dmar Po	Ch. Karma Rus Timantra
Ch. Karma Rumtek	Karma Tharpa
Karma Kosala	Ch. Karma Ami Chiri

Mrs. Cohen died early in 1977. The tributes in the June-July 1977 *Lhasa Apso Reporter* from the kennels which owed her a debt of gratitude also list and contain pictures of Lhasas resulting from her efforts.

Americal

In 1951 Mrs. Marie Stillman who lived in Beverly Hills, California before her death in 1976 bought her first female Lhasa Apso from Hamilton Farms. She, like the Cuttings, was originally a German Shepherd breeder. In all, Mrs. Stillman purchased five or six Lhasa Apsos from Hamilton Farms, four of which became champions. Her third purchase was the famous bitch, BIS Ch. Hamilton Torma. She won Best of Breed at the Westminster Kennel Club Show in 1955 and 1956, and was the first Lhasa Apso to place in the Non-Sporting group at that show. It has been said that her handler, Mitch Wooten, was one of the first to show a combed Lhasa.

Ch. Hamilton Torma made history in the United States on October 26, 1957 when she became the first Lhasa Apso in history to win an all-breed Best in Show.

These Hamilton dogs formed the foundation stock for Mrs. Stillman's kennel, named Americal after an American Army Division in World War II. Starting from that base Mrs. Stillman not only perpetuated the Hamilton Farms type but also added a substantial degree of elegance to it.

Ch. Americal's Torma Lu, son of BIS Ch. Hamilton Torma, won Best of Breed at the Westminster Kennel Club 1965 show. Mrs. Dorothy Benitez, who had served in the Hamilton Farm Kennel, was then his owner.

Some famous Americal Lhasa Apsos are:

Americal's Sandar of Pamu	Ch. Americal's Lha Lu
Ch. Americal's Moma	Ch. Americal's Leng Kong

Mrs. Marie Stillman, Americal, is shown here with Ch. Hamilton Chang Tang at 19 months of age.

A group of early day Lhasas—(left to right) Ch. Hamilton Tsang, Ch. Hamilton Torma, Hamilton Suchau, Ch. Americal's Nina and Ch. Hamilton Chang Tang.

Ch. Americal's Rika	Ch. Americal's Torma Lu
Americal's Lhasa ROM	Ch. Americal's Sing Song
Ch. Americal's Torma Tsing	Ch. Americal's Cho To
Ch. Americal's Licos Linga	Ch. Americal's Amo
Ch. Americal's Regent	Americal's Sandalwood of Pamu

Mrs. Stillman was a charter member of the American Lhasa Apso Club and served as a member of the ALAC Board of Directors from the first election of club officials in 1959 until the 1972 election. One of the pioneer Lhasa Apso breeders Mrs. Stillman will be long remembered for her contribution to the breed.

Licos

Mrs. Stillman gave Mrs. Grace Licos of Licos Lhasa Apsos, two puppies, Americal's Leng Kong and Americal's Rika. These two, half brother and sister, bred together produced the famous breed record holder BIS Ch. Licos Kulu La.

Mrs. Licos continued the Hamilton type with the added Americal excellence but is really famous for an indefinable extra charisma in the dogs she bred. She produced a higher level of elegance and refinement of type plus good movement, which evidenced good physical structure. In fact she bred a more nearly perfect Lhasa Apso than had been bred up to that time in this country. This also was done in the face of almost insurmountable obstacles and carping critics. Dogs which she bred

The foundation of Licos' Lhasa Apsos are (left to right) Ch. Americal's Leng Kong, Ch. Americal's Rika, Ch. Hamilton Pluti, Ch. Licos Nyapso La, Ch. Hamilton Katha, BIS Ch. Licos Kulu La and Ch. Licos Karo La.

Ch. Americal's Torma Lu shown winning Best of Breed at the 1965 Westminster KC show under judge Frank Landgraf with handler Frank Sabella. Torma Lu is owned by Dorothy Benitez and was alive and well at 19½ years of age in 1977.

Litter sisters, Ch. Licos Nojin La and Ch. Licos Namcha La, handled by Mrs. Grace Licos, their breeder and owner, to Best Non-Sporting Brace under Isidore Schoenberg at the Kennel Club of Beverly Hills 1973 show.

could win today. A Licos Lhasa was not dated; it was a dog for all time.

Some of the famous Licos dogs are:

BIS Ch. Licos Kulu La	Ch. Licos Chaplia La
Ch. Licos Nyapso La	Ch. Licos Cheti La
Ch. Licos Omorfo La	Ch. Licos Chulung La
Ch. Licos Kupl La	Ch. Licos Namni La ROM
Ch. Licos Namsi La	Licos Khung La
Ch. Licos Shingi La	Ch. Licos Shor Shan La
Licos Gia La	Ch. Licos Soji La
Ch. Licos Tseti La	Ch. Licos Karo La
Ch. Licos Naminka La	Can. Ch. Licos Yarto La

These four kennels, Hamilton Farms, Karma, Americal and Licos have had a very beneficial effect upon many of the newer kennels.

Gar Ten

The success of Mrs. Isabelle Loyd's Gar Ten Kennels, of Ontario, California, over the many years since its establishment can be credited to the combining of Hamilton-Licos-Karma bloodlines.

Mrs. Loyd has produced many champions but probably the most famous, not only in the show ring, but also as a producer is Ch. Kashgar of Gar Ten, the sire of more than 16 champions.

Gar Ten is noted for producing elegant, upstanding Lhasa Apsos of the proper type.

Milbryan

Mrs. Mildred Bryant, a popular, multi-breed judge, used Licos-Karma bloodlines through Ch. Licos Shor Shan La, Ch. Milbryan Karma Vegas and Ch. Milbryan Licos Gayla La.

The use of these bloodlines produced, to name a few, Ch. Milbryan Mei-Shan Tu of Gamac, Ch. Milbryan Dri-Mah-Tee-Nee, Ch. Milbryan Kim-Ly Shim and Ch. Milbryan Snazzi Nor for the Milbryan Kennels in Paradise, Texas.

Mrs. Bryant's activities as a Lhasa breeder greatly influenced the breed in her section of the country.

Shangri La

Shangri La Lhasa Apsos, located in Northern California, has over the many years since its establishment been the home of many influential Lhasa Apsos. The late Ruth Doty and her daughter, Marilyn Sorci, are noted for their successfully combining bloodlines of the very early imports in this country.

BIS Ch. Licos Kulu La winning Best of Breed at the 1962 Westminster KC show under the late Percy Roberts and handled by Maxine Beam.

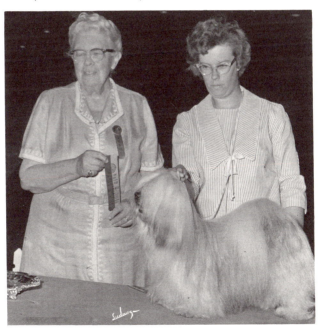

Ch. Kash Gar of Garten is shown winning Best of Breed and Group 2nd under Mrs. L. W. Bonney and shown by Nancy Tinker for owner Isabelle Loyd. Kash Gar is the sire of at least 16 champions.

Am., Mex. Ch. Licos Shor Shan La was a Westminster Best of Breed winner. A son of Ch. Hamilton Achok and Ch. Licos Nyapso La, he was owned by Mildred Bryant and bred by Grace Licos.

Ch. Hamilton Droma, Best in Show in Mexico City, 1964, was owned by Marilyn Sorci.

Shangri La was the home of the memorable Ch. Hamilton Droma whose show record was outstanding for her time. Ch. Hamilton Achok, who did not care to show as well as his kennel mate Droma, made his mark with his producing ability. Ms. Sorci says that two of the singularly finest specimens she ever owned were the dog, Ch. Tenzing of Lost Horizons, bred by Daisy Ellen Frazier in 1952 and the bitch, Lynchaven's Tangla, bred by Anita Lynch in 1955. From these two Shangri La started a distinct line using Ch. Hamilton Achok as an outcross.

Ch. Shangri La Sho George, sired by Tenzing and whose paternal grandmother is Tangla and maternal grandfather is Achok, is found in the pedigrees of many modern Lhasas. Demonstrating the longevity of the Lhasa Apso, George is still alive at this writing (1977) and is considered by Ms. Sorci to be a nearly perfect specimen.

While the Cuttings and later Mrs. Cohen, Mrs. Stillman and Mrs. Licos were developing the Hamilton line and type, three other kennels, Frank T. Lloyd Jr.'s Ming Kennel in New Jersey, and L. R. Liebmann's Miradel Lhasa Kennel and Mrs. Dorothy Sabine de Gray's Las Sa Gre Kennel, both of California, were developing a somewhat different bloodline and type.

Ming

Frank T. Lloyd Jr. owned the Ming Kennel of Merchantville, New Jersey. That kennel must be considered important not only on the East Coast but also throughout the country. He was the direct or indirect source of foundation stock for a number of the kennels which significantly influenced the breed during the period of the Lhasa Apso's meteoric rise in popularity.

Ming Kennel advertisements in the 1950s stated that it was established in 1943. It exhibited its Lhasa Apsos at the 1946 Westminster Kennel Club show held in New York City. Until then Hamilton Farm Kennels had been essentially the prime exhibitor of the breed. The bitch, Ming Lu, was the first Lhasa shown at Westminster by Ming Kennels and was also destined to be its first to become a champion. She was whelped August 26, 1943 and bred by William N. Hatch. Her sire was Ming Tai and Tai Ho was her dam.

Ming Kennel had the only exhibits at the 1948 Westminster show neither bred nor owned by Hamilton Farms. All three of the homebred Ming dogs shown were offspring of Ming Lu who by then was a champion and was shown as the only Lhasa Apso champion. Two of the dogs were littermates, Ming Changnopa and Ming Tsarong, sired by Pedro. That dog was the son of Chang Tso Lin and Mai Ling of

Ch. Hamilton Achok, owned by Marilyn Sorci of Shangri La
Lhasa Apsos, shown in a win under Col. E. E. Ferguson.

Judge Frank Lloyd with one of his
Ming Lhasa Apsos.

Boydon. Ming Tsarong was sold to Mrs. Elizabeth Campbell before the 1949 show where the brothers again were shown along with their mother.

The third Ming dog shown at the 1948 Westminster show was Wu Tai, sired by Hamilton Dakmar, also out of Ch. Ming Lu. Wu Tai sired the dog which Miradel Kennel later advertised as its foundation stud. That was Ch. Ming Tali II, CD.

At the May, l957 Trenton (New Jersey) Kennel Club show Ming Kennel showed the only three Lhasas neither bred nor owned by the Hamilton Kennel. None of them was of its own breeding. One was the bitch, Las Sa Gre's Fu La Somba, whelped July 13, 1955 and bred by Mrs. Dorothy Sabine de Gray of the Las Sa Gre Kennel. The other two bitches, Ming Taicha and Ming Teri, were littermates whelped June 25, 1956 and bred by Dr. and Mrs. Philip T. Newman.

The only dog not of Hamilton Farm lineage shown at the 1958 Westminster Kennel Club show was Raggs of Cornwallis, owned by Paul Williams. Raggs was a male littermate of Ms. Steinberg's Princess. They were whelped January 18, 1957 and bred by Paul Williams, now deceased, owner of Corwallis Kennel. Their sire was Yon Ton Senghi and their dam was Miradel's Ming Fu Dream Girl. Dream Girl was the daughter of Ch. Ming Tali II, CD.

Mrs. Anna Griffing's Ch. Ming Toy Nola, entered as a champion, was the third non-Hamilton Farm Lhasa Apso shown at the September, 1957 Westchester Kennel Club show and the sole Lhasa entered at the three New Jersey shows held in the fall of that year. That bitch was bred by Elbertine E. Campbell, handler for Ming Kennel, and was a daughter of Ch. Ming Changnopa and Americal's Chia Yang.

Ming Toy Nola was a veteran of about eight years of age at the time of the 1962 Westminster Kennel Club show. That year she won Best of Opposite Sex but previously she was the first Lhasa Apso to win a Non-Sporting Group in the East.

Mrs. Anna Griffing, who showed Nola, and her husband Robert started their Lhasa Apso Kennel under the name of Chig in 1954 at Mountainside, New Jersey. Their kennel was one of three to show their dogs as early as 1957 in shows held in the New York-New Jersey Metropolitan Area.

They bred and exhibited many Lhasa Apsos, including Ming Thudi and Linga Drog, children of Ch. Ming Toy Nola, who became champions late in 1962, Ch. Chig Chig and Ch. Chig Jo Mo whose picture was on the cover of the June 1976 issue of *Pure-Bred Dogs–American Kennel Gazette*.

Ch. Ming Tali II, bred by Judge Frank T. Lloyd and foundation stud for Miradel Kennel, is the sire of at least 11 champions.

An ad published in an early dog magazine describing the size of Miradel Lhasa Apsos.

Ch. Las Sa Gre's Manchado Dorado bred by Dorothy Sabine de Gray (Ch. Fu Al Tirito and Ch. Fu La Diablita).

52

The Griffings were active supporters of the American Lhasa Apso Club (ALAC) and of the Stewards Club of America. Mr. Griffing was the second President of ALAC from 1963 to 1967. He also became an active judge of numerous breeds. Mrs. Griffing was the Corresponding Secretary for ALAC for many years. The Griffings' vigorous support of ALAC in the early years helped the Club off to a good start. After Mr. Griffing's death in 1969 Mrs. Griffing, who died in 1976, was less active in the breed.

Judge Lloyd, unfortunately ill at the time of the 1962 Westminster Kennel Club show, could not witness his protegés success. By the time he died later that year, dogs which he had bred while his Ming Kennel was in operation, and their successors, had fanned out all over the country. They were not only in nearby New Jersey kennels, like Chig, but also throughout the country as far west as California.

Miradel

Miradel Lhasa Apso Kennel owned by Mr. and Mrs. L. R. Liebmann of Campbell, California was probably the most effective means of projecting the influence of Ming Kennel. It was originally established in 1947, only four years after Ming, and continued to operate until August 1967 when it sold its breeding stock. The contribution of the Miradel Kennel to the dissemination of Ming, Las Sa Gre and Rinpoche Kennels' dogs is summarized in its August 1962 *Popular Dogs Magazine* advertisement as follows:

"Foundation stud *Ch. Ming Tali II, CD,* sire of the above pups, will leave his mark of quality for many generations. Bred by the late Frank T. Lloyd, Jr., raised at Miradel, he sired 11 champions, 4 obedience degree winners, and is grandsire to nearly all 37 other champions from Miradel stock. *Miradel's Fa Li* whelped three champions by Ming. *Ch. Fu La Simpatica* whelped three champions with the Miradel prefix. Homebred *Al Wu Ting Ling,* in her first litter, produced *Ch. Lakeland's Ta Hsing of Miradel* and *Ch. Colarlie's Shan Bangalor,* both siring champions. We could go on and on."

No story of Ming or Miradel Kennels would be complete without reference to Las Sa Gre, mentioned in Chapter 2, and Rinpoche Kennels.

La Sa Gre

Las Sa Gre Kennel was established in 1945 by Dorothy Sabine de Gray of Encinitas, California. Unfortunately adequate information about her is not available to us but she is of vital importance to the

Two of Las Sa Gre's champions with their owner and handler Mrs. Dorothy Sabine de Gray. On the left is Ch. Fu Pacifiquito and on the right is Ch. Fu La Diablita.

Ch. Kham Te-Ran Rinpoche, CD and his breeder-owner Alice Parta-nen. Te-Ran's sire is Ch. Shangri La Sho George and his dam is Ron Si Rinpoche.

history of the breed. She imported the bitch Ch. Fardale Fu Ssi from England in July 1950 and was the owner of the bitch Las Sa Gre.

The three Lhasas Ming Kennel showed at the May 1957 Trenton Kennel Club show were a bitch Las Sa Gre's Fu La Somba, bred by Mrs. de Gray, and her two daughters, Ming Taicha and Ming Teri.

The Las Sa Gre Kennel, while an important part of the 1950 Lhasa Apso scene, has long since disappeared.

Rinpoche

Rinpoche Kennel or Rinpoche Lhasa Apsos founded in 1951 by John Partanen of San Francisco, California was a contemporary from that year of Ming, Miradel and Las Sa Gre Kennels. It outlived them and was revitalized in the late 1960s by the renewed activity of Mr. Partanen's daughter, Alice, following completion of her education.

The program then was to preserve the best of the well established line of Lhasas started in 1951 by Mr. Partanen. This was brought out and indelibly set in Ch. Kham Te-Ran Rinpoche, CD, born January 20, 1967, and owned by Miss Partanen. By April 1970 he had won 12 Bests of Breed, one Group first and three other Group placings. He was described as hailing "through his dam, Ron-Si Rinpoche" from the renowned Rinpoche stock and as "the type which in the past produced such fine dogs as Ch. Tashi Rinpoche, Ch. Kepa Rinpoche and Rincan of Kelea (Tashi's litter brother) who produced the fabulous Colarlie's Shan Bangalor—sire of 17 champions."

Lui Gi

Mrs. Albertram McFadden of Lui Gi Kennel originally in Palo Alto, California and later of Las Vegas, Nevada, acquired Ch. Chumpa of Furzyhurst, bred in the English Lhasa Apso Kennel of that name. He, as well as the Hamilton bloodline stock she had previously acquired, became part of her foundation stock. Thus she combined American and English bloodlines in her kennel.

Mrs. McFadden bred for soundness and substance. She always had the best interests of the Lhasa Apso in her heart, not only in her breeding program, but also in her relationships with others interested in the breed. Her views of the best interests of the breed did not, however, always coincide with those of others in the dog fancy. Also, her methods of fostering what she conceived to be such interests were frequently not conducive to success.

Ch. Lui Gi's Shigatzoo, grandson of Ch. Chumpa of Furzyhurst went to Mrs. B. K. Scott of San Saba Kennel, Harlingen, Texas. Mrs.

Scott bred him to Hamilton Chodon to produce BIS Am., Can., Mex. Ch. San Saba Chi Chi Jimi. She was the third Lhasa Apso bitch to win a Best in Show. Bred to her father, Jimi produced Ch. San Saba's Lori.

When Mrs. Scott dissolved her San Saba Kennel in 1966, Mrs. G. W. (Edna) Voyles of Cho Sen Kennel in Kentucky, acquired Jimi, who died in 1974, and her sire. As Mrs. Voyles is also an all-breed handler she was limited in her breeding to carry on the Lui Gi-Furzyhurst bloodline. She had, however, a half brother of Jimi, Ch. Yum Yum Chu Chu, a grandaughter, Ch. San Saba's Cho Sen Lee Sa and a great grandaughter, Ch. Cho Sen's Leesa Khan.

In addition to what for want of a better name might be called first echelon kennels—at least since they were first in time, there was a very important succeeding echelon. A third echelon of kennels closely connected with the second echelon will sometimes, for continuity of story, be discussed with it.

Zijuh

Mrs. Bea Loob, Zijuh Lhasa Apsos of Napa, California, bought her first Lhasa Apso in 1959. Very soon, however, she found that it was not of the quality of Mrs. Marie Stillman's dogs who were winning in the show ring. When Mrs. Loob sought to buy an Americal Lhasa, Mrs. Stillman did not have one available, but she helped Mrs. Loob to acquire a female from Hamilton Farm Kennel. That was Hamilton Shim Tru. Shim Tru had a total of ten puppies. Out of the ten came Ch. Zijuh Tsam, Ch. Zijuh Kata, Ch. Zijuh Seng Tru ROM and Ch. Zijuh El Torro.

Mrs. Loob's next purchase was another female, Donna Cardella's Tsng. Tsng, bred to Ch. Zijuh Tsam had a litter in February 1964 of four, including Ch. Zijuh Thori and Ch. Zijuh Jinda.

The first male Mrs. Loob purchased came from Mrs. Gloria Fowler of Everglo Kennel. Named Ch. Everglo's Zijuh Tomba by Mrs. Loob, he sired a litter from Ch. Zijuh Jinda all three of whom became champions. One was Ch. Zijuh Cha La.

Hamilton Shim Tru did not like the show ring, but with considerable effort Mrs. Loob showed her to her championship. She vowed, however, that she would not go through such an effort again. Hence when Ch. Everglo Zijuh Tomba indicated a distaste for the show ring, she gave him and Ch. Zijuh Jinda to Sharon Rouse, who had come looking for stud service. Mrs. Rouse put considerable effort into his training and eventually after a year handled Tomba to his championship. Jinda showed herself and readily earned her championship.

Ch. Lui-Gi's So-Nan, owned and bred by
Mrs. Albertram McFadden (Al Tabu of
Lhasarab and Ch. Lui-Gi's Melodi).

Ch. Zijuh Cha La, a daughter of Ch. Everglo Zijuh
Tomba and Ch. Zijuh Teri.

Multiple Group winner Ch. Everglo Zijuh Tomba shown winning the Stud Dog class at the Golden Gate
KC under J. G. W. Head, handler Sharon Rouse. His progeny are (center) BIS Ch. Sharbo Topguy, out of
Ch. Sharbo Zijuh Tsa Chu, handled by Darby McSorley and (right) Ch. Sharbo Me-Shanda Ba, out of
Everglo Flair handled by Lynn Morgan.

Both Ch. Everglo Zijuh Tomba born in June, 1965 and Ch. Zijuh Jinda born February, 1964, alive in the fall of 1977, show the longevity of the breed.

Shar Bo

Mrs. Sharon Rouse, Shar Bo Kennel of Danville, California, first met Mrs. Loob when she sought a mate for a pet bitch. The Shar Bo Kennel made a vast contribution to the breed by furthering the excellent program initiated by Zijuh Kennel. Mrs. Rouse apparently aimed at and succeeded in minor but desirable improvements to the already sound Zijuh stock.

Mrs. Rouse bred Ch. Zijuh Jinda to Ch. Chen Nyun Ti and from that first litter came four champions, including Ch. Shar Bo Zijuh Tsa Chu and Ch. Zijuh Shar Bo Spanggur. Her second litter from Jinda was sired by Tomba. That litter included the Best in Show winner Ch. Shar Bo Zijuh Zer Khan ROM and the Group winner Ch. Shar Bo Zijuh Kamaru. Mrs. Rouse's third litter resulted in four champions, one of whom was the Best in Show winner Ch. Shar Bo Topguy, the first black Lhasa Apso to win such an honor, and Int. Ch. Sharbo Tsan Chu who was a multiple Toy Group winner in Europe.

Pandan

Mrs. Onnie Martin, Pandan Lhasa Apsos, of Chico, California, stated that she would always be grateful to Marie Stillman, Bea Loob, Grace Licos and Pat Chenoweth for their help. Mrs. Martin is an American Lhasa Apso Club Register of Merit breeder, having bred at least 18 champions. Ch. Pandan Lhamo, CD was her first champion. Her most famous Lhasa Apso was Ch. Zijuh Seng Tru ROM, bred by Bea Loob. He sired BIS Ch. Potala Keke's Yum Yum ROM and her litter sister Ch. Potala Keke's Zin Zin ROM. Seng Tru is also the sire of Ch. Tabu's King of Hearts ROM, sire of more than 20 champions and is the grandsire of Ch. Pan Chen Tonka Sonan, the sire of at least 12 champions.

Mrs. Martin's breeding objective has been to advance the Hamilton type and also improve its structure to be evidenced by movement. As a breeder, Mrs. Martin has made substantial strides toward her objective; but, it is as a judge that she has made her biggest contribution to the breed. Her performance as a judge in the breed ring reflects her wealth of knowledge of both good Lhasa type and sound structure.

The physical location of the breeding programs which have developed the Lhasa Apso has shifted like a pendulum. Originally in the East

Ch. Hamilton Shim Tru, foundation bitch for Zijuh and dam of Ch. Zijuh Seng Tru ROM. She is the daughter of Ch. Hamilton Tatsienlu and Hamilton Dobra.

BIS Ch. Sharbo Zijuh Zer Khan ROM is a son of Ch. Everglo Zijuh Tomba and Ch. Zijuh Jinda. He is shown with his co-breeder Sharon Rouse, Sharbo.

at Hamilton Farms, it shifted to the West upon the closing of that kennel and the purchase of its dogs by Mrs. Cohen. Her Karma Kennel, joining with the already existing Americal, Licos and Lui Gi Kennels, centered the significant breeding programs in the far West.

Next the pendulum swung back to the East with the transfer of Mrs. Phyllis Marcy's Norbulingka Kennel from California, first to the Washington D.C. area, and later the New England area, and the rise of Paul Williams' Cornwallis Kennel in Cornwall, Pennsylvania.

Norbulingka

Mrs. Marcy's Norbulingka Kennel also is an American Lhasa Apso Club Register of Merit (ROM) breeder. She combined and extended the Karma and Licos elegance and type. The major contribution of this kennel was the development of BIS Ch. Kham of Norbulingka ROM. He may well be one of the greatest Lhasa Apso sires of modern times in bloodlines and producing ability as evidenced by the following excellent producing daughters:

Ch. Kinderland's Sang-Po ROM
Ch. Gindy of Norbulingka ROM
Ch. Arborhill's Lhana ROM
Ch. Kinderland's Mi Terra ROM
Ch. Keke's T'Chin Ting T'Chin ROM

Another notable dog produced by Norbulingka is the black Kham son, Ch. Mighty of Norbulingka, the sire of more than nine champions.

Mrs. Marcy also owned Ch. Willy of Cornwallis (litter brother to BIS Ch. Tibet of Cornwallis ROM) who sired several Norbulingka champions. Another sire at Norbulingka was the very typey Ch. Licos Shipki La. These four sires have greatly influenced the breeding programs of those kennels using their offspring.

Norbulingka is also the home of Group winning Am., Can. Ch. Lingkhor Bhu of Norbulingka, a Kham son, and BIS Am., Can., Bda. Ch. Blahapolos Norbulingka Ke Ko, a BIS Ch. Everglo's Spark of Gold ROM son.

Cornwallis

Paul Williams of Cornwallis Kennel had an exceptional eye for both type and structure. This enabled him, among other things, to cross the Karma and Licos bloodlines and by that means improve upon both of them. He combined Karma Tharpa with Ch. Licos Cheti La to produce BIS Ch. Tibet of Cornwallis ROM and Ch. Willy of Cornwallis. Mr. Williams bred Tharpa to Ch. Karma Kan Sa ROM to produce the 1967

Ch. Pandan Panchen bred by C. R. and Onnie Martin and owned by C. R. Martin and John Hylton is a daughter of Ch. Chen Nyun Ti ROM and Pandan Nangi. John Hylton is the handler.

Ch. Gindy of Norbulingka ROM is owned by Norman and Carolyn Herbel and bred by Phyllis Marcy. Gindy is the dam of more than eight champions; two are Group winners.

Karma Tharpa is the son of Karma Yon-Ten and Karma Kam-Bu. He was the Hamilton-bred foundation stud for Cornwallis Lhasa Apsos.

Ch. Licos Cheti La is the dam of BIS Ch. Tibet of Cornwallis ROM and Ch. Willy of Cornwallis.

Winners Dog at the Eastern ALAC Specialty, later to become BIS Am., Bda., Can. Ch. Ku Ka Boh of Pickwick, the 1969 Eastern ALAC Speciality Best of Breed winner. Tharpa was also bred to Ch. Miss Kim of Cornwallis, the 1971 Westminster Best of Opposite Sex winner, to produce Ch. Mae's Toiling of Cornwallis.

Paul Williams, now deceased, was a charter member of ALAC and proved himself a superb asset to Lhasa Apsos by providing valuable breeding stock for many East Coast breeders.

Tabu

The authors' Tabu Lhasa Apsos were originally located in Langhorne, Pennsylvania and currently are in Lucas, Kansas. Tabu is an American Lhasa Apso Club ROM breeder kennel having bred more than 22 champions.

We have sought to combine the best features of the Norbulingka and Cornwallis Kennels' type, including the elegance and charisma of Licos and the beautiful heads and coat texture of Karma.

When we turned to Lhasa Apsos from German Shepherds and Cairn Terriers, with the intention of breeding excellent animals, we searched for the best available to us.

We acquired 14 months old Tibet of Cornwallis. The same year his half brother, later to become BIS Am., Bda., Can. Ch. Ku Ka Boh of Pickwick, came to live at Tabu. The following year we obtained a female stud fee puppy later to become the multiple BIS winner, Am., Bda. Ch. Kinderland's Tonka ROM. To complete our foundation stock we also obtained a puppy bitch who became Ch. Gindy of Norbulingka ROM.

Tonka, a Tibet daughter out of a Ch. Kham of Norbulingka daughter, was bred to Ch. Zijuh Seng Tru ROM to produce the Group winner Ch. Tabu's King of Hearts ROM and Ch. Tabu's Kiss Me Kate. Later, Kate was bred to her grandsire, Tibet, and produced the Group winner Ch. Tabu's Gold Galaxy who is the dam of Am. Can. Ch. Tabu's Pacesetter.

Tibet, a Karma-Licos melding, was bred to Gindy, a Kham (Licos-Karma melding) daughter and this combination produced in several litters Ch. Tabu's Rhapsody in Red; Ch. Tabu's Raquel; Tabu's Rags To Riches; Ch. Tabu's Double or Nuthin and Ch. Tabu's Dresden Doll (both ALAC national Speciality point winners); Am. Can. Ch. Tabu's Appleseed Annie; Group Winner Ch. Tabu's Fame and Fortune (Winners Dog at Westminster) and his litter sister Tabu's Firebird.

We leased Ch. Taglha Muni, a Tibet daughter, and bred her to Ch.

BIS Am., Can., Bda. Ch. Ku Ka Boh of Pickwick (Karma Tharpa ex Ch. Karma Kansa ROM) was bred by Paul Williams, Cornwallis. Boh is pictured winning the 1969 Eastern ALAC Specialty under Henry Stoecker, handled by Jane Kay for owner Carolyn Herbel.

BIS Am., Bda. Ch. Kinderland's Tonka ROM owned by Norman and Carolyn Herbel and bred by Ellen Lonigro.

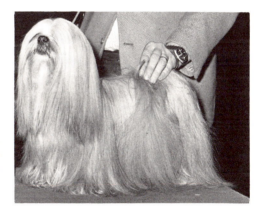

BIS Ch. Tibet of Cornwallis ROM is the sire of over 40 champions; among them at least seven Group winners and three BIS winners. He was born in March 1966 and is owned by Norman and Carolyn Herbel and bred by Paul Williams, Cornwallis.

Pan Chen Tonka Sonan. From this mating we produced Ch. Tabu's Make Mine Minx (dam of Ch. Tabu's Bronze Bonanza and Ch. Tabu's Bric A Brac); Ch. Tabu's Miss Chimney Sweep (Best of Winners at the 1975 Westminster show); Tabu's Mini Magic (dam of Am., Can. Ch. Tabu's Idle Time and Ch. Tabu's Indian Summer) and Tabu's Mr. Bo Jangles (sire of Am. Can. Ch. Potala Keke's Golden Gatsby). Tibet was the sire of both Minx's and Magic's litters.

Gindy and her daughter Dresden Doll were both bred to Ch. Pan Chen Tonka Sonan and produced Ch. Tabu's Jinger with A J and Tabu's Jazz Man and Ch. Tabu's Naturally Nutmeg, respectively.

No story of Tabu would be complete without crediting it as the home of BIS Ch. Tibet of Cornwallis ROM. Tibet was born on March 16, 1966 and his first litter was born July 10, 1967 containing the 1968 ALAC Specialty's Winners Bitch, Ch. Keke's Georgie Girl and Ch. Keke's Bamboo ROM, the dam of BIS and multiple Speciality winner Am. Can. Ch. Potala Keke's Yum Yum ROM. Tibet's last litter was born November 15, 1974 and contained Ch. Barcon's Wheeler Dealer.

During the seven years Tibet was used at stud, as of January 1, 1978, he produced 41 champions, among them three Best in Show dogs and seven Group Winners. Tibet's get includes the record holder for bitches, multiple BIS Am., Bda. Ch. Kinderland's Tonka ROM; multiple BIS Am., Can. Ch. Pon Go's Oddi Oddi, bred by Edmund and Carolyn Sledzik of Virginia; BIS Ch. Tulku's Yeti of Milarepa and his littermate, Group winner Ch. Tibs Tribulation of Milarepa, bred by Mary Carter, of Texas; Ch. Potala Keke's Gladiator who won a Group First from the classes; Ch. Tabu's Gold Galaxy who was Group first the first time shown as a champion and Group winner Ch. Tabu's Fame and Fortune.

With this as our foundation it is our privilege to help carry on the breeding programs of our predecessors—Hamilton Farms, Americal, Karma and Licos.

Chen

Contemporaneous with the upsurge of Hamilton bloodlines at Norbulingka and Cornwallis Kennels in the East, they were also being used at the Chen Lhasa Apso Kennel of Mrs. Patricia Chenoweth of Saratoga, California. She ranks high on the ALAC ROM Breeders list. Mrs. Chenoweth succeeded in extending the lovely Karma-Licos-Americal type and combining it with the soundness of Kyi Chu. One of Chen's most notable sires is Ch. Chen Nyun Ti ROM, the sire of more than 20 champions, among them numerous excellent daughters and three famous sons.

BIS Ch. Tulku's Yeti of Milarepa is a son of BIS Ch. Tibet of Cornwallis ROM and Carter's Tara of Everglo ROM. Yeti is owned by Ruth Barker, Tulku, and bred by Mary Carter, Milarepa.

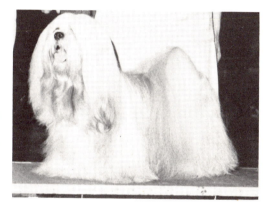

Multiple BIS winner Am., Can. Ch. Pongo's Oddi Oddi owned by Edmund and Carolyn Sledzik and Mary Slaby. He is a son of BIS Ch. Tibet of Cornwallis ROM and Ch. Pongo's Chi Kha.

Multiple BIS Am., Bda., Col. Ch. Chen Korum Ti ROM shown with his "Winky" the *Kennel Review* trophy for Top Non-Sporting Dog in 1972. Kori is owned by Patricia Chenoweth and co-bred with Frances Harwell.

Group winner Am., Can. Ch. Chen Krisna Nor ROM is a son of Ch. Chen Nyun Ti ROM and Chen Pho Nimo and is shown with his owner Wendy Harper. He is co-owned by Patricia Chenoweth and bred by Janet Seal.

Ch. Dolsa Yojimbo is a son of Am. Can. Ch. Chen Krisna Nor ROM and Cordova Sin Sa ROM and is owned by Elaine Spaeth, Yojimbo, and bred by Jean Kausch, Dolsa. He is the sire of multiple Best in Show winner Ch. Yojimbo Orion.

Multiple Group winner Ch. Karma Rus Tilopa, bred by Dorothy Cohen, and owned by Maria B. Aspuru. Tilopa is a son of Ch. Karma Rus Ti and Ch. Americal's Lha Lu.

Ch. Pan Chen Tonka Sonan who was bred by the late Mrs. Barbara Finnigan, of Pan Chen Kennel, combined the bloodlines of Pandan Kennel of Mrs. Onnie Martin with those of the Chen Kennel.

Group winning Am., Can. Ch. Chen Krisna Nor ROM is the sire of many exceptionally fine females and more than 16 champions. His show record, although impressive, should have been much greater because of his excellence.

Multiple Best in Show Am., Bda., Col. Ch. Chen Korum Ti ROM has an enviable show and producing record being the sire of more than 21 champions.

Mrs. Chenoweth, a breeder for more than 20 years, continues to be in the forefront of Lhasa Apso breeders, with more than 26 homebred champions to her credit.

Tsung

The influence of the West Coast Hamilton bloodlines extended to and were carried forward by the Tsung Lhasa Apso Kennel of Miss Maria Aspuru of Hialeah, Florida. She is another American Lhasa Apso Club ROM Breeder. Miss Aspuru added the bloodlines of the Everglo Kennel to those of Karma and Licos.

The Tsung Kennel made its major contribution through the sire BIS Ch. Karma Frosty Knight O Everglo ROM. He produced more than 12 champions, among them were Ch. Everglo Zijuh Tomba, a Group winner and the 1970 Western ALAC Specialty Best of Breed winner; Ch. Everglo's Charlie Brown ROM and multiple Group winner Ch. Daktazl Tsung, the 1975 Eastern ALAC Specialty Best of Breed winner.

Miss Aspuru purchased the Tomba son BIS Ch. Shar Bo's Zijuh Zer Khan ROM from Mrs. Rouse and has his young homebred son multiple Group winning Ch. Banji Bang Bang Tsung as well as Ch. Azabache Hen Tsung, a Zer Khan daughter.

Miss Aspuru also has Ch. Karma Rus Tilopa. He was bred to Ch. Karma Cordova Tsung to produce from one litter: Ch. Jack Pot Yen Tsung, Ch. Ciclon Yen Tsung, Ch. Amapola Yen Tsung and Ch. Tornado Yen Tsung.

Another male at Tsung is multiple Group winning Ch. Tabu's Chubby Checkers, the result of a Frosty Knight grandson bred to a Kham daughter.

Over the years the Tsung Kennels has been the home of BIS Ch. Drax Ne Ma Me ROM, BIS Ch. Karma Frosty Knight O Everglo ROM, BIS Ch. Shar Bo Zijuh Zer Khan ROM, multiple Group winner

Ch. Chen Karakorum, the dam of BIS Ch. Chen Korum Ti ROM.

Ch. Daktazl Tsung, winner of the 1975 Eastern ALAC Specialty was bred by Maria B. Aspuru and Angela O. Rossie and owned by Miss Aspuru and co-owned and handled by Leonard Ripley.

Multiple Group winner Ch. Tabu's Chubby Checkers is a son of Ch. Kublai Khan Tsung and Ch. Gindy of Norbulingka ROM. Chubby is owned by Maria B. Aspuru and was bred by Mr. and Mrs. Norman Herbel.

Manop Jen Tsung, multiple Group winner Ch. Tabu's Chubby Checkers, Group winner Ch. Kwan Ting Tsung, multiple Group winner Daktazl Tsung and multiple Group winning Ch. Banji Bang Bang Tsung.

Potala

Mrs. Keke Blumberg of Rydal, Pennsylvania, has used the names Keke's, Potala's and Potala Keke's to prefix the Lhasa Apsos bred at her Potala Lhasa Apso Kennel. She has led the American Lhasa Apso list of Register of Merit Breeders since its inception in 1973. According to the most recent listing of the ALAC Mrs. Blumberg has bred 41 champions.

Previously interested in a number of different breeds and in obedience rather than the conformation ring Mrs. Blumberg turned to Lhasas late in 1963. She has been unusually successful in selecting different stud dogs to develop championship caliber get. Some of these stud dogs are: BIS Ch. Kham of Norbulingka ROM, BIS Ch. Tibet of Cornwallis ROM, Ch. Ramblersholt Verles Rham Tru, Ch. Zijuh Seng Tru ROM, Ch. Everglo's Zijuh Tomba, BIS Ch. Chen Korum Ti ROM, Ch. Daktazl Tsung, Ch. Licos Tseti La, Ch. Mr. Kay of Cornwallis, Ch. Karma San Po, Ch. Kinderland's Bhu Sun, Tabu's Mr. Bo Jangles and her own homebred Ch. Potala Keke's Tomba Tu ROM.

Keke purchased her first Lhasa, a bitch later to become Ch. Keke's T'Chin T'Chin, who was bred by William and Janet Smedley and sired by Ch. Hamilton Namsa ROM. T'Chin was bred to Ch. Kham of Norbulingka ROM and a daughter of that mating, Ch. Keke's T'Chin Ting T'Chin ROM, was bred to Ch. Tibet of Cornwallis ROM to produce Ch. Keke's Bamboo ROM. When bred to Ch. Zijuh Seng Tru ROM, Bamboo produced the litter sisters BIS Ch. Potala Keke's Yum Yum ROM and Ch. Potala Keke's Zin Zin ROM. Zin Zin, when bred to Ch. Chen Korum Ti ROM produced Best in Show winner Ch. Potala Keke's Zintora. Yum Yum was bred to Ch. Everglo Zijuh Tomba and produced multiple Group winning Ch. Potala Keke's Tomba Tu ROM who, when bred to his grandmother, Bamboo, produced Ch. Potala Keke's Mistique.

Yum Yum also produced Ch. Potala Keke's Kelana, Ch. Potala Keke's Nyana and Ch. Potala Keke's Kal E Ko when bred to Tomba. When Yum Yum was bred to Ch. Daktazl Tsung she produced Ch. Potala Keke's Andromeda, Winners Bitch at the 1974 Eastern ALAC Specialty.

Yum Yum as well as being the dam of six champions is the winner of an all-breed Best in Show and in 1976 won Best of Breed at both the Eastern and Western ALAC Specialities.

BIS Am., Can. Ch. Potala Keke's Yum Yum ROM (Ch. Zijuh Seng Tru ROM ex Ch. Keke's Bamboo ROM). She is owned and bred by Keke Blumberg and is shown winning the Group under Gwladys Groskin, Carolyn Herbel handling.

Multiple Group winner Ch. Potala Keke's Tomba Tu ROM, owned and bred by Keke Blumberg, is shown winning the Group in Clearwater Florida under Frank Landgraf, handler Carmen Herbel.

BIS Am., Can. Ch. Potala Keke's Zintora shown winning Best in Show at the Wilmington KC, April, 1974, under John Ward Brady, Jr. and handled by Robert Sharp. Pictured on the left is his breeder, Keke Blumberg. He is a son of BIS Ch. Chen Korum Ti ROM and Ch. Potala Keke's Zin Zin ROM and is owned by Dorothy Schottgen, Dor Thi.

Potala was also the home of BIS Ch. Kyi Chu Shara ROM the dam of six Potala champions.

Another Potala champion of Canadian fame is Can., Am. Ch. Potala Keke's Golden Gatsby, a son of Tabu's Mr. Bo Jangles and Ch. Potala Keke's Sharabara (Ch. Karma San Po ex Ch. Karma Rus Timala).

Everglo

Mrs. Gloria Fowler of Bakersfield, California, who uses the name Everglo Lhasa Apsos for her kennel has had essentially two different breeding programs.

During her first program she used Ch. Kai Sang's Clown of Everglo as one of her studs.

Mrs. Fowler bred the Clown first to Ruffway's Hun-Nee-Bun to produce Tibetan Cookie of Everglo and then back to Cookie to produce BIS Ch. Everglo's Spark of Gold ROM.

The Clown's grandsires were the brothers, Ch. Las Sa Gre's Manchado Dorado and Las Sa Gre's Hijo D' Altiro. His paternal grandmother was Ch. Miradel's Nima. She was the daughter of Ch. Ming Tali II, CD out of Miradel's Fa Li. The Clown's maternal grandmother was Chika Rinpoche. Her sire was Ch. Hamilton Sandur and her dam was Ch. Yay Sih of Shebo.

Ruffway's Hun-Nee-Bun was sired by Ch. Miradel's Ming Fu Tzu out of Ch. Glenflo's Girja. Ming Fu Tzu was the son of Ch. Miradel's Kahn Dee. She in turn was the daughter of Ch. Ming Tali II, CD and Miradel's Fa Li. Ch. Glenflo's Girja was the daughter of Las Sa Gre's Hijo D' Altiro and Ch. Miradel's Nima.

Spark of Gold was sold as a puppy to Mrs. Joan Kendall Lohmann of Orlane Kennel where he made an illustrious record.

Later Mrs. Fowler acquired foundation stock from Karma Kennel and continued the type of her Hamilton-Karma progenitors, but with special emphasis on red coats. The Best in Show winner Ch. Everglo Sundance exemplifies the efforts of Mrs. Fowler's second breeding program. Sundance's sire is Everglo Red Regent and his dam is Everglo Red Cricket.

Orlane

Mrs. Joan Kendall Lohmann's Orlane Kennels, formerly of Iowa and currently located in Newark, Delaware is another successful establishment on the American Lhasa Apso Club Register of Merit Breeders list having bred in excess of thirty champions.

She started in Lhasas in 1962 and has had a tremendous impact upon the breed initially in the Midwest when there were few such breeders in

Ch. Kai Sang's Clown of Everglo, the sire of BIS Ch. Everglo's Spark of Gold ROM.

Am., Can. Ch. Karma Bandido of Maru (Karma Sha-Do of Everglo ex Ch. Karma Bidang), owned by David Marshall and Jack Russell, finished his American championship at eight months and his Canadian title at ten months.

BIS Am., Mex. Ch. Everglo Sundance, a son of Everglo Red Regent and Everglo Red Cricket, is owned by Lisabeth C. and E. Kiefer Labenberg. Sundance was bred by Gloria Fowler and is shown with Marvin Cates.

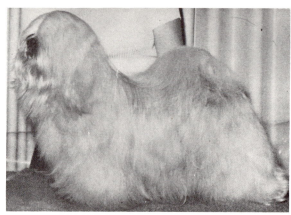

BIS Ch. Everglo's Spark of Gold ROM, by Ch. Kai Sang's Clown of Everglo ex Tibetian Cookie of Everglo, is the sire of over 40 champions. He was owned by Dorothy Lohmann.

Ch. Orlane's Dulmo ROM is a son of BIS Ch. Everglo's Spark of Gold ROM and Ch. Orlane's Chitra of Ruffway ROM. Photographed at 10 years of age, he is the sire of over 21 champions. Dulmo is owned by Larry Smith, Yat Sen and bred by Dorothy Lohmann.

Multiple BIS Am., Can. Ch. Orlane's Be Sparky of Al-Mar ROM is a son of Ch. Orlane's Dieh Bieh and Orlane's Holly Berry. Be Sparky was bred by Dorothy Kendall Lohmann and is owned by Marjorie Lewis.

that region, and later throughout the country. Her success story is the typical one of a good product available at the time that the demand for it was beginning to expand. Orlane dogs became available at a time when there was a great need for an improvement in topline and rear quarters. Her dogs were and are characterized by good, high withers, good rears and good toplines.

Orlane is also a success story of a top producing dog. In 1962 Ms. Lohmann bought her first Lhasas. They were a three-month-old puppy who was to become the famous sire, BIS Ch. Everglo Spark of Gold ROM, and his half sister who became Ch. Kai Sang's Flame of Everglo, as her foundation stock.

Sparky, shown sparingly in the Midwest, won Best in Show at Springfield, Illinois over 1200 dogs and then at Cedar Rapids, Iowa over 800 dogs. Unfortunately he suffered heat stroke on the way home from a match so that after recovery he was not shown as much as he probably otherwise would have been.

While he was young Sparky was not used much at stud but he showed promise of being a top producer.

His first litter consisted of one male puppy who became Int. Ch. Orlane's Golden Puppet.

Bred to Ch. Arborhill's Lee-Sah ROM with bloodlines of Ch. Cherryshores Bah Bieh Boi (Ch. Kyi Chu Kaliph Nor ex Cherryshores Mah Dahm), Sparky produced the well known winner Ch. Arborhill's Rapso Dieh who was seven times a Best in Show winner. He was bred by Sharon Binkowski of Arborhill Lhasa Apsos and is owned by Janet Whitman, Ja Ma, Spring Valley, New York.

Sparky is the sire of BIS Ch. Ruffway Mashaka owned, bred and handled by Georgia Palmer of Ruffway Kennels.

Another of Sparky's Best in Show sons is BIS Am., Can., Bda. Ch. Blahapolos Norbulingka Ke Ko, out of Secunda Kye. He was bred by Megan Shirley, Blahapolo Lhasa Apsos in Houston, Texas and is owned by Phyllis Marcy, Norbulingka.

Sparky also is the sire of the record holding multiple Best in Show winner Ch. Barcon's The Avenger, owned and bred by Mr. and Mrs. Barry C. Tompkins of Barcon Kennels.

At the time of Sparky's death in the fall of 1976 the list of his get read like the "who's who" of Lhasadom. It included the names of 43 champion children and 94 champion grandchildren. He had four BIS sons and eight BIS grandsons; Ch. Arborhill's Rah Kieh ROM, Ch. Brush's Alvin of Samara, Ch. Orlane's Be Sparky of Al-Mar ROM, Ch. Joi San's Happieh Go Luckieh, Ch. Joi San's Golden Mocca of Ky, Ch. Orlane's Vindicator and Ch. Tiffany's Qua-La-Ti.

When Sparky died the records of the top producing Lhasa Apso sires were only available through the year 1975. On that basis he was the leader with 43 champions.

With the heritage of the sons, daughters and grandchildren left behind him, Sparky will have a significant influence on the breed for years to come.

Yat-Sen

Yat-Sen Kennel of Louisville, Kentucky, is the home of Ch. Orlane's Dulmo ROM, champion producing son of BIS Ch. Everglo's Spark of Gold ROM. Dulmo has sired more than 21 champions.

Arborhill

Sharon Binkowski, Arborhill Kennels of Ann Arbor, Michigan, is the breeder of BIS Ch. Arborhill's Rapso Dieh, BIS Ch. Arborhill's Rah Kieh ROM and Ch. Arborhill's Bhran Dieh ROM. Arborhill is the home of these homebred Register of Merit bitches: Ch. Arborhill's Lee-Sah ROM, dam of seven champions; Ch. Arborhill's Karoling Karolyn ROM, dam of six champions and Ch. Arborhill's Lhana ROM, dam of five champions.

Ruffway

Mr. E. R. and Mrs. Georgia E. Palmer of Addison, Illinois originally had a kennel for Rough Collies which they called Ruffway Kennels. In 1956-57 they bought their first Lhasas, Ch. Glen Flo's Girja and Ch. Miradel's Ming Fu Tzu, both black and white particolors. From them came Ch. Ruffway Solitare. They also bought Ch. Miradel's Dinah Might.

Although they continued in Collies after they started breeding Lhasas, the Palmers were out of Collies by 1965.

Mrs. Palmer handled Karma Frosty Knight of Everglo to his championship title.

The Palmers are on the American Lhasa Apso Club Register of Merit List having bred more than 20 champions. Some of these 20 champions are Ch. Ruffway Chogal, Ch. Ruffway Kamet, Ch. Ruffway Kara Shing ROM, Ch. Ruffway Kham Chung, Ch. Ruffway Lolung, Ch. Ruffway Chudar, Ch. Ruffway Tsong Kappa, Ch. Ruffway Nor-Pa, BIS Ch. Ruffway Mashaka and his littermate brothers Ch. Ruffway Marpa ROM and Ch. Ruffway Norru, and Group winner Ch. Ruffway T'Ang Chu ROM.

Ch. Arborhill's Lee Sah ROM, owned and bred by Sharon Binkowski.

BIS Am. Can. Ch. Arborhill's Rapso Dieh is a son of BIS Ch. Everglo's Spark of Gold ROM and Ch. Arborhill's Lee Sah ROM. Rapso Dieh is owned by Janet Whitman.

BIS Ch. Maraja's Tsering Momo, owned and bred by Jane N. Bunse, Maraja, is a son of Ch. Ruffway Tsong Kapa and Miradel's Yung Chen of Ruffway.

BIS Ch. Ruffway Mashaka, bred, owned and handled to a BIS win in 1971 by Georgia Palmer, is a son of BIS Ch. Everglo's Spark of Gold ROM and Ch. Ruffway Kara Shing ROM.

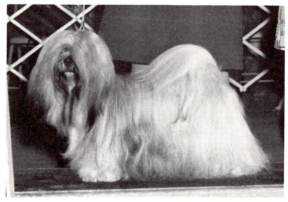

Ch. Ruffway T'Ang Chu ROM, bred and owned by Georgia Palmer, is a son of Ch. Reiniet's Roial Chanticleer and Ch. Ruffway Kham Chung.

Kinderland

Mrs. Ellen Lonigro of Kinderland Kennels moved from the Midwest to the East Coast and is now located in Culpepper, Virginia. Originally in German Shepherds, she bought her first Lhasa in the 1950s as a pet for her daughter. That led to a decision to breed better Lhasas. As good bitches were hard to get she decided to concentrate on males. Her first one was Ch. Jigme of Carycliff, a Hamilton line male which she finished and was the sire of several champions. When Jigme died prematurely due to heat prostration she bought Ch. Larrmar De-Tsen, a son of the great BIS Ch. Licos Ku Lu La. Her foundation bitch, Ch. Kinderland's Sang-Po ROM, purchased in 1965, was bred by Sherry and Alexander Holser and is a daughter of BIS Ch. Kham of Norbulingka ROM.

When Sang Po was bred to BIS Ch. Tibet of Cornwallis ROM she produced the famous BIS Am., Bda. Ch. Kinderland's Tonka ROM, who has won more Bests in Show than any other Lhasa Apso bitch in the history of the breed. Sang Po is also the dam of Group Winner Ch. Potala Kinderland's Goliath and Grand Futurity winner Ch. Kinderland's L'oo-Ky.

Mrs. Lonigro not only is high on the list of ALAC ROM Breeders but her Ch. Kinderland's Sang-Po has led the list of Register of Merit Dams for four consecutive years.

In 1969, Mrs. Lonigro purchased an eight months old puppy who became Ch. Ruffway Norru and the next year bought his littermate Ch. Ruffway Marpa ROM. Marpa when bred to Sang Po produced Group winner Ch. Potala Kinderland's Goliath, Ch. Kinderland's Tim-Pa, Ch. Kinderland's L'oo-Ky, Ch. Kinderland's Tonka-Tu and Ch. Kinderland's Grundoon.

Mrs. Lonigro has bred at least 27 champions; among them are Group winner Ch. Kinderland's Zimba, Group winner Ch. Potala Kinderland's Goliath, Ch. Kinderland's Mi Terra ROM, Ch. Kinderland's Ginkgo, Ch. Kinderland's Sonan, Ch. Kinderland's Nicola, Ch. Kinderland's Gayla, as well as BIS Am., Bda. Ch. Kinderland's Tonka ROM.

Kyi Chu

Mrs. Ruth Smith of Boise, Idaho who bred first under the name of Colarlie and later as Kyi Chu had a breeding program which stressed the basic soundness of the dog and the dog's ability to move well as proof of that fact. She did not let minor details obscure her basic concepts. Her emphasis upon the proper size of the Lhasa was also a keynote of her program.

Ch. Kinderland's Sang-Po ROM and her owner Ellen Lonigro. Sang is the dam of at least nine champions. She is a daughter of BIS Ch. Kham of Norbulingka ROM and Ch-Ha-Ya-Chi.

Ch. Ruffway Marpa ROM, owned and handled by Ellen Lonigro, sire of twelve champions.

Ch. Ruffway Norru and his owner Ellen Lonigro. He was bred by Georgia Palmer and is a son of BIS Ch. Everglo Spark of Gold ROM and Ch. Ruffway Kara Shing ROM.

Mrs. Smith is the breeder of the famous Ch. Colarlie's Shan Bangalor, the sire of 17 champions and both the paternal great-grandfather and maternal grandfather of the breed record holder BIS Am., Can., Bda., Mex. Ch. Kyi Chu Friar Tuck ROM.

Mrs. Smith and Mrs. Jay Amann bred Ch. Quetzal Feyla of Kyi Chu. His sire was Ch. Hamilton Jimpa and his dam was Ch. Colarlie's Miss Shandha ROM, dam of eight champions and the daughter of Ch. Colarlie's Shan Bangalor ROM. Feyla is the sire of at least six champions, among them BIS Ch. Kyi Chu Friar Tuck ROM also out of Ch. Colarlie's Miss Shandha ROM.

Other notable Lhasas carrying the Kyi Chu prefix are: Ch. Kyi Chu Kira CD, the dam of BIS Am. Can. Ch. Kyi Chu Shara ROM; Ch. Kyi Chu Kara Nor ROM, the top producing dam for Chen Kennel; Group winning Ch. Kyi Chu Tukki Dar, Ch. Kyi Chu Impa Satan, Ch. Kyi Chu Kum Nuk, Ch. Kyi Chu Inshalla CD, Ch. Kyi Chu Shufi and Ch. Kyi Chu Whimsi of Sharbet.

Dzong

Dzong Lhasa Apso Kennel, owned by Mrs. Beverly Garrison of Kathleen, Georgia is on the ALAC list of ROM breeders. Her kennel is the home of the famous Ch. Colarlie's Miss Shanda ROM, daughter of the famous sire, Ch. Colarlie's Shan Bangalor ROM. Other notable producing Dzong dogs are Dzong Sassy Cookie ROM, Ch. Dzong Firelight ROM and Ch. Quetzal Fun Tu of Kyi Chu ROM.

A number of the Dzong dogs from the 1960s were Ch. Dzong Bamboo Pete by Ch. Colarlie's Shan Bangalor ROM out of Ch. Quetzal Fun Tu of Kyi Chu ROM; Ch. Dzong Yogi by Ch. Dzong Firelight ROM ex Jakana's Tutu of Dzong; Ch. Dzong Panda by BIS Ch. Drax Ni Ma Me ROM ex Ch. Colarlie Miss Shandha ROM; Ch. Dzong Merry Mop by Ch. Colarlie's Shan Bangalor ROM ex Ch. Quetzal Fun Tu of Kyi Chu ROM.

Robert Sharp

Robert Sharp of Albany, New York who has bred Lhasa Apsos under the names of Sharbet, Sharp's, Agra and Sharpette has bred many champions but is best known for the many Lhasas he has handled to their titles.

Mr. Sharp who became involved in Lhasas in the early 1960s has had the honor of piloting BIS Am., Can., Bda., Mex. Ch. Kyi Chu Friar Tuck ROM to his breed record. He also handled BIS Am., Bda., Col. Ch. Chen Korum Ti ROM to his eight Bests in Show as well as

Ch. Colarlie's Shan Bangalor ROM at 14 months, owned by Ruth Smith. Shan Bangalor ultimately sired 17 champions.

Group winner Ch. Kyi Chu Whimsi of Sharbet, a full brother to BIS Ch. Kyi Chu Shara ROM, was bred by Terry Smith.

Group winner Ch. Colarlie's Dokki, CD is a son of Ch. Colarlie's Shan Bangalor ROM and Miradel's Ming Fu Chia, CD. Dokki was the first black Lhasa Apso to win a Group. He was bred and owned by Ruth Smith.

BIS Am., Can. Ch. Rimar's J. G. King Richard, shown with handler Robert Sharp, is a son of Ch. Tabu's King of Hearts and Ch. Rimar's Tipit, bred by Stephen Campbell.

accumulating enough wins to make him the Number 1 Non-Sporting Dog (*Kennel Review* System) for 1972 and winning the Ken-L Award for 1972 by having won the most Non-Sporting Groups; that being 42.

Mr. Sharp handled BIS Am., Bda. Ch. Kinderland's Tonka ROM to her record-making Best in Show and Group wins as well as her son Ch. Tabu's King of Hearts ROM to his multiple Group wins, and his son, BIS Am., Can. Ch. Rimar's J. G. King Richard to a Best in Show win and many Group and Best of Breed wins.

The Ch. Chen Korum Ti ROM son, Ch. Potala Keke's Zintora was shown to his Best in Show by Mr. Sharp. He also handled the Group Winning Ch. Kyi Chu Tukki Dar, a Friar Tuck son.

Some Lhasas that carry Mr. Sharp's prefixes are: Ch. Sharpette's Gaylord (Best of Breed winner at the 1973 Western ALAC Specialty); Ch. Sharpette's Number One Son; Ch. Sharpette's Maya Maya; Ch. Sharpette's Bobette; Ch. Sharpette's Galahad; Ch. Agra's Imprecious; Ch. Sharpette's Hasty Pudding, Ch. Sharp's Bee Gee ROM; Ch. Sharpette's Lady Godiva and Ch. Kyi Chu Whimsi of Sharbet.

To list any of the many, many champions that Mr. Sharp has finished for other breeders would risk missing some of importance; however, it is safe to say that this number is well into the hundreds.

Drax

Mrs. Winifred Drake's Drax Kennels in Hialeah, Florida, is another ALAC ROM kennel listed. Drax has been active on the Lhasa Apso scene almost as long as the club itself. Originally a breeder of Cocker Spaniels, she has combined American and English bloodlines to produce dogs of quality.

Early in the 1960s Mrs. Drake advertised stud service from Ramblersholt Le Pon and puppies from Ch. Ramblersholt Shahnaz ROM acquired from the English Lhasa Apso Kennel of that name.

In 1967 Ch. Drax Ni Ma Me, came out, after a short retirement under Tsung Kennel guidance to win two Groups and a Best in Show in successive weekends. By August 1967 he had 99 Bests of Breed, 51 Group placements, 14 Group Firsts and one Best in Show.

Drax winners in the spring of 1968 were Ch. Drax Do Sa La Dkar Bo and her sire Ch. Drax Bonpo Zan-Po. Other Drax champions by that time were Ch. Drax Kamba Dzong, Ch. Drax Ka-U ROM, Ch. Drax Ron Cun Wa, Ch. Drax Chen Chen Tsung, Ch. Drax Ka Ba Kol Ba and Ch. Dhuphyz Nor Bu.

Drax's advertisement in 1970 for Drax Bye Pa Mkar Pa shows how the kennel combined American and English bloodlines. In that dog's background are Ch. Licos Namni La, Ch. Colarlie's Shan Bangalor

Ch. Panda Bear Sing of Kyi Chu, bred by Ruth Smith and owned by Patricia and Tom Chenoweth. He is a son of Ch. Colarlie's Shan Bangalor and Colarlie's Pitti Sing.

Multiple Group winner Am., Can. Ch. Chok's Joker, sired by Ch. Tabu's King of Hearts ROM out of Chok's Joppa Bu-Mo ROM, is owned by Susan Gehr.

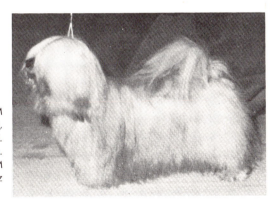

BIS Ch. Drax Ni-Ma Me ROM was bred by Winifred Drake, Drax, and owned by Maria B. Aspuru. Ni-Ma is a son of Ch. Colarlie's Shan Bangalor ROM and Ch. Ramblersholt Shahnaz and the sire of five champions.

ROM, Ch. Ramblersholt Shahnaz ROM and Ch. Drax Ne Ma Me ROM as well as other Drax champions.

Drax Kennel advertised puppies for sale in 1974 and has continued to be active since then principally in conjunction with other kennels.

Dandi

Mrs. Diane R. Dansereau of Dandi Lhasa Apsos in River Ridge, Louisiana was interested in purebred dogs as a young girl. Her first two were Cocker Spaniel bitches. These led her to study about dogs and then to train her second dog for obedience.

About 1963 she and her husband Raymond bought four Lhasa Apsos. Only ten years later they had a fully equipped kennel house but, as Mrs. Dansereau said, "we operate on a limited budget" and they do their own work. In spite of these restrictions Dandi Lhasa Apsos is listed as an ROM kennel having bred at least 11 champions.

Their first dog to finish was Ch. Sugarplum's Number One Son. He sired four of Dandi Kennel's champions. Mrs. Dansereau's special pet, Ch. Crest O Lake Kin Go, sired five of their champions. Each of those dogs is a grandsire and great grandsire of a number of Dandi champions. The list includes Ch. Dandi Jim Rik'i, CDX, Ch. Penbois Tilu Khan, Ch. Dandi Dapper Dan Dan Dandi, Ch. Dandi's Wa Hoo, Ch. Dandi's Shu Gah Cookie, Ch. Dandi Jimm Jimm Dandi, Ch. Dandi Fanci Dandi, Ch. Dandi's Dipsey Doodle Dandi, Ch. Dandi's Golden Sheba and Ch. Dandi's Golden Nugget. Their Dandi Golden Gypsy of Everglo ROM received her Register of Merit Award in 1974.

The quality of these dogs is ample evidence that Mr. and Mrs. Dansereau's efforts to improve the breed have not been limited.

Canadian Contributions

This completes our list of Lhasa Apso breeders, including all of those on the American Lhasa Apso Club's Register of Merit Breeders List. It would unduly lengthen this chapter to discuss in detail the contributions of Canadian kennels to the United States but the story would be incomplete if we did not mention at least two which have added to our history.

Abbotsford Kennel of Mr. and Mrs. James Roberts in British Columbia, whose Ch. Teako of Abbotsford won the 1969 Western ALAC Specialty has contributed foundation stock to several United States Lhasa Apso kennels such as San Jo, located in the Seattle Area.

Marianne Nixon, San Jo Lhasa Apsos, states that Group winner Ch. Gyal Kham-Nag of San Jo ROM was the foundation sire for San Jo. He

Ch. Sugarplum's Number One Son, by Miradel's Chu Cha of Sugarplum ex Sugarplum's Jewel of Barbara, is the sire of four champions. He is owned by Diane Dansereau.

Dandi Golden Gypsy of Everglo ROM is the daughter of BIS Ch. Karma Frosty Knight O Everglo ROM and Ch. Kyima of Everglo ROM, owned by Diane Dansereau.

Group winner Ch. Dandi's Wahoo is the daughter of Dandi's Apso Lute Lee Dandi and Dandi's Chu Cha Cha. She was bred and owned by Diane Dansereau.

Multiple BIS Ch. San Jo's Torgi was born in 1967 and was the first Lhasa Apso to win Best in Show in the Pacific Northwest, with a total of two Best in Shows and nine Group firsts, always amateur handled.

BIS Ch. San Jo's Torgi is a son of Ch. Gyal Kham-Nag of San Jo ROM and Am., Can. Ch. Kyi Chu Kissami ROM. Torgi is owned by Gayle Fristad, Raaga, and was co-bred by Marianne Nixon and Ruth Smith. He is photographed with Marianne Nixon, San Jo.

is a son of Am., Can. Ch. San Yu Ti of Abbotsford and Ch. Jomo Dkar-Po of Abbotsford. Bred and owned by Mrs. Nixon he was shown at an early age and attained his championship with a Group First from the classes.

Kham-Nag is the sire of nine champions; one is Ch. San Jo's Torgi who became a multiple Best in Show winner.

The other Canadian kennel is Dr. Ellen Brown's Balrene Kennel in Ontario whose Can., Am. Ch. Balrene Chia Pao won the 1971 Eastern ALAC Specialty.

Since only concentrating on the kennels which we believe to have been most influential to the breed has resulted in a long list, we must be forgiven for mentioning a comparatively small number of kennels and individuals. Hindsight will probably reveal some which should have been included even though they have not yet become part of the Register of Merit list.

BIS Ch. Licos Kulu La, winner of four all-breed Bests in Show. Kulu La was and still is considered by many judges and breeders the epitome of the breed. He was bred and owned by Grace Licos and handled to his record by Maxine Beam.

4

The Lhasa Apso
Record Holders

IN THE SPRING OF 1935 the American Kennel Club sanctioned Lhasa Apso participation in all-breed shows. Twenty-two years later, on October 26, 1957, at the Twin Cities Kennel Club, Yuba City, California, Ch. Hamilton Torma became the first Lhasa Apso to win Best in Show at an all-breed show. Mitch Wooten handled her this day as he had to many other wins in her long, successful career.

Ch. Hamilton Torma

Torma was whelped on February 6, 1952 at Hamilton Farm Kennel. She was bred by Mr. and Mrs. C. S. Cutting and was owned by Mrs. Marie Stillman of Americal Kennel. Her sire was Ch. Hamilton Tatsienlu and her dam was Hamilton Lachen.

During her career she won sixty Bests of Breed including two at Westminster, and had 35 Group placings.

Ch. Licos Kulu La

Torma's record stood until 1961 when her grandson BIS Ch. Licos Kulu La, sired by Ch. Americal's Leng Kong out of Torma's daughter, Ch. Americal's Rika, under the capable handling of Maxine Beam, won four Bests in Show including one at the large Ventura, show. Born May 26, 1956, Kulu La died May 21, 1963. Although 1961, when he won four

Bests in Show, was his big year, he also won Best of Breed at both the 1962 and 1963 Westminster Kennel Club shows. During his career he won 24 Groups, including the Group at the International Kennel Club show in Chicago, and numerous other Group placements.

Ch. Kham of Norbulingka

BIS Ch. Kham of Norbulingka ROM set a new record with five Bests in Shows in 1966, only five years after BIS Ch. Licos Kulu La had set his record. Kham, bred by Mrs. Phyllis Marcy of Norbulingka Kennel and sired by Licos Khung La out of Karma Kosala, was whelped in June 1961 and died in August 1974. He was also twice Best of Breed at Westminster and the International as well as Best of Breed at the first ALAC Specialty in Trenton, New Jersey. His Best in Show wins were made at the Lakes Region, Lancaster, Trumbull, Delaware County and Champlain Valley Kennel Club shows. He had 21 Group wins and about 42 other Group placements.

Ch. Karma Frosty Knight O Everglo ROM

BIS Ch. Karma Frosty Knight O Everglo ROM followed Kham as the winner of most Bests in Show. He was bred by Mrs. Dorothy Cohen of Karma Lhasa Apsos. His sire was Ch. Karma Kushog and his dam was Ch. Hamilton Sha Tru. Mrs. Cohen sold him to Mrs. Gloria Fowler of Everglo Kennel. Mrs. Georgia Palmer of Ruffway Lhasa Apsos guided Frosty Knight to his championship for Mrs. Fowler. He was purchased by Misses Aspuru and Rossie of Tsung Kennel, who campaigned him to his first six Bests in Show which set a new record. Frosty Knight won alternate Bests in Show on the January 1970 Florida Circuit and then retired with 11 Best in Show awards.

Frosty Knight later received an American Lhasa Apso Club Register of Merit Stud Dog award and is on the Top Twenty listing.

Ch. Kyi Chu Friar Tuck ROM

BIS Am., Bda. Can. Mex. Ch. Kyi Chu Friar Tuck ROM was the next Lhasa to set the record for most Best in Show wins. He was bred by Mrs. Jay Amann and Mrs. Ruth Smith. Friar Tuck, born January 30, 1965, was a son of Ch. Quetzal Feyla of Kyi Chu and Ch. Colarlie's Miss Shandha ROM. He earned his first points at eight months of age and finished his championship while still a puppy. Robert Sharp who handled Friar Tuck so effectively during his career bought him during 1967.

BIS Ch. Hamilton Torma made history for the breed by being the first Lhasa Apso to win an all-breed BIS. The show was the Twin Cities KC, Yuba City, California, October 26, 1957. Torma was bred by Mr. and Mrs. C. S. Cutting and proudly owned by Marie Stillman. Torma was handled by Mitch Wooten to the history-making win under judge Maurice Baker.

BIS Ch. Kham of Norbulingka ROM, owned and bred by Phyllis Marcy, the winner of five all-breed Bests in Show and the Best of Breed winner at the first ALAC Specialty. He is shown here winning a BIS under Heywood Hartley, handled by Jane Kay.

The following year Friar Tuck won Best of Breed at the American Lhasa Apso Club Specialty in Trenton, New Jersey.

In 1969, then owned by Marvin Frank, Friar Tuck won several Bests in Show and added enough in 1970 to make his final record 13 Bests in Show, 100 Group firsts, 280 Group placings and 312 Bests of Breed. He also won Best of Breed at the 1970 Eastern ALAC Specialty in Trenton, New Jersey.

Friar Tuck is still the top winning parti-color in the history of the breed. He is an ALAC ROM stud dog and is on the Top Twenty list.

Ch. Barcon's The Avenger

BIS Ch. Barcon's The Avenger became the current Best in Show record holder in 1974 by amassing 14 victories in less than two and one half years. Mr. and Mrs. Barry C. Tompkins bred and owned him and Ms. Dorothy Kendall Lohmann, owner of his sire, BIS Ch. Everglo's Spark of Gold ROM, co-owned and handled him. His mother is Barcon's Madam Eglantine. Her paternal grandparents were BIS Ch. Tibet of Cornwallis ROM and BIS Ch. Kyi Chu Shara ROM.

The Avenger, called "Rastus", finished his championship in January 1972. His intensive campaigning began in May 1972 and in July of that year he won two Bests in Show. During his career he appeared in half of the states in the Union, frequently two or more times, during a year. He won at least three times as many Groups as he did Bests in Show and more than a hundred Group placements.

With the completion of his extensive campaigning in 1974 he retired to the Barcon Kennel of his breeders and owners at Fulton, New York.

He already has sired enough champions so that his name should very shortly appear on the ALAC Register of Merit Stud Dog Award list. Among these champions are the Best in Show winner, Ch. Tiffany's Qua-La-Ti and Group winner Ch. Orlane's Suntoy of Geodan.

Ch. Yojimbo Orion

When any record is set, conjecture always arises about the possibility of it being broken and how soon that is likely to occur. That is a question that can never be answered.

We know, however, that BIS Ch. Yojimbo Orion has, at this writing tied the breed record for Bests in Show and is making a concerted effort to create a new record. He was Best of Breed at the 1977 Westminster Kennel Club show and then, for the first time in history for a Lhasa Apso, won the Group at that show. He also won Best of

BIS Ch. Karma Frosty Knight O Everglo ROM was bred by Dorothy Cohen and used in the kennels of Everglo and Ruffway before he was finally purchased by Tsung Kennel. It was Tsung that campaigned Frosty to his history-making record.

BIS Am., Bda., Can., Mex. Ch. Kyi Chu Friar Tuck ROM is the winner of 13 Bests in Show and two ALAC Specialties. Tuck is a past record holder for the breed and the top-winning parti color of all time. He was shown by Robert Sharp for owner Marvin Frank.

BIS Ch. Barcon's The Avenger, winner of the 1973 and 1974 Eastern ALAC Specialties is the son of BIS Ch. Everglo's Spark of Gold ROM and Barcon's Madam Eglantyne and is owned and bred by Barry and Connie Tompkins. He is shown winning one of his 14 Bests in Show this one under Dr. Malcolm Phelps, handled by his co-owner Dorothy Lohmann.

BIS Ch. Yojimbo Orion shown winning Best in Show at the San Gabriel Valley KC under Derek Rayne and handled by John Thyssen for breeder-owner Elaine Spaeth. "Ryan" is the son of Ch. Dolsa Yojimbo and Blackbay Sass A Fhrass. He won Best of Breed at the 1977 Western ALAC Specialty, and is the first Lhasa Apso to win the Group at Westminster.

Lhasa Apsos have been held in high esteem by Tibetan holy men for centuries. Even in modern times the breed is the special pet of Tibetan Buddhists. Here is the *Tara Tulku,* head of the Buddhist Tantric College, Dalhousie, India, with his Lhasa.

Kristen Wanni
Wannisky, CD

Hamilton Maroh in a playful mood at Hamilton Farms.

Europasieger (European champion) Dolsa Red Alert.

Three ge
Melodye H
UD, Cana
CD and C

102

Ch. Daktazl Tsung.

Ch. Yojimbo Orion (Ch. Dolsa Yojimbo ex Blackbay Sass A Fhrass), owned and bred by Elaine Spaeth, was the breed's standout winner during 1977 and into 1978. "Ryan's" record includes 14 Bests in Show, tieing the breed record, the 1977 Western ALAC Specialty and numerous Group 1sts and other placements. He is the first Lhasa to win the Group at Westminster, this historic achievement taking place in 1977 under judge C. L. Savage. He was also the winner of the Ken-L Award in 1977 for winning the most Non-Sporting Groups in the United States that year. This outstanding campaigner has been handled throughout his brilliant career by John R. Thyssen.

BIS Am. Can. Ch. Potala Keke's Yum Yum ROM was the winner of both the 1976 Eastern and Western ALAC Specialties. She is shown here with judge Robert Berndt, her handler Carolyn Herbel and her breeder-owner Keke Blumberg.

BIS Am., Can. Ch. Kyi Chu Shara ROM shown winning a Group under Heywood Hartley, handled by Jane Kay. Shara was bred by Terry Smith and owned by Keke Blumberg. She was Best of Breed at the 1967 ALAC Specialty, is a daughter of Ch. Karma Kanjur and Ch. Kyi Chu Kira, CD and is the dam of six champions.

Breed at the 1977 Western ALAC Specialty in Houston, Texas. He repeated his Westminster win in 1978 and went on to a Group 3rd.

Orion's sire is Ch. Dolsa Yojimbo bred by Jean Kausch, Dolsa Lhasa Apsos. Yojimbo's sire is Am., Can. Ch. Chen Krisna Nor ROM and his dam is Cordova Sin Sa ROM. Orion's dam is Blackbay Sass A Fhrass out of Ch. Orlane's Dulmo ROM and Tumuch Tusoon of Yin Hi I. Q. Orion's breeder and owner is Elaine Spaeth of Yojimbo Lhasa Apsos in Canoga Park, California. He has been handled throughout his illustrious career by John Thyssen.

The Best in Show Bitches

The story of the record holders for Bests in Show by bitches has been radically different from that of the males.

BIS Ch. Hamilton Torma won the first Best in Show in 1957 and even when her grandson BIS Ch. Licos Kulu La broke her record for any Lhasa Apso in 1961 her record for most Best in Shows for bitches remained. It was not even matched until 1966. Then in three successive years it was matched but not surpassed by three bitches.

BIS Can., Am. Ch. Kyi Chu Shara ROM owned by Mrs. Keke Blumberg went Best in Show at the Camden County Kennel Club show in December 1966.

She was whelped July 4, 1964. Her sire was Ch. Karma Kanjur of Hamilton background and her dam was Ch. Kyi Chu Kira, CD. Shara's maternal grandparents were Ch. Hamilton Jimpa and the productive Ch. Colarlie's Miss Shandha ROM. Shara has six champion offspring.

BIS Am., Can., Mex. Ch. San Saba Chi Chi Jimi won Best in Show on September 3, 1967 at the Mid Kentucky Kennel Club show.

Jimi, owned and handled by Mrs. Edna Voyles, was bred by Mrs. Bettye K. Scott. Her sire was Ch. Lui Gi Shigatzoo and her mother was Hamilton Chodon.

BIS Am., Can. Ch. Orlane's Good as Gold was the fourth to become a joint holder of the then record for bitches of one Best in Show. Mrs. Dorothy Kendall Lohmann owned and handled "Goody" who was whelped May 8, 1965. She won Best in Show at the Burlington Iowa Kennel Club show.

Her sire was Ch. Quetzal Feyla of Kyi Chu and her dam was Ch. Kai Sang's Flame of Everglo, the foundation bitch of Orlane Kennel. Flame's sire was Ch. Kai Sang's Clown of Everglo and her dam was Hamilton Norden.

Goody won Best of Breed at the 1969 Westminster Kennel Club show and also won four Bests in Show at Canadian shows.

BIS Ch. Kili's Katara of Ke-Tu is shown winning Best in Show at the Oakland Kennel Club show. She was handled by Marvin Cates for her breeders-owners Lisbeth C. and E. Kiefer Labenberg.

BIS Am., Can., Mex. Ch. San Saba Chi Chi Jimi is a daughter of Ch. Lui Gi's Shigatzoo and Hamilton Chodon. Jimi was bred by Bettye Kirksey Scott and was handled and owned by Mrs. Edna Voyles.

Torma's record, matched by Shara, Jimi and Goody, remained until June 1972 when BIS Ch. Kili's Katara of Ke Tu won Bests in Show on successive weekends at the San Joaquin and Contra Costa Kennel Club shows in California.

In the fall of that year BIS Am., Bda. Ch. Kinderland's Tonka ROM won three Bests in Show to become the new record holder.

Katara won a third Best in Show at the Oakland Kennel Club show in the spring of 1973 to tie Tonka. Later in the fall of that year Tonka won a fourth Best in Show at the Mohawk Valley Kennel Club show to become the undisputed record holder for bitches.

Katara was bred and owned by Lisbeth C. and E. Kiefer Labenberg of San Mateo, California. Her sire is Ch. Choshe Ke Tu of Pandan and her dam is Kili's Fol Dol.

Tonka was bred by Ellen Lonigro of Kinderland Kennel and owned by the authors. She was sired by BIS Ch. Tibet of Cornwallis ROM and her dam is Ch. Kinderland's Sang Po ROM.

Tonka's ROM title attests to her ability to produce. She is the dam of Group winning Ch. Tabu's King of Hearts ROM.

BIS Am. Can. Ch. Potala Keke's Yum Yum ROM was bred and owned by Mrs. Keke Blumberg and handled by Carolyn Herbel. Yum Yum was the top winning bitch for 1974, 1975 and 1976. She won Best of Breed at the 1974 Westminster Kennel Club show and at both the Eastern and Western 1976 American Lhasa Apso Club Specialties.

Ch. Tabu's Kiss Me Kate, litter sister to Ch. Tabu's King of Hearts ROM.

Multiple BIS Am., Can. Ch. Joi San's Gol-Den Mocca of Ky by Ch. Arborhill's Bhran-Dieh ex Chu Shu's Kiri, bred by Joyce Stambaugh, Joi San. He is pictured winning a Best in Show under Dr. T. Allen Kirk, Jr. He is owned by Jim and Annette Lurton (handling). His litter sister, Ch. Joi San's Khan Dieh, is the dam of over five champions, one a Group winner.

Multiple BIS Ch. Joi San's Happieh-Go-Luckieh, littermate of BIS Ch. Joi San's Gol-Den Mocca of Ky, owned and bred by Joyce and Jim Stambaugh, Joi San, is pictured winning Best of Breed at the Kentuckiana Lhasa Apso Club Specialty under Emil Klinckhardt, handled by Annette Lurton. It is believed that these two brothers are the only Best in Show littermates in the history of the breed.

109

Ch. Sharpette's Gaylord winner of the 1973 Western ALAC Specialty with his owner and handler Murray Teitelbaum. He was bred by Lucy C. Joyce and is the son of BIS Ch. Kyi Chu Friar Tuck ROM and Ch. Karma Ja Lu.

This record-making brace won eight Groups and six Best Brace in Show awards in 1977. They are Group winner Am., Can. Ch. Anbara's Abra-Ka-Dabra and Ch. Anbara's Ruffian shown winning under Mrs. Nicholas Demidoff and handled by their owner and co-breeder Barbara Wood. Their sire is multiple Group winner Am., Can. Ch. Rimar's Rumpelstiltskin and their dam is Ch. Rgyal Khetsa-Po ROM. They were co-bred by Stephen Campbell.

110

Multiple Group winner Ch. Everglo Zijuh Tomba with his handler John Brown. Tomba is the son of BIS Ch. Karma Frosty Knight O Everglo ROM and Kambu of Everglo. He is shown here winning a Group under the late Clara Alford. Tomba was the Best of Breed winner at the 1970 Western ALAC Specialty.

BIS Ch. Sharbo Topguy, a son of Group winner Ch. Everglo Zijuh Tomba and Ch. Sharbo Zijuh Tsa Chu, is the first black Lhasa Apso to win an all-breed Best in Show. Topguy is owned by Darby McSorley and shown with Carol Smith.

111

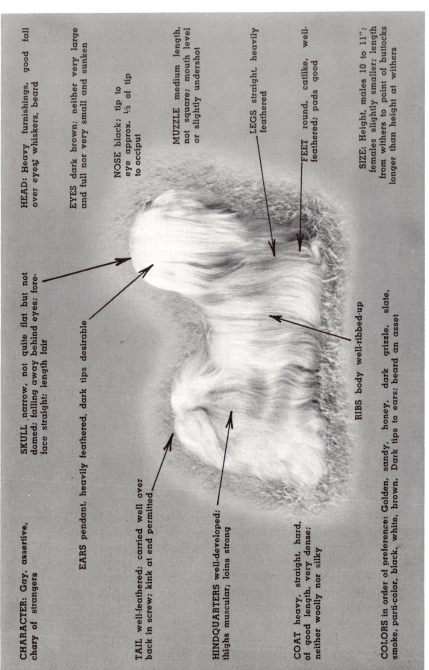

CHARACTER: Gay, assertive, chary of strangers

SKULL: narrow, not quite flat but not domed; falling away behind eyes; fore-face straight; length fair

HEAD: Heavy furnishings, good fall over eyes; whiskers, beard

EARS pendant, heavily feathered, dark tips desirable

EYES dark brown; neither very large and full nor very small and sunken

NOSE black; tip to eye approx. ⅓ of tip to occiput

MUZZLE medium length, not square; mouth level or slightly undershot

TAIL well-feathered: carried well over back in screw; kink at end permitted

LEGS straight, heavily feathered

HINDQUARTERS well-developed: thighs muscular; loins strong

FEET round, catlike, well-feathered; pads good

RIBS body well-ribbed-up

COAT heavy, straight, hard, of good length, very dense; neither woolly nor silky

SIZE: Height, males 10 to 11"; females slightly smaller; length from withers to point of buttocks longer than height at withers

COLORS in order of preference: Golden, sandy, honey, dark grizzle, slate, smoke, parti-color, black, white, brown. Dark tips to ears; beard an asset

Visualization of the Lhasa Apso Standard, reprinted with permission from Dog Standards Illustrated, © 1975, Howell Book House Inc.

112

5

Official Standard
of the Lhasa Apso

A BREED STANDARD is a definition of the ideal specimen of the breed described. It is a word pattern by which dogs of that breed are judged at shows. The American Kennel Club view is that a Standard of a given breed is not aimed at a person who has never seen a specimen of that breed. It is meant as a guide to help the person who has some familiarity with dogs in general and with the breed in particular.

Conversely, it is not an anatomical study which would enable one who had never seen a specimen of the breed to know exactly what that breed looks like.

When you read a Standard, remember that it is only an elementary description of a breed. It points out qualities that make the breed unique. It also indicates areas where judges should be alert for problems. Some detail may be necessary but too much detail is confusing. Judges find too much detail difficult to remember. Overemphasis may even cause unexpected problems.

Background of the Standard

The American breed Standard for Lhasa Apsos, approved April 9, 1935 and revised July 11, 1978 by the American Kennel Club, defines the ideal specimen of the breed for the United States of America. The Canadian Kennel Club Standard, currently in effect, is virtually the same as its American counterpart (except that measurements are expressed in the metric system). The Apso Standard on which many countries based their own Standards was the British version approved by the Kennel Club in 1934 when the Tibetan Breeds Association defined the various Tibetan breeds of dogs. The current British

113

Standard is the revised edition issued in 1973 by the English Lhasa Apso Club.

To clarify the significant similarities and differences in the two Standards, they are presented here in parallel columns. The sequence of the paragraphs is that of the American Standard. The paragraphs of the English Standard have been transposed so they are adjacent to their American counterparts.

The American Standard

Character—Gay and assertive, but chary of strangers.

Size—Variable but about 10 inches or 11 inches at shoulder for dogs, bitches slightly smaller.

Color—All colors equally acceptable with or without dark tips to ears and beard.

Body Shape—The length from point of shoulders to point of buttocks longer than height at withers, well ribbed up, strong loin, well-developed quarters and thighs.

Coat—Heavy, straight, hard, not woolly nor silky, of good length, and very dense.

Mouth and Muzzle—The preferred bite is either level or slightly undershot. Muzzle of medium length; a square muzzle is objectionable.

Head—Heavy head furnishings with good fall over eyes, good whiskers and beard; skull narrow, falling away behind the eyes in a marked degree, not quite flat,

The English Standard

Characteristics—The Apso should give the appearance of a well-balanced, solid dog. Gay and assertive, but chary of strangers. Free and jaunty in movement.

Size—Ideal height-10 inches at shoulder for dogs; bitches slightly smaller.

Colours—Golden, sandy, honey, dark grizzle, slate, smoke, parti-colour, black, white or brown.

Body—The length from point of shoulders to point of buttocks greater than height at withers. Well ribbed up. Level topline. Strong loin. Well balanced and compact.

Coat—Top coat heavy, straight and hard, not woolly or silky, of good length. Dense under-coat.

Mouth—Upper incisors should close just inside the lower, i.e., a reverse scissor bite. Incisors should be 'nearly' in a straight line. Full dentition is desirable.

Head and Skull—Heavy head furnishings with good fall over the eyes, good whiskers and beard. Skull moderately narrow, falling away behind the eyes in a marked

but not domed or apple-shaped; straight foreface of fair length. Nose black, the length from tip of nose to eye to be roughly about one-third of the total length from nose to back of skull.

Eyes—Dark brown, neither very large and full, nor very small and sunk.

Ears—Pendant, heavily feathered.

Legs—Forelegs straight; both forelegs and hind legs heavily furnished with hair.

Feet—Well feathered, should be round and catlike, with good pads.

Tail and Carriage—Well feathered, should be carried well over back in a screw, there may be a kink at the end. A low carriage of stern is a serious fault.

degree; not quite flat, but not domed or apple shaped. Straight foreface, with medium stop. Nose black. Muzzle about 1½ inches long, but not square; the length from tip of nose to be roughly one-third the total length from nose to back of skull.

Neck—Strong, well covered with a dense mane which is more pronounced in dogs than in bitches.

Eyes—Dark, medium sized, eyes eyes to be frontally placed, not large or full, or small and sunk. No white showing at base or top of eye.

Ears—Pendant, heavily feathered. Dark tips an asset.

Forequarters—Shoulders should be well laid back. Forelegs straight, heavily furnished with hair.

Hindquarters—Well developed with good muscle. Good angulation. Heavily furnished. The hocks when viewed from behind should be parallel and not too close together.

Feet—Round and cat-like, with good pads. Well feathered.

Tail—High set, carried well over back and not like a pothook. There is often a kink at the end. Well feathered.

Note—Male animals should have two apparently normal testicles fully descended into the scrotum.

Approved July 11, 1978

The Significance of Type

Now that you have seen the Lhasa Apso Standard in effect in the United States, Canada and England, it is necessary for you to understand how they relate to the term *type*.

The general definition of the word *type* is, "a kind, class or group that is distinguished by some particular characteristic; the general form, structure, style or characteristic common to or distinctive of a particular kind, class or group; a person or thing embodying the characteristic qualities of a kind, class or group; a representative specimen."

The biological definition of the word *type* is, "a form of being having the morphological (the form and structure of an organism considered as a whole) and physiological (the functions of the organs and parts of a living being) characteristics by which a number of individuals may be classified together."

Possibly a simpler sounding definition of the word *type* is "a genus or species that most nearly exemplifies the essential characteristics of a higher group; the one or more specimens on which the description and naming of a species is based."

We have labored to define the word because, in the language of the dog world, one of the most misused words is *type* perhaps because many fanciers and breeders *interpret* the word rather than *define* it. This is a polite way of saying that many who use the word really do not know what it means. More frequently than not the word is improperly used. All too often we hear the expression "that dog is not *my* type" or "is *my* type", as though the speaker were the authority specifying the essential characteristics of the breed. Sometimes correct movement is said to be "good type" or "typey". At other times elegance is equated to soundness or proper type. Those phrases conceal the fact that *at most* the speaker is stating *his preference* which may or may not coincide with the official description of the essential characteristics of the breed. Obviously a statement of preference is of value only to the extent of the speaker's knowledge, information and experience and all the other words on that subject hidden in the cliche "expertise."

Before written Standards, dog owners used to assemble and pit their dogs in a contest to determine their ability to perform the function for which they were bred (i.e. herding cattle, locating birds, flushing game, etc.). The dog which most consistently had the qualities to perform his allotted function had *type*. Time moved on and more people became interested in the different breeds so that it was no longer possible to rely on oral statements. Hence written statements or Standards came into use.

6

Blueprint of the
Lhasa Apso Standard

INTERPRETATION of the Standard is necessary to assist the novice to understand and the expert to recall all the component parts. The comments which follow are intended for that dual purpose.

Character

The first paragraphs of both the American and English Standards describe the character of the Lhasa Apso as *"gay and assertive, but chary of strangers."* Placement of this paragraph at the beginning of both Standards, when the *American Kennel Club Guide for Writing Standards* lists temperament last, shows that the character of the breed is of paramount importance.

The Standard states that the Lhasa Apso is *chary*. That word borrowed from the English Standard has caused confusion among Americans unaccustomed to the English precise use of language. The word has a multiplicity of connotations.

It means (1) careful, (2) wary, (3) shy of, but not shy, (4) fastidious and (5) sparing.

Any assumption that it means shy or cowardly is erroneous and overlooks some fine shades of meaning complimentary to the dog.

Careful has two basic but different definitions. Concern for something is one meaning. Watchfulness is the other. Lhasas have great concern and solicitude for their masters. They also exhibit watchfulness and caution with strangers, not out of concern for themselves, but from need of assurance that their masters will not be harmed.

As the word *wary* indicates, Lhasas are watchful and on their guard. Characteristically they are alert and cautious with strangers and their actions show it. They are not, however, shy in the sense of timid or afraid of strangers, but *shy of* or *wary* of them. They could not at the same time be both *assertive* on the one hand and timid on the other.

Fastidiousness is the fourth and often overlooked quality included in the term *chary*. Lhasas do exhibit that quality and like to keep clean.

Sparing, the fifth meaning of chary, has two different meanings (1) saving and (2) frugal. Frugality is well understood and more applicable to humans than dogs. *Saving* in addition to its religious meaning and its similarity to frugality means to rescue from danger, and to preserve and guard from destruction or loss. It emphasizes what has already been said about the breed.

It is necessary to track the meanings of the word *assertive* through a dictionary to obtain a clear understanding of the term. When this is done, it is evident that the draftsmen of the Standard meant to convey the idea of a fully assured animal prepared to defend its rights.

The Lhasa Apso is *gay* in the traditional sense of merry, bright and lively.

If our synopsis of the meaning of gay and assertive, but chary of strangers has not been as detailed as you would like, you will find that consultation of a large dictionary and Roget's Thesaurus as to these words and their synonyms will clear up all lingering doubts.

Size

Both the American and English Standards specify only the height objective under the heading of size.

The English Standard states the "Ideal height" is "10 inches at shoulder for dogs; bitches slightly smaller." Size, or rather height, in the American Standard is "variable, about 10 or 11 inches at shoulder for dogs; bitches slightly smaller."

This slight difference permits personal preference. Apparently, the English like a 10-inch dog and the Americans like one a little larger. Weight is not mentioned but is to be commensurate with a well muscled, strong, small, but not Toy-sized dog.

The language of both Standards shows that they only specify an objective and that there is permissible tolerance above and below the numbers specified. Precise size is of secondary importance as long as the dog has the other attributes of the breed. The Lhasa should not,

Group winner Ch. Gyal Kham-Nag of San Jo ROM is owned and bred by Marianne Nixon. He was born in 1960 and died in 1974. He was a multiple Best of Breed winner and the foundation sire for San Jo.

Ch. Ruffway Nor-Pa is a son of BIS Ch. Karma Frosty Knight O Everglo ROM and Ruffway Khambu. Nor-Pa was owned by Mildred Bryant and bred by Georgia Palmer and is the sire of at least five champions.

Ch. Milbryan Licos Gayla La was owned by Mildred Bryant and bred by Grace Licos and is the daughter of Ch. America's Leng Kong and Dama Lu's Country Fair.

BIS Am., Can. Ch. Arborhill's Rah-Kieh ROM is the son of BIS Ch. Arborhill's Rapso Dieh and Ch. Arborhill's Lhana ROM. He is owned by Darrell Smith and Dick Brown and bred by Sharon Binkowski.

however, vary more than one inch larger or smaller than the ideal stated in the Standard.

There is substantial range between the American Lhasa Apso's 10 to 11 inch height and the Tibetan Terrier's 14 to 16 inches. The current trend seems to be toward larger Lhasas. Our hope is that it will not continue and that the substantial range between the Lhasa Apso and Tibetan Terrier will be maintained. If we were given our preference, we would select one about 10½ inches which is an acceptable height within the American Standard.

Color

The words of the first phrase in the American Standard and the only phrase in the current English Standard are identical. They are:

"Golden, sandy, honey, dark grizzle, slate, smoke, parti-color, black, white or brown."

The second and third sentences of the American color paragraph read as follows:

"This being the true Tibetan Lion dog, golden or lion-like colors are preferred. Other colors in order as above."

The 1973 amendment to the English Standard deleted the second and third sentences calling for color preference and made all colors equally acceptable.

There is a movement to make a comparable change in the American Standard.

The color preference provision in the original English and current American Standard is confusing because it states that golden or lion-like colors are preferred because the Apso is the true Tibetan Lion dog.

In *Hutchinson's Dog Encyclopedia* part 31c, pages 1142–1146, published in England about the time the American and English Standards were being drafted, the Editor said:

The English fanciers who brought Apsos from China knew the breed there as Lion Dogs. That name is never used in Tibet.

Colour is not of primary importance. The pure golden is the most sought after and is very rare, next in favor is the honey colour, and then almost anything except black, except a little black on the tips of ears and beard is an asset.

These are statements of fact without a reason for them. They could have been completely true and needed no explanation.

Whatever the reason, the original draftsmen, being intelligent and informed individuals, probably had some basis for believing that the Tibetans had a preference for golden Apsos. It is our opinion that color preference should not take precedence over sound structure and breed type.

Ch. Cherryshore's Bah Rich Boi, the son of Ch. Kyi Chu Kaliph Noi and Ch. Cherryshore's Mah Dahm, is the sire of at least 26 champions.

Ch. Ruffway Kamet, bred and owned by Georgia Palmer, is the son of Americal's Sandar of Pamu and Karma Tagan.

Ch. Zijuh Seng Tru ROM was bred by Bea Loob and owned by C. R. and Onnie Martin. Seng Tru was the foundation sire for the Martins' Pandan Lhasas.

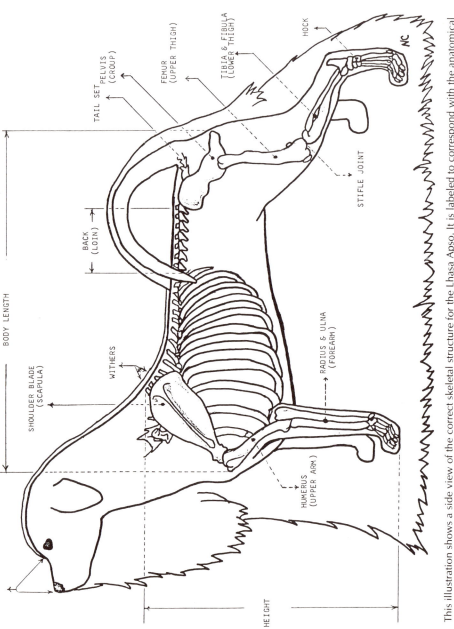

This illustration shows a side view of the correct skeletal structure for the Lhasa Apso. It is labeled to correspond with the anatomical terms as explained in sections of the Blueprint of the Standard.

122

Body Shape

The American Standard provides:

"The length from point of shoulders to point of buttocks longer than height at withers, well ribbed up, strong loin, well developed quarters and thighs."

In 1973 the amendments to the British Standard (1) made grammatical changes that need not concern us, (2) substituted the word "greater" for "longer" in the description of length, (3) added the phrase "level topline" and (4) made "well balanced and compact" an absolute requirement.

Body shape involves us in a study of the anatomy and locomotion of a Lhasa Apso. The Standard assumes that the reader has a substantial knowledge not only of the words used but also of dogs and other quadrupeds. We cannot look at Lhasa Apsos with tunnel vision and make any informed judgment about them. The Standard only sketches unique features of the breed against an assumed background of knowledge of dogs and other animals. Many Standards were written by men with a broad knowledge of dogs and horses who borrowed terms from the paddock and omitted express reference to concepts they thought were self-evident. Sadly, today many of those interested in particular breeds lack not only such knowledge but also an understanding of other breeds of dogs. This results in current misunderstanding of words included in Standards, words generally used by the dog fancy and of elementary concepts of animal structure and locomotion. Our purpose is to give you an elementary understanding of the Lhasa Apso's anatomy as a dog and not merely as a unique breed.

Turning back to the Body Shape paragraph of the Standard, it describes the length of the Lhasa measured from the *point of shoulders* to *point of buttocks* as longer than height at *withers*.

The *withers* is the highest point of the shoulders immediately behind the neck. The *point of the shoulders* is the articulation of the upper arm (humerus) and the shoulder blade (scapula). *Buttocks* are the hips or articulation of the pelvis and femur.

The Size paragraph has established the ideal height at that point as 10 to 11 inches, with further provision for variation and bitches slightly smaller. We prefer the ratio of 7.5 to 10. This means that our preference for height of 10½ inches at the withers requires the length to be 14 inches.

The American Kennel Club Guide for Writing Standards suggests that the size of a dog should be described in inches at the highest point of the shoulder blades, as the Lhasa Apso Standard does, rather than in pounds. Hence any attempt to conjecture concerning ideal weight is

Ch. Americal's Leng Kong, 1953, Grace Licos' first Lhasa Apso and the sire of the famous record holder BIS Ch. Licos Kulu La. He is a son of Ch. Hamilton Tsang and Hamilton Suchau.

Ch. Dixie's Beau of Everglo, a son of Ch. Licos Chulung La and Everglo Buttercup, is owned by David Marshall and Jack Russell, Maru.

Ch. Hamilton Katha, full sister of Ch. Hamilton Sandupa, was Best of Breed at the 1960 Westminster KC show.

gratuitous; however, overweight dogs tend to have more difficulty functioning than do trim, well-muscled dogs.

The English, but not the American Standard, also calls for the dog to be "well balanced and compact." *Compact* according to the AKC Glossary means "*short-bodied* or cobby." Since the American definition of compact is contrary to our present Standard requirements it would be undesirable here and is properly omitted from the American Standard. Without full knowledge of English usage of those words no comment is made on their propriety in the English Standard.

Next, both Standards call for the dog to be *well ribbed up*. That phrase comes from the paddock and applies to the last or floating rib. If the last rib springs well from the spinal column, angles backward at 45 degrees and has good length, the other ribs usually follow the same pattern. The arc formed by a well sprung rib should be similar to the arc formed by a football shape rather than a basketball shape. The circle or basketball shape represents the undesirable barrel chest.

The 1973 amendment of the Body paragraph of the English Standard added the phrase *level topline* apparently as a matter of structure and not as a description of appearance during motion. Again no comment is made on that phrase as used in the English Standard. In America it is inexact and misleading from the point that the AKC has not defined the term. If the phrase *level topline* was to be included in the American Standard it would have to be clarified so that it meant to call attention to the improper rise and fall of the withers of a defectively built dog. It should be made clear that the words were not used to describe structure standing, but to specify a characteristic of movement.

A *strong loin* refers to the "region of the body on either side of the vertebral column between the last ribs and the hindquarters." That is between the thoracic section and the pelvis or croup. The loin has seven vertebrae with their processes slanting forward to support the muscles of that part which pull rearward. The shoulder muscles pull forward. The drive of the back legs passes through this section. Hence strong muscles are needed here to prevent an undesirable roach or soft back.

Finally, the American Standard calls for *well developed quarters and thighs*. The word *thigh,* according to the AKC Glossary, means hindquarters from hip to stifle. That subject in the Hindquarters paragraph of the English Standard will be discussed here.

To understand the thigh it is necessary to consider the combined assemblies of the back legs and croup. The foundation of the back leg drive is the pelvis or croup. The function of the rear assembly is not weight support but power generation.

From the top down the rear assembly is: (1) pelvis or croup (sacrum vertebrae), (2) upper thigh (femur), (3) stifle joint or knee (patella), (4) lower thigh (tibia and fibula), (5) hock assembly and (6) foot.

The pelvis consists of three bones fused together on each side of and fastened to the spinal column where it forms the *croup*. The proper slope of the croup to develop the greatest power is thirty degrees to the horizontal.

The femur is attached to the pelvis in a ball and socket joint. The femur extends downward and forward to the stifle joint. The stifle joint is the dog's knee. It is the joint between the upper thigh and lower thigh. A well bent stifle is one in which the inside angle between the upper thigh and lower thigh is about 90 degrees, regardless of the croup angle.

The lower thigh consisting of the tibia and fibula, extends from the stifle to the hock joint.

The hock is the area between the lower thigh and the foot; the dog's true heel. It should be perpendicular to the ground. Hocks that are well let down, a term synonymous with hocks close to the ground, means

BIS Ch. Windsong's Gusto of Innsbrook is the son of Ch. Annie's Golden Fluff ROM and Cajohn's Buf-Fieh of Windsong ROM and is owned by Dr. and Mrs. John Lang, Innsbrook, and bred by Shirley Ruth, Windsong. He is shown winning Best of Breed at the Lhasa Apso Club of Greater Houston Specialty under Dorothy Nickles, handler Dorothy Kendall Lohmann.

Multiple Best in Show winner Am., Can., Bda. Ch. On-Ba Khabhul Khan of Sharbo is a son of BIS Ch. Sharbo Zijuh Zer Khan ROM and Zijuh On-Ba Zim Zim. He is co-owned by Dorothy O'Connor (pictured) and Noel Benson and is handled by John Murdock.

there is a relatively short distance between the hock joint and the ground, which reduces the leverage on the Achilles tendon and lessens fatigue.

The foregoing summarizes the meaning of well developed thighs and their relationship to the rest of the rear assembly.

You will note the English Standard states, "Hocks strong and parallel when viewed from behind." The American Standard does not include this phrase, which is apparently designed to make clear that hocks should not be turned in or out. No comment is made upon its use in the English Standard. Its limitations to the standing animal may be understood in that country.

A standing dog is supported by all four legs with the pads planted at the corners of a quadrangle. The support by all four legs does not appear at any time when the dog is moving. As the speed of a moving dog increases the legs gradually angle inward until the pads are finally falling on a line directly under the longitudinal center of the body. Its hind legs form a "V" with the hips as the upper points and the pad marks as the apex of the "V" on the ground. The legs slant from the hips to the ground as the dog moves faster but the hocks should turn neither in nor out.

As the result of the 1973 amendments to the English Standard the phrase *good angulation* was added only to the Hindquarters section.

127

Coat

The coat section of the American Standard reads as follows:
"Coat-Heavy, straight, hard, not woolly nor silky, of good length, and very dense."

It is one of the few sections in the Standard which does not use a single word that has a special meaning to the dog fancy or presuppose some background acquired only after interest in dogs has developed. Here the words speak for themselves.

Originally the American and English Standards were the same. The English Standard has, however, been amended to call for two coats, a top coat described as in the original Coat section and a dense undercoat. A similar amendment was discussed in this country in late 1976 and early 1977 but apparently has been abandoned. Calling for a double coat as a new requirement more than forty years after the breed Standard was issued places a heavy burden of justification upon those who would urge it.

Ms. Ellie Baumann has stated the problem very well in *Lhasa Tales* (September 1974 pages 8–9):

We should be wary of producing animals whose greatest asset is also their greatest liability . . . My feeling is that we should breed for the long coats that are heavy enough to weigh themselves down straight, and yet hard enough to groom easily. As for density, I feel that the next step is "impossibility!" We want to keep something comfortable for those loving pet companions. We must take serious thought about the practicality of breeding for more and denser coat or owning a Lhasa will become a burden instead of a pleasure.

Mouth and Muzzle

The first sentence of the Mouth and Muzzle section of the current American Standard reads as follows:
"Mouth level, otherwise slightly undershot preferable."

In England the original Mouth section read substantially the same. The amended English Standard revised this section to insure that the dog would be slightly undershot so that such bite was given the name, reverse scissors bite, and made the only permissible bite for an English Lhasa Apso.

It is incorrect to assume that the word *mouth* is always synonymous with the word *bite*. There is strong evidence that the phrase *mouth level,* standing alone, connotes that scissors and level bites are both acceptable under the full meaning of that term. Only when there is an acceptable variation will there be an inclusion of that variation.

Canadian BIS Am., Can. Ch. Balrene's Chia Pao is the son of Ch. Carroll Panda and Ch. Licos Yarto La. He won Best of Breed at the 1971 Eastern ALAC Specialty handled by his breeder-owner Dr. Ellen Brown.

Ch. Licos Namni La ROM, a younger brother of Ch. Licos Cheti La, owned by Raena Wilks.

It is the belief of the authors that the phrase, "Mouth level, otherwise slightly undershot preferable." means:

Mouth level, (i.e. level or scissors bites equally acceptable), if these bites are not present, then a slightly undershot bite is preferable to a grossly undershot or overshot bite.

Found in the Head section of the current English Standard, immediately following "muzzle about 1½ inches long", is the phrase "but not square." The American Standard states, "a square muzzle is objectionable." These statements in both Standards agree that a square muzzle is undesirable.

According to the AKC Glossary the definition of muzzle is:

"The head in front of the eyes—nasal bone, nostrils, and jaws. Foreface."

According to the dictionary square means:

"A four sided plane figure having all its sides equal and all its angles right angles."

We conclude from these definitions that no matter what view one takes (top, frontal or side) the muzzle should not appear square. This means the underlying bone structure and should not be confused with the illusion given by good whiskers and beard.

Head

The italicized words in the Head paragraph quoted below have a special meaning in the AKC Glossary. We have followed the quotation with such definitions.

The paragraph reads as follows:

"Heavy head furnishings with good *fall* over eyes, good *whiskers* and *beard;* skull narrow, falling away behind the eyes in a marked degree, not quite flat, but not *domed* or *apple-shaped;* straight *foreface* of fair length. *Nose* black, about 1½ inches long or the length from tip of *nose* to eye to be roughly about one-third of the total length from *nose* to back of skull."

Here are the definitions of the underlined words:

"*Fall:* Hair overhanging the face."

"*Whiskers:* Longer hairs on muzzle sides and underjaw."

"*Muzzle:* The head in front of the eyes—nasal bone, nostrils, and jaws. Foreface."

"*Beard:* Thick, long hair growth on the underjaw."

"*Domed:* Evenly rounded in topskull; convex instead of flat. Domy."

"*Apple head:* An irregular roundedness of topskull; in greater or less degree humped toward its center."

"*Foreface:* The front part of the head, before the eyes. Muzzle."

"*Nose:* Organ of smell."

There are two significant differences between the American and English Head paragraphs.

Ch. Licos Omorfo La, son of BIS Ch. Licos Kulu La and Ch. Hamilton Pluti, is the sire of at least eight champions.

Ch. Shenji's Miss Kachika of Chen ROM is another of the Chen Register of Merit bitches with four champions to her credit.

Ch. Milbryan Snazzi-Nor now owned by Jan Seamans of Dallas is a daughter of Ch. Ruffway Nor-Pa and Ch. Quizas Shanzzi Tu.

Licos Gia La is the dam of Ch. Chen Nyun Ti ROM. She is a daughter of Ch. Licos Chulung La and Ch. Hamilton Pluti. Her breeder is Grace Licos and she is owned by Patricia Chenoweth.

First, the English Standard has included the word "moderately" in the phrase, "skull moderately narrow" by the 1973 amendment. Inclusion of that word makes it clear that the English prefer a broader skull than the American Standard requires.

Second, the 1973 amendment to the English Standard included the phrase "medium stop." We reserve comment on that inclusion as we are not familiar with its relation to current English problems.

It is, however, the opinion of the authors that ambiguous words such as medium and moderate are not precise enough to add any degree of clarification.

Both the current English and American Standards ask for the muzzle to be about 1½ inches long. The Standards not only state an ideal length but also with the word *about* make provision for a slight variance. The 1½ inch requirement has two very significant implications: (1) it further distinguishes the Lhasa Apso from the Tibetan Terrier and the Shih Tzu, and (2) it states a definite measurement which is designed as a safety valve to control size.

Nature tends to produce balance and symmetry; therefore, if the length of muzzle changes the remainder of the animal tends to follow that change. It is especially important in the case of the Lhasa Apso since in its country of origin there was evidence of a variation in size in the Apso breed. The Western World has attempted to make the Lhasa Apso a specific breed and the 1½ inch muzzle requirement is an integral part of the Lhasa Apso Standard.

We found the comparative chart on pages 134-5 of the Standards' paragraphs relating to the head of the Lhasa Apso, Tibetan Terrier, Shih Tzu and Pekingese helps to differentiate the Lhasa Apso from the other breeds.

Ch. Karma Ami Chiri is the daughter of Hamilton Shi Pon and Ch. Hamilton Karma. Bred by Dorothy Cohen and owned by Robert Sharp.

Ch. Dandi's Golden Nugget is the son of Ch. Crest-O-Lake Kin Go ROM and Dandi's Blu Voo Doo and is owned and bred by Diane Dansereau.

Ch. Kye Ho of Everglo, daughter of Ch. Karma Frosty Knight O Everglo and Hamilton Norden.

Ch. Dandi Jin Rik'i, CDX, by Ch. Sugarplum's Number One Son out of Dandi Golden Gypsy of Everglo ROM, is owned and bred by Diane Dansereau. Rik'i was obedience trained and handled by Mrs. E. Schulman.

A COMPARISON OF HEADS BY THEIR STANDARDS

Lhasa Apso

Mouth and Muzzle—The preferred bite is either level or slightly undershot. Muzzle of medium length; a square muzzle is objectionable.

Head—Heavy head furnishings with good fall over eyes, good whiskers and beard; skull narrow, falling away behind the eyes in a marked degree, not quite flat, but not domed or apple-shaped; straight foreface of fair length. Nose black, the length from tip of nose to eye to be roughly about one-third of the total length from nose to back of skull.

Eyes—Dark brown, neither very large and full, nor very small and sunk.

Ears—Pendant, heavily feathered.

Shih Tzu

Head—Broad and round, wide between the eyes. Muzzle square short, but not wrinkled, about one inch from tip of nose to stop. *Definite Stop. Eyes*— Large, dark and round but not prominent placed well apart. Eyes should show warm expression. *Ears*—Large, with long leathers, and carried drooping; set slightly below the crown of the skull; so heavily coated that they appear to blend with the hair of the neck. *Teeth*—level or slightly undershot bite.

Faults—Narrow head, overshot bite, snikiness, pink on nose or eye rims, small or light eyes, legginess, sparse coat, lack of definite stop.

134

A COMPARISON OF HEADS BY THEIR STANDARDS

Pekingese

Skull—Massive, broad, wide and flat between the ears (not dome-shaped), wide between the eyes. *Nose*—Black, broad, very short and flat. *Eyes*—Large, dark, prominent, round, lustrous. *Stop*—Deep. *Ears*—Heart-shaped, not set too high, leather never long enough to come below the muzzle, nor carried erect, but rather drooping, long feather. *Muzzle*—Wrinkled, very short and broad, not overshot nor pointed. Strong, broad underjaw, teeth not to show.

Faults—Protruding tongue, badly blemished eye, overshot, wry mouth.

Disqualifications

Dudley nose.

Tibetan Terrier

Skull and Head—Skull of medium length, not broad or coarse, narrowing slightly from ear to eye, not domed but not absolutely flat between the ears. The malar bones are curved, but should not be overdeveloped so as to bulge. There should be a marked stop in front of the eyes, but this must not be exaggerated. The head should be well furnished with long hair, falling forward over the eyes. The lower jaw should carry a small but not over-exaggerated amount of beard. Jaws between the canines should form a distinct curve The length from the eye to tip of nose should be equal to that from eye to base of skull, not broad or massive.

Nose—Black. Any color other than black shall disqualify.

Eyes—Large, dark, neither prominent nor sunken; should be set fairly wide apart. Eyelids dark.

Ears—Pendant, not too close to the head "V"-shaped, not too large; heavily feathered.

Mouth—Level by preference but a slight undershot should not be penalized.

Faults—Poor coat; mouth very undershot or overshot; a weak snipy foreface.

Disqualification

Nose any color other than black.

The current English Standard contains the following section: "Neck-strong, well covered with dense mane which is more pronounced in dogs than in bitches." We make no comment because we are not aware of the significance of this statement.

Eyes

The American and the original English Standards are substantially the same. Each called for "eyes dark, neither very large and full, nor very small and sunk." The American Standard also described the eyes as dark *brown*.

In 1973 the English Standard was amended to require "no white showing at base or top of eye" and the eyes "to be frontally placed."

It is the opinion of the authors that these changes, in America, would be insignificant, and by their inclusion, would be elevated to a position of importance that they do not warrant. Possibly there are needs for such changes in England, but we are not aware of them.

Ears

Both the American and English Standards describe ears as, "pendant, heavily feathered."

The AKC Glossary defines feathering as a longer fringe of hair on ears, legs and tail. Little can be added to the Standard's language.

Legs

The American Standard states:
"Forelegs straight; both forelegs and hind legs heavily furnished with hair."

In 1973 the Forequarters section of the English Standard was amended to provide also that the forelegs must not only be straight but also the shoulders must be well laid back.

We assume that the inclusion of this phrase is referring to the proper 45 degree angle of the shoulder blade.

The American Standard states that the forelegs are to be straight. This reference to bone structure tells us that the front of a Lhasa Apso is a normal canine front rather than a low center of gravity front like that of a Dachshund or Bulldog.

Feet

Both the American and English Standards call for feet which are round and catlike with good pads and well feathered. According to the AKC Glossary a cat foot is, "The short, round, compact foot like that of a cat. The foot with short third digits."

Int. Ch. Troubadour de Gandamak (France) on a 17th Century prayer table.

Ch. Sharbo Topguy with handler Carol Smith.

Ch. Chen Krishna Nor with co-owner Wendy Har

Ch. Everglo Sundance with handler Marvin Cates.

Ch. Ahisma A Tantras with handler Carolyn Herbel.

Ch. Karma Kushog with Darby McSorley.

ʰ. Tabu's Appleseed Annie with owner Susan Gehr.

Ch. Tabu's Bric A Brac, owned by Charles and Barbara Steele and handled by Carmen Herbel, is shown winning under judge Leota Vandeventer.

Ch. Anbara's Abra-Ka-Dabra and Ch. Anbara's Ruffian, owned and handled by Barabara Wood, were Best Brace in Show six times during 1977. They are shown making one of these wins at the Farmington Valley KC under judge Lorna B. Demidoff.

Ch. Arborhill's Bhran-Dieh, owned by Shirley Ruth, shown in a win under judge George Payton, handler Thelma Sloan.

Ch. Tabu's Miss Chimney Sweep, owned and handled by Nancy Clarke, was BW at Westminster enroute to her championship. The judge was Edd Embry Bivin.

Ch. Potala Keke's Tomba Tu, owned and bred by Keke Blumberg, is shown winning BB at Queensboro under Katherine E. Gately, handler Carmen Herbel.

Ch. Balrene Chia Pao with his owner-breeder-handler, Ellen Brown.

Ch. Potala Keke's Golden Gatsby, owned by Barbara Chevalier, is shown winning the Non-Sporting Group at Quebec under judge A. Peter Knoop, handler Garrett Lambert.

Tabu's Jazz Man, bred, owned and handled by Carolyn Herbel.

Ch. Potala Keke's Kelana, owned by Jeanne and John Hope and shown with handler Carolyn Herbel.

Ch. Tabu's Fame and Fortune, owned by Gerri and Ann Goldberg, shown winning under Dr. Harold Huggins, handler Carmen Herbel.

Ch. Everglo Zijuh Tomba (left) winning a stud dog class under judge Graham Head. Tomba was handled by Sharon Rouse. His progeny shown are Ch. Sharbo Topguy (center) with Darby McSorley and Ch. Sharbo Me-Shanda Ba with Lynn Morgan.

144

The front view illustrates the correct position of the legs standing and the broken lines illustrate the position of the legs during movement. Note converging pattern.

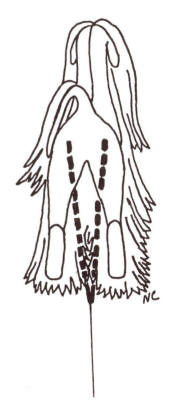

The rear view illustrates the correct position of the legs and hocks standing, and the broken lines illustrate the position of the legs during movement.

145

Tail and Carriage

The American Standard states: "Well feathered, should be carried well over back in a screw, there may be a kink at the end. A low carriage of stern is a serious fault."

The English Standard states: "Tail-high set, carried well over back and not like a pothook. There is often a kink at the end. Well feathered."

Both Standards provide that the tail should be carried well over the back and may have a kink at the end. The American Standard further states that the tail should be carried well over the back in a screw. The English Standard, although also requiring the tail to be carried well over the back, further specifies that it shall not be like a pothook. The American Standard finally provides that low carriage of stern is a serious fault. Apparently the American Standard has used the word "stern", which usually means the tail of a sporting dog or hound, to describe the tail of a Lhasa.

Movement in the Lhasa Apso

The American Standard's silence on describing movement means that the Lhasa Apso should have normal canine movement as judged by the trot. The normal canine movement is not restricted by exceptions like the slight roll required for the Pekingese; the short, stilted gait of the Chow Chow; the slightly rolling gait of the Shih Tzu; the ambling or pacing movement of the Old English Sheepdog or the Hackney gait of the Miniature Pinscher. These variances from the norm are created by exceptions to the normal canine structure which are not provided for in the Lhasa Apso Standard.

The perfect Lhasa Apso does not exist and perfection is somewhat in the eyes of the beholder. However, we hope that this blueprint of the Standard will help readers recognize the more nearly perfect specimens of the breed.

Comments on the July 1978 Revision of the Standard

Color:

The July 1978 revision to the American Lhasa Apso Standard has made all colors equal. It is the opinion of your authors that this change was good because it correctly places emphasis on sound structure and breed type rather than on color.

146

Mouth and Muzzle:

The July 1978 revision to the American Lhasa Apso Standard has substituted the word bite for mouth, therefore, eliminating any description of the jaw or mouth. It has also stated the two *preferred* bites but in doing so has made all bites, including the overshot bite (pig jaw) acceptable. It is the opinion of your authors that this change should have been accompanied with a statement of fault for the overshot or pig jaw.

Head:

The July 1978 revision to the American Lhasa Apso Standard has deleted the words, "about 1½ inches long, or". It is the opinion of your authors that this change could have a bad effect on the head structure of the Lhasa Apso, one of the most important characteristics distinguishing the breed's type. Lhasa Apso breeders must be careful not to let the one-third measurement be distorted so that we have Lhasa Apsos with ½ inch muzzles and one inch skulls or two inch muzzles and four inch skulls.

Ch. Chulung of Garten is a son of Ch. Kash Gar of Garten and Ch. Chu Chu La of Garten, a daughter of Ch. Licos Chulung La, bred and owned by Isabelle Loyd.

Ch. Tabu's Bronze Bonanza owned by Martin and Elaine Fisher is the proud mother of this week-old litter.

Lhasa Apso puppies at two weeks of age.

7

Choosing a Lhasa Apso Puppy

SELECTING A PUPPY for your family requires careful research. The puppy you select will hopefully be a member of your family for at least ten years or more. The more carefully you plan before making your selection the more likely it is that you will avoid the disappointment of having to live with a dog that does not suit your household.

Before you look at any puppies, look at your environment and try to visualize it containing an adult dog of the breed you are considering.

First Considerations

If the Lhasa Apso is the breed of your choice consider its characteristics so that your final selection will not be a mistake. The responsibility of maintaining the long coat may be a liability to an extremely busy, active family. The Lhasa is a hardy breed but should not be considered either a stuffed toy or a wrestling partner for young children. Although a small dog, the Lhasa will require the same discipline and training as a large dog. If, after considering these characteristics, you and your family have decided upon the Lhasa Apso it is time to select your individual puppy.

149

Mrs. Mildred Bryant, Milbryan, with an armful of Lhasa Apso puppies. These are about a month old.

Ch. Americal's Torma Lu pictured here at eight weeks. This picture appeared on the cover of the October, 1967 *American Kennel Gazette.*

Ch. Licos Namni La ROM at six weeks of age. Namni La is owned by Miss Raena Wilks of New York City. His breeder is Mrs. Grace Licos.

150

A litter of six golden nine-week-old puppies by Ch. Licos Omorfo La ex Ch. Kyi Chu Kara Nor ROM.

These puppies are between 12 and 13 weeks old. They are out of Ch. Tabu's Rags to Riches and Goldmere Dharma.

This litter is by Ch. Chen Krisna Nor ROM ex Cordova Sinsa ROM. This is the typical look of a Lhasa puppy between 12 and 16 weeks.

151

Finding the Right Puppy

It is advantageous and enjoyable to be able to see one or both of a puppy's parents and at some kennels you may even see grandparents, aunts, uncles and cousins. Observation of its relatives can give you an insight as to the temperament and stableness you may expect from your puppy.

The Lhasa Apso is a breed noted for longevity, therefore, it is usually slower to mature than many other breeds. Because of slow maturity Lhasa puppies should not go to new homes until they are at least twelve weeks old.

Male or Female

Your selection of sex is not important as both sexes make excellent pets and companions. Assuming that you are buying your Lhasa as a family pet it may be advisable to have him castrated or her spayed. The altering of your female pet will eliminate the twice-yearly job of keeping her confined for three weeks while she is in season. A male will not be inclined to roam in search of a female if he has been altered.

The matter of reproducing the Lhasa Apso should be the responsibility of the experienced, knowledgeable and properly equipped breeder.

What to Look For

It is difficult to tell much about a very young puppy except that it appears to be healthy. A healthy puppy should be alert, lively, and plump, but not pot-bellied. A pot-belly may be a sign of poor nutrition or worms. The healthy puppy will have clear eyes with no discharge. His ears should be clean and free of irritation. The skin and coat should be clean with no signs of parasites. Beware of the puppy that has a runny nose and eyes.

Temperament is very important and should be considered strongly when making your selection. The proper attitude for young Lhasa puppies is happy, friendly and outgoing. As the puppies get older they will begin to show the aloof reserve with strangers that is typical of the adult Lhasa Apso temperament.

Sometime between twelve and sixteen weeks you can catch a glimpse of what the puppy promises to be structurally; but you must have considerable knowledge of and experience with dogs generally and the breed specifically to be able to make a lasting evaluation as to show quality.

For the next few months the puppy goes through a series of constantly changing, somewhat awkward stages. Then between eight

Tn Hi Hapki Barnaby at nine months of age. He is by Ch. Tn Hi Lammi Po Kah and Ch. Tn Hi Pahti Shyshy. Barnaby is owned and bred by Joyce Hadden of Tn Hi Kennel.

Tabu's Beau Raintree at just under six months of age.

and twelve months an expert can give you a reasonably valid opinion about the dog's structural potential as a show dog.

If you are looking for a show puppy, you will obviously want to wait until the puppy is at least twelve to sixteen weeks old and will not make a choice then without help. Preferably you will wait until the puppies you are considering are between eight and twelve months old.

While it is true that the older the puppy the higher the price may be, the increase in price is what you are paying for more probability of success when you begin to show.

If you are buying Lhasa Apso with the intention of your conformation showing, we suggest that you check the animal against the breed Standard set forth in Chapter V and the Blueprint in Chapter VI and try to make an informed judgement as to how he or she measures up to the Standard requirements.

For your convenience we have listed some of the ratios, measurements and angles we use in evaluating the structure of our Lhasa Apsos.

The following is meant as a guide to be used in conjunction with the Standard and to evaluate adults or nearly full grown puppies while standing still. (Illustration A)

1. Height of 10½ inches at top of shoulder (withers) for a dog, a bitch slightly smaller.

2. Ratio of the length of body from point of shoulders to point of buttocks to the height at withers is 10:7.5.

3. Muzzle about 1½ inches long.

4. Ratio of length of muzzle (from tip of nose to eye) to length of skull is 1:2.

5. Ratio of length of head from muzzle to back of skull to length of body is 1:3.

6. Length of neck and head from point of attachment of neck to body is slightly less than height at the withers.

7. Length of neck from point of attachment of neck to body to base of skull slightly less than length of head.

8. Angle of neck approximately 90 degrees to shoulder blade.

9. Angle of layback of the shoulder blade 45 degrees to a horizontal.

10. Angle of upper arm 90 degrees to shoulder blade.

11. Length of upper arm nearly as long as length of shoulder blade.

12. Front legs perpendicular to a horizontal base.

13. Angle of tibia and fibula 90 degrees to femur. (i.e. stifle joint)

14. Hock perpendicular to ground.

15. Tail set straight above articulation (joint) of pelvis and femur.

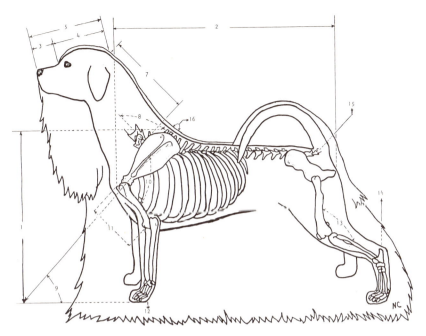

Illustration A: Ratios, angles and measurements used in evaluating structure.

Illustration B: A Lhasa Apso with proper structure should give this appearance.

16. Withers is the highest point in the top line which slopes gradually back to the croup.

The final test for proper structure is to observe the dog moving at a trot. If he appears to move like the dog in Illustration B it means that he has the proper ratios, angles and measurements enumerated above.

Essential Documents

Purchasers of a show puppy generally are looking into the future to the time their Lhasa will be bred. For this reason it is important to request the explanation of the puppy's pedigree. You should be supplied with this document, along with the official American Kennel Club registration form, when you buy your puppy.

The pedigree is not an official document of registration but is a record of your puppy's ancestors. When the time comes for mating your Lhasa, the pedigree will be an invaluable aid in the selection of a proper mate. You should, however, learn as much as possible about the dogs appearing in the pedigree long before breeding; their strong and weak breeding points.

Do not forget to ask for health records so that you can supply your veterinarian with this information and keep his records complete for your dog.

Whether you are selecting your Lhasa Apso puppy for a pet, a show dog or both, remember that a healthy, structurally and mentally sound puppy will be more easily trained to fit into your environment as the companion dog the Lhasa Apso was developed to be.

When you buy a dog that is represented as being eligible for registration with The American Kennel Club, you are entitled to receive an AKC application form properly filled out by the seller, which—when completed by you and submitted to the AKC with the proper fee—will enable you to effect the registration of the dog. (*See Pages 157 through 159.*) When the application has been processed, you will receive an AKC registration certificate.

Under AKC rules, any person who sells dogs that are represented as being AKC registrable, must maintain records that will make it possible to give full identifying information with every dog delivered, even though AKC papers may not yet be available. *Do not accept a promise of later identification.*

The Rules and Regulations of The American Kennel Club stipulate that whenever someone sells or delivers a dog that is said to be

owner of dog. Fee ($4.) must accompany application. Use this form for recording ORIGINAL transfer only - for subsequent transfers, use Supplemental Transfer Statement (see p. 18).

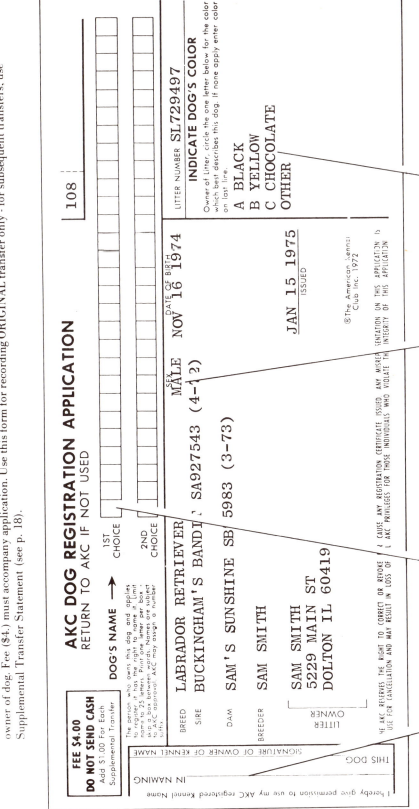

| | 108 |

AKC DOG REGISTRATION APPLICATION
RETURN TO AKC IF NOT USED

FEE $4.00
DO NOT SEND CASH
Add $1.00 For Each
Supplemental Transfer

DOG'S NAME →

The person who owns this dog and applies to register it has the right to name it. Limit name to 25 letters. Print one letter per box - skip a box between words. Names are subject to AKC approval. AKC may assign a number suffix.

1ST CHOICE

2ND CHOICE

If you own a registered name prefix and are granting permission to use the prefix, complete this section. If your prefix is not registered, leave this section blank.

BREED   LABRADOR RETRIEVER

SIRE   BUCKINGHAM'S BANDIT   SA927543   (4-72)

DAM   SAM'S SUNSHINE   SB 5983   (3-73)

BREEDER   SAM SMITH

LITTER OWNER

SAM SMITH
5229 MAIN ST
DOLTON IL 60419

Person who registers dog has right to name it. Indicate TWO unique name choices. Choices may not contain a Roman or Arabic numeral; AKC reserves right to assign Roman numeral if necessary.

SEX
MALE (4-12)

DATE OF BIRTH
NOV 16 1974

JAN 15 1975
ISSUED

©The American Kennel Club Inc. 1972

[...] CAUSE ANY REGISTRATION CERTIFICATE ISSUED ANY MISREPRESENTATION ON THIS APPLICATION IS [...] AKC PRIVILEGES FOR THOSE INDIVIDUALS WHO VIOLATE THE INTEGRITY OF THIS APPLICATION

THE AKC RESERVES THE RIGHT TO CORRECT OR REVOKE [...] USE FOR CANCELLATION AND MAY RESULT IN LOSS OF

Litter owner should check sex specified on the face of the application. to be sure it corresponds to sex of dog being transferred.

LITTER NUMBER SL729497

INDICATE DOG'S COLOR

Owner of Litter, circle the one letter below for the color which best describes this dog. If none apply enter color on last line.

A BLACK
B YELLOW
C CHOCOLATE
OTHER

Litter owner should indicate color by circling color that most closely resembles PRESENT color of dog.

SIGNATURE OF OWNER OF KENNEL NAME

IN NAMING
THIS DOG

I hereby give permission to use my AKC registered Kennel Name

Reverse side of blue application form. In buying a dog, do not accept an application that has not been properly completed in Section "A" by the litter owner.

INSTRUCTIONS: PLEASE TYPE – OR USE PEN. NO PENCIL. Erasures or Corrections may cause return of application for an explanation.

SEC. A

MUST BE COMPLETED IN FULL and SIGNED BY OWNER OF LITTER (AND CO-OWNER, IF ANY) SHOWN ON REVERSE SIDE.

ONE box MUST BE checked

☐ I (we) still own this dog, and I (we) apply to The American Kennel Club to register it and have ownership recorded in my (our) name(s).

☒ I (we) certify that this dog was transferred DIRECTLY TO THE FOLLOWING PERSON(S) ON FEB   4   75
                                                 mo.   day   year

MUST be filled in by owner(s) of Litter

PRINT NAME(S) OF PERSON(S) TO WHOM MR. & MRS. JAMES JOHNSON
DOG WAS DIRECTLY TRANSFERRED

ADDRESS 631 HARRIS ST. LOUIS, MO 63120

Signature _Sam Smith_
    OWNER OF LITTER AT BIRTH   Signature   CO-OWNER (IF ANY) OF LITTER AT BIRTH

SEC. B

TO BE COMPLETED and SIGNED BY THE PERSON(S) NAMED IN SEC. A ABOVE, PROVIDED the person(s) owns the dog at the time this application is submitted to the A.K.C. If the person(s) named in SEC. A has transferred the dog to some other person(s). DO NOT COMPLETE SEC. B. Instead - obtain a Supplemental Transfer Statement form the A.K.C. Instructions for its completion and use are on the form.

I apply to The American Kennel Club to have Registration Certificate for the dog issued in my (our name(s), and certify that I/we acquired it DIRECTLY from the person(s) who Signed Sec. A above, and that I/we still own this dog. I agree to abide by American Kennel Club rules and regulations.

New Owner's Signature _James A Johnson_

PRINT
Name James Johnson   New Co-Owner's Signature _Joan Johnson_

Address 631 Harris   PRINT Name Joan Johnson

City St. Louis   State MO   Zip 63120   Address 631 Harris

                                                 City St. Louis   State MO   Zip 63120

REGISTRATION FEE MUST ACCOMPANY APPLICATION. MAKE your MONEY ORDERS PAYABLE TO THE AMERICAN KENNEL CLUB. DO NOT SEND CASH.

FEE: $4.00 plus $1.00 for each additional transfer of dog represented by Supplemental Transfer Statement. (Separate and individual signatures of all co-owners are required.)
FEES SUBJECT TO CHANGE WITHOUT NOTICE

When completed and submitted, this Application becomes the property of the American Kennel Club

Mail to: THE AMERICAN KENNEL CLUB 51 Madison Avenue, New York, N. Y. 10010

If new owner named in Section "A" intends to keep dog and register it in his ownership, he should sign and complete Section "B". (Separate and individual signatures of all co-owners are required.)
If the dog is to be transferred again do not complete Section "B". See page 18 for instructions on completing a supplemental transfer state-

Litter owner must complete Section "A" by indicating date of transfer and printing name and address of person(s) to whom he is directly transferring the dog.

Litter owner must sign Section "A" verifying details of transfer. Separate and individual signatures of ALL co-owners are required. Husband and wife must sign separately.

SUPPLEMENTAL TRANSFER STATEMENT (gray). Only the first transfer by the litter owner is recorded on the blue form shown on Pages 157 & 158. If further transfer of the dog is to be made before the application is submitted for registration, the former AND new owner(s) must complete this Supplemental Transfer Statement, and attach it to the completed blue form. A fee of $1. (in addition to $4. fee required with blue form) must accompany each transfer application.

SUPPLEMENTAL TRANSFER STATEMENT
NOT VALID unless attached to the AKC Dog Registration Application

SEC. A MUST BE **COMPLETED** AND **SIGNED** PERSONALLY BY PERSON OR PERSONS WHO TRANSFERRED THE DOG. *

I certify that on (month) FEB (day) 28 (year) 75 I delivered or shipped the (breed) LABRADOR RETRIEVER

(sex) M (color and markings) YELLOW from litter No. SL729497 DIRECTLY TO:

PRINT NAME(S) JOHN JONES

ADDRESS 123 BROADWAY, AKRON OH 44322

SIGN *James Johnson* — FORMER OWNER — PERSON TRANSFERRING DOG

SIGNED *Joan Johnson* — FORMER CO-OWNER (if any)

INVALID IF SIGNED IN BLANK

SEC. B MUST BE **COMPLETED** AND **SIGNED** PERSONALLY BY NEW OWNER (AND NEW CO-OWNER, IF ANY) NAMED IN SEC. A ABOVE, provided he still owns the dog and wants registration certificate issued in his name. If the dog has again been transferred, do not use this Sec. B, but make out Sec. A on another of these forms.

I apply to The American Kennel Club to have registration Certificate for this dog issued in my/our name(s), and certify that I/we acquired it DIRECTLY from the person(s) who signed Sec. A above, and that I/we still own this dog. I agree to abide by American Kennel Club Rules and Regulations.

New owner's personal signature *John Jones*

Print Name JOHN JONES

Address 123 BROADWAY

City, State AKRON, OH 44322

Co-Owner's Signature If Jointly Owned

Print Name _____

Address _____

City, State _____

*READ INSTRUCTIONS ON REVERSE SIDE

R48-10 (10-74)

Former owner(s) must complete Section "A", indicating date of transfer, breed, color, sex, and litter number of dog, and must print name and address of *person(s) to whom dog is being directly transferred.* Former owner(s) must sign Section "A" verifying details of transfer. (Separate and individual signatures of all co-owners are required.)

New owner(s) of dog who apply to register it, should complete Section "B". (Separate and individual signatures of all co-owners are required.)

registrable with the AKC, the dog must be identified either by putting into the hands of the buyer a properly completed AKC registration application, or by giving the buyer a bill of sale or a written statement, *signed by the seller*, giving the dog's full breeding information as follows:

—**Breed, sex,and color of the dog**
—**Date of birth of the dog**
—**Registered names of the dog's sire and dam**
—**Name of the breeder**

If you encounter any problems in acquiring the necessary registration application forms, it is suggested that you write The American Kennel Club, 51 Madison Avenue, New York, N.Y. 10010, *giving full particulars* and the difficulty will be reviewed. All individuals acquiring a dog represented as being AKC registrable should realize it is their responsibility to obtain complete identification of the dog as described above sufficient to identify in AKC records, or <u>THEY SHOULD NOT BUY THE DOG</u>.

Ch. Hamilton Jimpa poses with a puppy to demonstrate the difference in appearance between the Lhasa puppy and adult.

8

How to Groom
the Lhasa Apso

THE LHASA APSO'S profuse coat is one of the hallmarks of the breed. You are apparently attracted to "hairy dogs" or you would not have chosen it. If you decided on the Lhasa Apso because you saw a beautiful specimen with a floor length coat in a photo or at a dog show, you should realize the dog did not just happen to look like that. Many hours of grooming and care were spent by his owner, handler or both to make the coat beautiful.

Proper grooming is not difficult. In fact, it is quite easy if done correctly, and can be fun for both you and your dog. Learning from a book can readily be done if you read the description carefully and think about what the words suggest, not just what they say. With the proper tools, patience and common sense, much can be accomplished in a few hours of grooming each week.

Tools

Here is a list of the necessary equipment for grooming your Lhasa Apso.

The Mason Pearson brush	Good quality barber's scissors
Slicker brush	Knitting needle
Fine and medium tooth steel comb	Hair dryer
Hemostat	Spray applicator
Nail clipper	Small latex bands & barrettes

Styptic powder

The Mason Pearson brush is manufactured in England and is expensive and hard to obtain. It has a combination of natural bristles and nylon pin bristles. It is highly prized for show grooming because it effectively removes tangles without damaging the coat. It may be substituted by a cushioned metal pin brush and there are many serviceable imitations of the Mason Pearson brush on the market.

The right Grooming equipment for a Lhasa Apso can usually be obtained from a well-stocked dog supply shop or at dog shows from a concession stand.

Preparation for General Grooming

Grooming can be fun if your Lhasa Apso is trained to allow it without a struggle. This training should start as early as possible. One of the first things a puppy should learn is to lie quietly on his side on a grooming table or flat surface. This surface should be comfortable for you while standing, or sitting if your prefer.

You should be comfortable while grooming or you tend to rush the job. Do not try to groom your Lhasa Apso from a disadvantageous position on the floor or on your bed. Neither you nor the dog will be comfortable and the grooming results will be disappointing.

Allow him to relieve himself before you start grooming to avoid restlessness. Give him a "break" frequently if his coat condition requires a long session.

To lay a Lhasa Apso on his side, stand him sideways in front of you on the grooming surface. Now grasp the front and back legs on his opposite side, (Photo 2) lift him slightly and push him over and away from your body (Photo 3). At the same time, lean over him and hold him while speaking softly until he relaxes (Photo 4). Then, gently and slowly slip your hands and body away so he lies still without being held (Photo 5). If he struggles and stands up, repeat the process until you have convinced him that he will not be hurt while lying on his side. You may have to use a little force to hold him down the first few times he struggles. Otherwise, he will assume he can get up any time he desires. Practice lying him on his side until he will stay there without being held. This frees your hands for grooming. When you have finished a practice session, praise him and play with him to make him feel rewarded for having pleased you. The early grooming sessions are more for the benefit of training than grooming.

In the beginning you will spend more time teaching him to be quiet than grooming him. A puppy's coat mats very little the first few months. By the time he starts the matting-tangling change of coat, at 6 to 9 months, he has been trained to lie still while you brush.

162

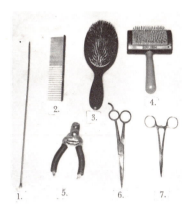

Photo 1. Grooming Tools—1. Knitting needle; 2. Fine and medium tooth comb; 3. The Mason Pearson Brush; 4. Slicker brush; 5. Nail clipper; 6. Scissors; 7. Hemostat.

Photo 2. Grasp the front and back legs on his opposite side.

Photo 3. Lift him slightly and push him over and away from your body.

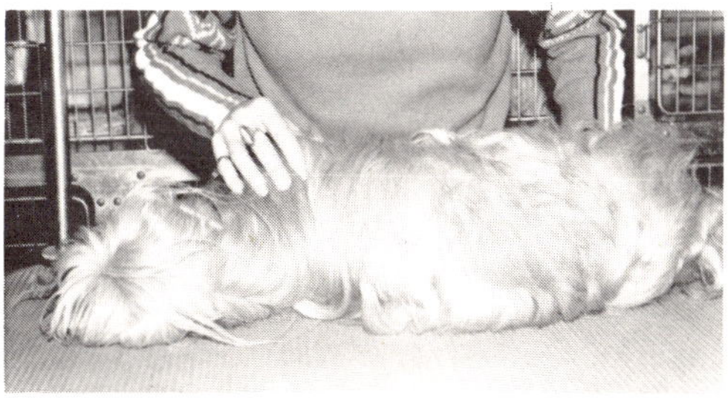

Photo 4. Lean over him while speaking softly until he relaxes in the desired position.

Photo 5. Slip your hands and body away so he lies still without being held.

163

Some Lhasa Apsos during grooming will try to bite or growl. This is a NO NO and must be stopped immediately by any method necessary. Try a sharp, loud NO, a slap on the table with NO or if necessary a sharp slap on the muzzle or the rump with a NO!

General Grooming

When your Lhasa Apso has learned to lie down without struggling or getting up, the real grooming process begins.

Start by pushing all the hair away from you, exposing the skin of the stomach. Having a starting point helps to avoid getting the hair caught in your brush or comb, and allows you to see the area to be groomed. The exposed skin of the stomach forms a horizontal part in the hair (Photo 6). The part need not be perfectly straight, but if you do not make a part, you may not get to the skin or you may miss some areas entirely.

Before brushing, spray with a fine mist of water or a commercial coat conditioner. This will help to lubricate the dry coat, protect the ends and help to control the static electricity, thus making the coat more manageable.

After spraying the coat, use the Mason Pearson brush to brush it down. Keep the brush flat on the hair avoiding any twisting, turning or flipping action which tends to break the ends of the hair (Photo 7). Brush a small portion of hair down toward the stomach continuing horizontally from the front to the back of the body. Take care to brush only a small amount of hair thus moving the part a fraction of an inch up the side of the body.

After moving the part up about an inch with the brush, use a medium tooth steel comb on the same area making sure there are no tangles or mats that were missed with the brush. Do not flip, twist or turn the comb either but simply pull it gently straight through the hair. If the comb is stopped by a snarl, simply lift it straight up and out of the hair and start over very gently working the tangle to within a few inches of the ends of the hair. Use the brush to gently work the snarl out the last few inches. Continue this inch by inch grooming process until you have groomed the entire body on one side of your Lhasa Apso, including tis chest and rear.

If you discover a mat too large to work out with the comb or brush, use your fingers to spread the mat apart. After separating the mat with your fingers, use the brush to work out the mat. Plenty of patience is a definite asset when working out mats. The more you separate the mat into smaller mats or tangles the less damage you will cause to the hair.

Another way to remove a large mat is to use the corner of a slicker

Photo 8. Grooming the leg requires you to hold the foot and most of the leg hair in one hand while brushing with the other.

Photo 6. The horizontal part that moves up the side of the body as you brush small amounts of hair.

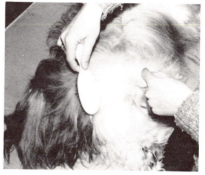

The proper way to hold the leg and brush when brushing the front of the leg.

Photo 7. Keep the brush flat on the hair avoiding any twisting or flipping action which tends to break the ends of the hair.

Photo 10. The proper way to brush the sensitive area under the leg next to the body.

165

brush in a "picking" action, gently pulling hair bit by bit loose from the mat.

Grooming the legs requires you to hold the foot and most of the leg hair at the same time (Photo 8). Start at the base of the leg next to the body. Brush the hair away from the foot and toward the body. By following the same technique as you did on the body the part should appear completely around the leg (Photo 9). The area under your Lhasa Apso's leg next to the body tends to mat quickly so be sure to get all the mats from this area. As this area is one of the most sensitive areas to groom, be gentle to prevent hurting your Lhasa (Photo 10). Brush the leg until you have reached the foot. Be careful not to use long brush strokes that damage the body coat. After all the leg hair has been completely brushed and detangled, lightly brush the coat downward toward the foot so it falls in its natural direction.

The whiskers and beard, another sensitive area, should be groomed with care. The facial area requires special attention because food particles may adhere to the hair around the mouth and matter accumulates under the eyes. Brush the ends of the beard carefully to avoid harming the eyes or scratching the lips or nose. After brushing the beard and whiskers thoroughly, use the fine toothed steel comb close to the eye, pulling gently away from the eye (Photo 11). Remove all eye matter with the comb. If the matter has dried, use a wet cotton swab to moisten it before combing. A toothbrush is also a good tool for cleaning this area. Two drops of eye wash solution in each eye will help to rinse away any matter in the eyes. Cleaning this facial area should be done frequently to eliminate a build-up of eye matter or food particles. Cleaning this area also helps to eliminate odor, infection and a generally untidy appearance.

The head, ears and tail should be groomed with special care because this portion of your Lhasa's coat can suffer damage more readily than the rest of the coat as it is usually of different texture. It also tends to be longer and the ends break more easily.

The head is groomed the same as the body by using the part, brush and comb method. Be sure to groom under the chin and neck too.

The ears may be sticky from being dragged in food. It may be necessary to spray their ends until wet and then gently brush to remove residue. After brushing the ears, gently comb to be sure no tangles have been missed. Be careful not to scratch the ear leather or damage the hair ends with the teeth of the comb.

The tail should be groomed by taking all the tail hair from the base of the tail to its end and making a part down one side (Photo 12). Fold all the hair over to one side and then spray and brush. After gentle brushing, comb near the tail but never comb the hair ends.

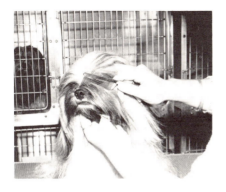

Photo 11. Use the fine-toothed comb close to the eye; pulling gently away from the eye to remove eye matter.

Photo 12. The tail should be groomed by taking all the hair from the base of the tail to its end.

Photo 13. While holding the ear leather with one hand, to expose the ear canal, use the hemostat to pull the hair from the ear.

167

Cleaning Ears

Because the Lhasa Apso is a long coated dog, it has hair in its ears. This hair can easily become embedded with dirt, causing infection or odor. It should be removed about once each month or as needed. Frequent ear hair removal helps eliminate irritation to the skin. A hemostat is ideal for pulling hair from the ears. With your Lhasa lying on his side the task will be much easier as it enables you to use both hands.

By holding the ear leather with one hand, the ear canal can be exposed and made accessible. Use the hemostat to pull a few hairs with one stroke; do not jerk (Photo 13). A steady pull is less painful as the ear canal does not have a great deal of sensitivity. Do not try to pull too much hair with one stroke. Instead, make several attempts to remove all the hair. Don't probe too deep into the ear canal; allow the hair to grow out long enough to grasp.

After the hair has been removed place a piece of cotton on the end of the hemostat. Dip the cotton in alcohol and swab the ear (Photo 14). This process should be repeated until the cotton is clean when removed from the ear. The cotton should not be stained after more than three times if the ear is healthy. The alcohol helps to remove any infectious particles from the ear and dissolves accumulated ear wax. The ears should be cleaned with alcohol every time your Lhasa is groomed.

Clipping Toenails

Your Lhasa's toenails should be clipped frequently enough to keep the nails short. The nails should never be allowed to grow long enough to absorb the pressure of walking. This pressure should be absorbed by the toes. If the nails are allowed to grow too long, they can cause splaying of the feet and discomfort to your Lhasa. The frequency of clipping depends on the kind of surface your Lhasa runs on. A Lhasa that runs on concrete will tend to wear his nails short, and a Lhasa exercised on grass or a soft surface will have longer nails from lack of abrasive contact to wear them short.

Lay your Lhasa on his side and grasp one of his feet in your hand. Use your index finger to push the hair away from the nails and place your thumb between his pads. With the nail clipper in your other hand, clip the tip off the nail a little at a time until the blunt end of the nail appears pink or, in the case of a black nail, moist (Photo 15). If you clip too deep the nail will bleed. The bleeding can be stopped by applying pressure on the end of the nail. Keep styptic powder available and apply it to stop the bleeding immediately.

168

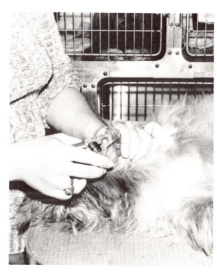

Photo 15. The proper way to hold the foot and clippers while clipping nails.

Photo 14. Swab the ear with a piece of cotton, on the end of the hemostat, that has been dipped in alcohol.

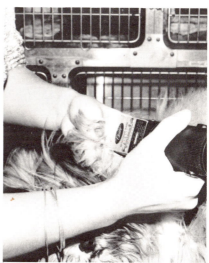

Photo 16. Clipping the hair from between the pads with an electric clipper.

Special Cleaning

If your Lhasa messes his genitals or anus, you will want to clean them as part of regular grooming and on special occasions. Spray the area until it is fairly wet. Sprinkle a little baby powder on the area and brush until it is fairly dry. The powder helps to absorb moisture, removes stain and controls odor. If your Lhasa is too messy in either area, bathe it. Dirt makes him uncomfortable and causes problems, infections and work for you. Check your Lhasa each time he eliminates for any fecal material that may adhere to his coat. Lhasas often report such problems to their owners; they really do not like to be untidy!

Trimming

The Lhasa Apso should have the hair between his pads trimmed approximately every two or three weeks. Lay him on his side and, using a pair of scissors or an electric clipper with a #15 blade, trim all excess hair that is between the pads (Photo 16). Do not trim on top of the feet or between the toes. Trim only the bottom of the foot between the pads. Sometimes it is desirable to *even* the hair on the top of the feet if it grows so long as to flop under the feet and create a handicap to the dog when he is moving. This trimming should be done with care and never too close to the feet. A rounded, neat appearance is desired.

The hair growing within one quarter inch of the anus may be trimmed to eliminate the collection of fecal material.

Trimming the hair under the eyes or on the muzzle may result in irritation to the eyes especially as it grows out. The hair under the eyes, if allowed to grow long enough, will drape down the side of the muzzle and will not irritate the eyes (Photo 17). Sometimes puppies will have excessive tearing when their hair has not grown long enough to drape down the muzzle away from the eyes. During this stage the puppy's eyes should be cleaned often. Keeping the area under the eyes clean helps promote the growth of the hair.

Finish Grooming

Your Lhasa has been thoroughly brushed. His ears, eyes and genitals are clean. His toenails and pads are trimmed. Now he is ready to have his hair parted neatly from the tip of his nose to the base of his tail and to have his topnot put up.

To get the part centered and straight, your Lhasa should be standing in a four square position facing you. Use a knitting needle to make the part down the back. Starting at the nose, center the part between the

Photo 17. This Lhasa's muzzle hair has grown long enough to drape down the side of the muzzle so that it does not irritate the eyes.

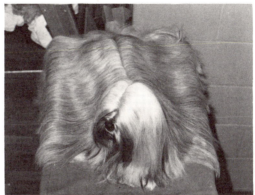

Photo 18. BIS Ch. Potala Keke's Yum Yum ROM models the proper part; straight from the tip of her nose to the base of her tail.

Photo 19. These Lhasa puppies are modeling the one topknot style. The puppy on the left is wearing a barrette and the other one an elastic band.

eyes and over the skull, aiming for the base of the tail. Attempt only about four inches with each stroke of the needle. Continue a straight line from the skull down the neck and back to the base of the tail, following the spinal column to center the part. Spray the part lightly and brush the hair straight down on both sides of the body (Photo 18).

This part is rather difficult to keep straight in puppies. In the longer, adult coat the part tends to remain orderly for several days.

Before putting up the topknot you must determine if your Lhasa Apso has enough headfall for one or two topknots. The longer, thicker headfall requires two topknots. With less headfall one will stay up better.

If you use one topknot, make a part from the outer corner of the eye to the back of the skull or occiput, just above the ear. Do not make the part below the eye or ear because it will stretch the skin and cause discomfort, and your Lhasa will probably scratch the topknot. Use the same process on each side of the head. Brush the two portions of hair straight back from the face to the top of the head making one strand or "pony tail" of hair. Secure this strand of hair with a latex band or barrette. Do not tie the hair too tight as it will pull his skin causing discomfort and scratching again (Photo 19).

When using two topknots, follow the same process as above except that the portions on each side of the head are kept separate, leaving the part in the center of the skull. Each side is secured in a strand or pony tail just above the ear, allowing the hair to hang down over the ear. Be careful not to catch any hair on the ears in the latex band or barrette as this may also cause discomfort and scratching (Photo 20).

Either style of topknot should be taken down and redone several times a week. Do not allow the topknot to remain up for more than one week or skin irritation resulting in sores may occur.

In the show ring for conformation and obedience the Lhasa must be shown without tying the hair back from the face; however, most Lhasa exhibitors prefer to keep the hair secured away from the eyes and face when their dogs are not in the show ring, to allow for better vision and for cleanliness. Securing the headfall in topknots prevents the Lhasa from chewing on the long hair and reduces eye irritation.

When introducing the Lhasa to a topknot, do something to take his attention away from the strange new thing on his head. One fairly successful plan is to tie the hair up just before going for a walk or a ride.

Bathing

Your Lhasa Apso should be bathed as often as needed to keep him tidy. The frequency of bathing will depend on the environment he lives

172

Photo 20. Ch. Thang-Ka Simhanada shows the proper two topknot style with barrettes.

in. A Lhasa running on a big concrete or gravel patio will not need bathing as often as one walked on oily city streets.

Prepare your Lhasa for his bath by performing a routine general grooming as described before. When all his mats and tangles have been removed, place him in a sink or bathtub. Keep the bathtub drain open and, using a spray attachment or dipping container, completely saturate the coat. Be careful not to get water in the ears. Apply a recommended dog shampoo to the coat with a squeeze bottle, keeping soap out of the eyes. You may wish to use a tearless shampoo for the head and around the eyes. Do not rub the shampoo into the coat. Squeeze it in as you would in washing a fine sweater. Rinse the shampoo out of the coat and apply a second time if needed. Always rinse *all* shampoo out of the coat. Otherwise, skin irritation and problems may result. After rinsing, apply a creme rinse according to directions, if desired. Creme rinse helps when brushing tangles from the wet coat but will not alone demat a coat. Dematting should be done before the bath as getting mats wet makes them tighter and harder to remove.

If there are any fleas or ticks on your Lhasa, this is the time to use a flea or tick rinse on him. Be sure to follow mixing directions to avoid irritation to your Lhasa by too strong a mixture. Ask your veterinarian to recommend a flea and tick rinse. This rinse should not have an offensive odor and may be used if you anticipate having your Lhasa in a location, such as a park, dog show or wooded area, where fleas or ticks are present. Do not use a flea and tick rinse routinely after every bath.

After the rinses have been applied and your Lhasa is ready to be dried, wrap him in a large terry cloth towel to blot all excess moisture. You may want to use two towels but never rub your Lhasa to dry him. To do so will create tangles and mats that are difficult to remove.

Now remove the towel and lay your Lhasa on his side on the grooming surface. Turn the hair dryer on warm and direct it toward the stomach. Start to brush as you dry, following the method used in general grooming, forming the horizontal parting of the coat and brushing until dry down to the skin.

After your Lhasa is dry, put the finishing touches on him by making a straight, neat part from his nose to his tail and securing his headfall into one or two topknots.

Patience is a virtue at all times during a grooming session. With practice your judgment and knowledge will increase and your Lhasa will look better and better. If you groom your Lhasa regularly and thoroughly, his beautiful coat will make you proud.

Ch. Astra Traba Ling A Tantras models the proper style for the head fall in the show ring.

Wrapping the Coat

Wrapping your Lhasa to obtain a long, luxurious, floor length coat is not necessary. There are some circumstances, however, where it might be desirable. Wrapping does not make the hair grow faster but keeps the ends from being damaged by the Lhasa's normal activity. If your Lhasa is exercised on a rough surface the ends of the hair will be damaged. Some Lhasas step on their coats while playing and pull out hair or break it off. Observing your Lhasa's daily routine will help you decide if wrapping will be beneficial.

Before wrapping your Lhasa groom him very thoroughly, making sure he is clean and free of mats and tangles.

The use of coat oil before wrapping is optional. If you use oil, it should be applied according to directions. Commercial coat oil helps promote a healthy coat and improves the coat texture. Apply the oil only to the coat. Do not saturate the skin as excessive oiling of the skin causes it to flake and peel as though it had been sunburned.

Wrappers are made of many different materials. Some popular materials are: paper towels, Handi-Wipes, silk squares, waxed paper, bakery tissues or plastic bags. You should experiment with different materials and choose the one you find easy to work with and that holds the coat best. The size of each wrap varies with the length of the coat. Ten inches square is the average.

With your Lhasa standing four square on the grooming surface in front of you, make the first section to be wrapped by parting the coat. Assuming that you have the part straight down your Lhasa's spine, make a perpendicular part from just in front of the withers to the bottom of the shoulder blade. Holding this part, make another part from the bottom of the shoulder blade across to just above the elbow. Finish parting this section by making a part perpendicular to the spine (Photo 21). You should have approximately one-third of your Lhasa's body coat above the elbow and below the spine in this square. Avoid getting any leg hair in this section as this causes discomfort. Brush the hair together into one strand and fold the wrapper in half lengthwise around the strand of hair (Photo 22). Making sure the hair stays together in the first fold, fold the now doubled wrap in half lengthwise (Photo 23). You may wish to make a third and fourth fold to make the wrap smaller (Photo 24). With the strand of hair securely wrapped in the lengthwise folded wrapper, fold this wrapper in half crosswise (Photo 25) and then in half again crosswise forming a neat little package with the strand of hair tucked securely inside. Take a rubber band and wrap it horizontally around the package so that it holds firmly but not tightly (Photo 26). Grasp the finished wrap and gently pull to loosen the

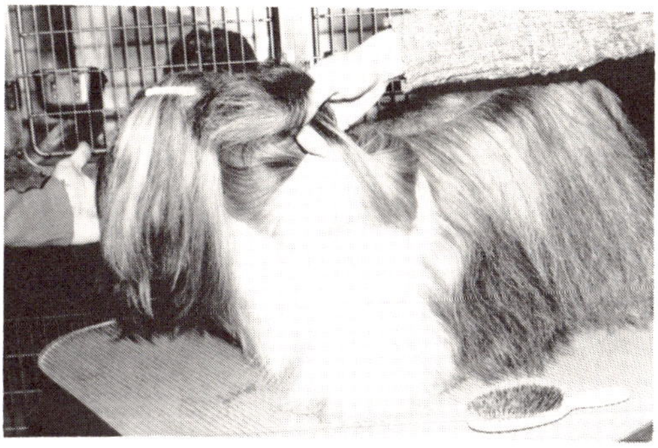

Photo 21. The first of coat section for wrapping.

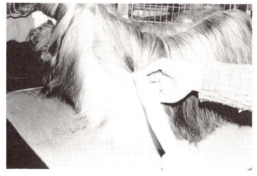

Photo 22. The hair brushed together into one strand with the lengthwise folded wrapper around it.

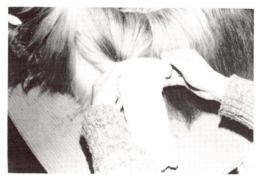

Photo 23. The second lengthwise fold of the wrapper.

Photo 24. A third and fourth lengthwise fold of the wrapper.

tightness all over but not so hard as to pull or loosen the hair from the wrap. This is done to ease uncomfortable tension on the skin.

To form the next section make a horizontal part straight across from above the elbow to the loin or flank area and perpendicular up to the spine (Photo 27). Wrap this section as described above.

The third and final section on this side of the Lhasa is formed by making a horizontal part from the loin area across to meet a perpendicular part straight down from the anus (Photo 28). When making the perpendicular part down from the anus do not get any hair from the opposite side. If you do, it will cause a pocket that will catch fecal material. Do not catch any hair attached to the genitals or beyond the base of the tail.

Repeat the wrapping process on the other side of your Lhasa (Photo 29).

If your Lhasa has never been wrapped, introduce him to wearing wraps slowly. Keep him wrapped only when you can observe him closely. If he tries to chew them out or scratches at them, reprimand him and draw his attention away from them. Never allow a wrapped Lhasa to run free where there are objects that can catch the hair above the wraps.

Braids may be substituted for wraps (Photo 30). If you feel that you are not satisfied with the results of wrapping your Lhasa's coat, you may want to try braiding. Some types of coat will respond better to braids. In making the decision between wraps or braids, experiment to see which is most satisfactory for you.

If braids are preferred, secure them with latex bands because rubber bands will damage the coat.

Use the same method for braiding as in wrapping by parting the hair into sections. After braiding each section secure the end with a latex band and fold it in half crosswise and then in half crosswise again. Secure this folded braid with a latex band.

The wraps or braids on your Lhasa should be changed when the underside of the hair, just above the wrap or braid, begins to tangle. This could be as often as every other day for some Lhasas.

Wrapping or braiding your Lhasa entails a considerable amount of time and effort. It should be done only under controlled conditions and after a considerable amount of grooming experience is obtained.

Wrapping or braiding the coat prevents wear to the ends of the coat caused by dragging on the surface your Lhasa walks on. Sometimes it is necessary to trim the body coat when it grows long enough to interfere with the Lhasa's movement (Photo 31). Trimming this coat should be done with care so that it does not look trimmed. When

178

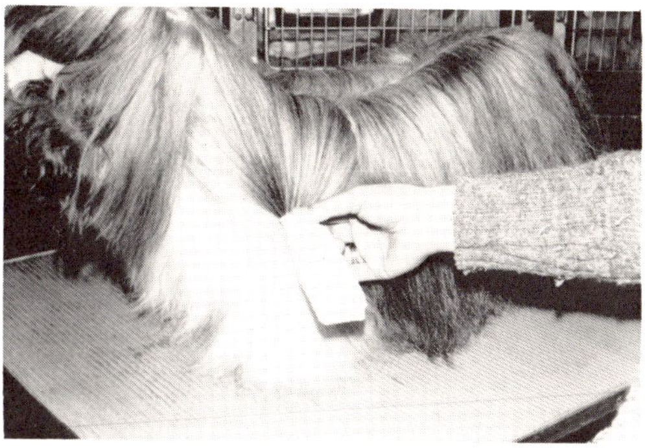

Photo 25. The lengthwise folded wrapper folded in half crosswise.

Photo 26. The first wrap finished and secured with a rubber band.

Photo 27. Section of coat for the middle wrap.

Photo 28. The third and final section for wrapping one side.

179

Photos 29 and 30. The Lhasa Apso above is modeling wraps used to protect the ends of his coat. For contrast, the model below wears braids. Note that the braid on the right is not folded to show where it begins and how the end is secured.

Photos 31 and 32. Multiple Group winner Ch. Potala Keke's Tomba Tu ROM before trimming (above) and after trimming (right).

trimming, your Lhasa should be standing as in the show ring. Trim so that the coat is not just touching the floor but is one inch longer (Photo 32). Improper trimming can ruin a Lhasa so have it done by an expert the first time to see the proper way.

Pet (or Necessity) Clipping

If you have difficulty keeping your Lhasa properly groomed or live where your dog picks up brambles and burrs, you may wish to have your Lhasa clipped. Lhasa Apsos are long coated and much of their initial charm is in their coats. They do have wonderful personalities, and with the proper clip lose none of their charm. Any professional grooming shop can probably clip your Lhasa or you may learn to clip him yourself.

There are several ways to clip your Lhasa and your choice depends on your taste and the reason he is being clipped. If you clip him because you do not want to cope with the long coat, clip the hair on the back and sides short and leave the legs, tail, ears and whiskers longer. This clip is much the same as a pet Schnauzer clip and is very attractive and easy to maintain.

Another style is to clip all the hair on the back and legs the same length. This is good for Lhasas that walk with their owners in fields and woods where stickers, leaves and brambles catch in a long coat. It also serves as a necessity clip, if your Lhasa gets extremely matted, instead of brushing. Trying to brush a very badly matted coat is painful to your Lhasa and the end result can be disappointing and leave him with a thin, straggly, unkept look.

Whether you choose one of these clips or choose one styled especially for your Lhasa, a clipped Lhasa can be handsome and easy to care for.

Ch. Keke's Georgy Girl demonstrates how appealing a girl can be with a short haircut.

Multiple Group winner Ch. Little Fir's Shel Ari of Chiz with his co-owner and junior handler, Joanne Baker. Shel Ari is a son of Ch. Ruffway Marpa ROM and Ch. Orlane's Meling of Ruffway.

Ch. Kinderland's Tim-Pa shown with junior handler, Mary Kuendel who finished him with five major wins. Tim-Pa is a son of Ch. Ruffway Marpa ROM and Ch. Kinderland's Sang-Po ROM.

Group winner Ch. Pan Chen Tonka Sonan (1 year) with his handler Marvin Cates (right) and his sire Ch. Chen Nyun Ti ROM (2 years) handled by Lynn Martin. Tonka Sonan's dam is Ch. Pandan Chose Tsen. Both are shown with the late Marjorie Siebern.

9

How to Show
a Lhasa Apso

In THIS CHAPTER we will tell you of the special techniques customary in showing a Lhasa Apso in the conformation ring. You will derive more benefit from our suggestions if you study them after you have read at least one good general text on showing dogs, such as *The Forsyth Guide to Successful Dog Showing* by Robert and Jane Forsyth, 1976, Howell Book House Inc., New York, N.Y. It will also help to have attended at least one dog show where you can watch the handling of Lhasa Apsos, the conduct of the judge and stewards and general ring routine.

After you and your dog have practiced at home, enter a few match shows so that you can practice your showing technique under simulated show conditions. With this preliminary practice you will feel more confident when you enter an AKC point show.

These are the special techniques customary in showing a Lhasa Apso in the conformation ring.

Posing

To set your Lhasa in a show pose, first place the front legs squarely under and supporting the front assembly. The front feet should not toe in or out.

Next stretch the rear legs back enough to express angulation with the hocks perpendicular to the ground and parallel to each other approximately four inches apart. If your Lhasa has a proper structure and is posed correctly, the topline should be slightly higher at the withers sloping to the croup without a sag or a roach. The head should be held proudly with its position straight ahead or slightly away from you. The tail should be held over the back naturally; however, you may hold it. If you hold the tail, it should be done in a manner so as not to detract from the dog's natural appearance.

After you have your dog posed, use a brush or comb to give the coat a neat, just-groomed appearance.

You may find it difficult to see your Lhasa set up as others see him when you are the handler. This problem can be easily solved by practicing the above procedure in front of a mirror. When he looks good to you in the mirror then look down on him and make a mental note of how he looks when viewing him from your angle.

Ch. Karma Rus Tikuli, owned and bred by Dorothy Cohen, is the son of Ch. Karma Rus Ti and Karma Keri. He was Best of Breed under Virginia Sivori at the Mid-Hudson Kennel Club show in 1971, handled by Allan Lieberman.

184

Proper way to set up a Lhasa Apso in the show ring.

Improper way to set up a Lhasa Apso in the show ring.

Improper way to set up a Lhasa Apso in the show ring.

Ch. Licos Chulung La is the sire of at least 12 champions. He was born December 25, 1959 and was shown undefeated to his championship.

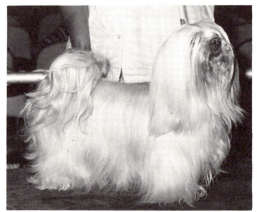

Ch. Karma Talung, a daughter of Ch. Karma Kushog and Hamilton Lug-Tru, born in 1963, was bred by Dorothy Cohen.

Ch. Ruffway Kara Shing ROM is the daughter of Ruffway Chogal and Ch. Ruffway Lholung. She is the dam of three champions, the litter brothers, Ch. Ruffway Norru, BIS Ch. Ruffway Mashaka and Ch. Ruffway Marpa.

186

Gaiting

Before gaiting your Lhasa be sure to speak to him, pat him, or both so he knows that it is time to move. Because Lhasas are shown with their head fall free, sometimes they are unable to see all of your movements, therefore, a communication other than visual should be established.

Lhasas should not be "strung up" (an extremely tight lead) when gaited as this will hamper natural movement. However, because of their obstructed vision many will move more confidently with the security of a firmly held lead to guide them.

Developing a Showman

A Lhasa Apso that is to be shown should be introduced to strange sights, sounds and surprise conditions and be introduced to strange people and dogs as early in his life as possible. We are not suggesting that you take an unimmunized baby puppy out among the public. Neither are we suggesting that you send an older Lhasa out alone and ignore him. We are advising that you familiarize him with situations away from home so that he does not become shy and unhappy when away from the security of the environment and things he is most accustomed to.

Remember your Lhasa should be, according to the standard, gay and assertive but chary of strangers. Therefore he may need a little more socializing than some of the other breeds. If he is like most Lhasas, he will learn to enjoy these outings. His tail is a good barometer of his feelings. It will be down when he is unhappy or afraid and up well over his back when he is happy and confident.

Showing your own Lhasa can be fun and enjoyable if you keep him groomed properly and practice showing techniques so that you feel comfortable in the ring.

Ch. Brush's Abbi of Samara and BIS Ch. Brush's Alvin of Samara a Best in Show brace. This brother and sister owned, bred and handled by Sami Brush are grandchildren of BIS Ch. Everglo's Spark of Gold ROM.

Mary Cole and her winning brace, Ch. Cole's Sunnee of Maru and Ch. Dolsa Maru Topaz. Sunnee is a son of Ch. Everglo Blaze and Ch. Everglo Ma-La-Bu. Topaz is a daughter of Ch. Karma Bandido of Maru and Ch. Chamdo's Tsering.

10

Special Care and Training of a Lhasa Apso

THE SUBJECT of care and training of dogs is so broad that a chapter in this breed book can only sketch instructions relating specifically to the Lhasa Apso and rely upon you to refer to other books which cover the subject in greater depth.

You probably bought or are considering buying a Lhasa Apso because you liked the way he looked or his personality and underlying character appealed to you.

These characteristics create the need for special care and training for your Lhasa.

Living with a Born Sentinel

As you have read a number of times in this book the Lhasa Apso was developed as a companion and warning sentinel. Hence he is friendly with those he knows but wary of unknown sights and sounds, and of strangers. That is not to say he is aggressive or bites. Simply that everything strange alerts him and you are informed of it by his barking and scurrrying around.

If your Lhasa develops the tendency to be overzealous in sounding alarms, discipline is necessary. Decide which warnings are not valid and give him the voice command *no*. In the early stages of training you may need to enforce the voice command with a physical reprimand such as a gentle shake or a stamp of your foot to get his attention. Generally as your Lhasa puppy develops his mature personality he will have better judgment as to what you need to be warned about.

The Coat

Because your Lhasa Apso is a long-coated breed he requires special care not required for many other breeds. In Chapter 8 we have completely explained how to groom your Lhasa Apso; however, we have listed below some hints that will help to make that grooming easier.

1. Do not allow him to run in lawns covered with leaves, weed patches or tall grass as his coat will become embedded with burrs, grass seed and dried leaves. If he runs into such an area the debris should be brushed out immediately so as not to cause irritation.

2. Do not allow him to run in the rain or snow. If he does be sure to immediately dry him with a hair dryer; brushing at the same time to eliminate matting and tangling. If he is muddy, rinse the mud from his coat before drying.

3. Your Lhasa's excessive rear coat can become soiled with fecal material so check him after his exercising periods.

Because your Lhasa is not only comparatively small but also has heavy, long hair he is usually not a good fighter even though the spirit is there. He is independent and will not back down from any dog so protect him from the risk of injury by preventing him from fighting.

Keep your Lhasa away from swimming pools, fish ponds or horse troughs. Even though he may like the water his long coat will weigh him down and cause his stamina to be drained quickly. Unless he can walk out of the pool or is rescued at the first sign of weakness he may drown.

Do take him driving with you as often as you can but observe the weather so as not to submit him to extremes of temperature while left in the car. Always lock the car with the windows open, only far enough so that he cannot jump out, to allow ventilation in warm weather. Although the car is not burglar proof with the windows open the locked doors will deter an accidental opening of the doors that may allow your Lhasa to jump out.

On Small Children

Children find it very tempting to pull the long hair of a Lhasa, particularly the attractive topknots. If you have a small child, teach him or her early to respect your Lhasa's rights. Teach the child to be gentle and loving and the Lhasa will reciprocate.

Ch. Milbryan Dri-Mah-Tee-Nee was Winners Dog at Westminster in February 1969 under Joseph Faigel and handled by his owner, Mildred Bryant. Tee Nee is a son of Ch. Ruffway Nor-Pa and Milbryan Merry Muffin.

Ch. Karma Gyapso is a full sister to Ch. Karma Getson, shown with her handler, George Payton.

191

Three puppies that made good—(from left) Ch. Kyi Chu Friar Tuck (8 months), Ch. Kyi Chu Impa Satan (9 months) and Ch. Kyi Chu Whimsi of Sharbet (14 months). All finished their championships in 1965 when this photo was taken.

Veterinary Concerns

If your Lhasa Apso must be tranquilized or anesthetized we suggest that you inform your veterinarian that some Lhasas have a tendency to react erratically to such treatment. The tendency is to react to the drug slowly and then not to regain conciousness as soon as they should. Also, repeated anesthesia is crucial as there may be retention within the body from one time to the next.

Do not worm your Lhasa Apso as a matter of routine. Worm him only when the veterinarian has made a diagnosis and determined that parasites exist. Frequent worming can cause a build up of the drugs within the body causing improper functioning of vital organs.

One final word regarding care. Keep your Lhasa Apso trim and muscular, *not overweight*. This will make him a healthier, happier animal and will allow him to use his structure properly.

Additional Reading

Problems common to other breeds, regardless of size and coat may arise in connection with your Lhasa. For that reason we have appended a list of books which you may find helpful in dealing with any general dog problems that may arise.

Howell Book of Dog Care and Training by Elsworth S. Howell, Milo G. Denlinger and A. C. Merrick, DVM, 1963, Howell Book House Inc. New York, N.Y.

The Complete Book of Dog Care by Leon F. Whitney, DVM, 1963, Doubleday & Co. Inc., Garden City, N.Y.

Dog Care and Training for Boys and Girls by Blanche Saunders, 1962, Howell Book House Inc. New York, N.Y.

New Knowledge of Dog Behavior by Clarence Pfaffenberger, various editions, Howell Book House Inc., New York, N.Y.

Understanding Your Dog by Michael W. Fox, PhD, B. Vet. Med., MRCVS, 1972, Coward, McCann and Geoghegan Inc., New York, N.Y.

Your Dog His Health and Happiness by Louis L. Vine DVM, 1971, 2nd printing 1974, Arco Publishing Co., Inc., New York, N.Y.

Current Veterinary Therapy Vol 5, by Robert V. Kirk, DVM, 1974, W. B. Saunders Company.

Dog Psychology by Leon F. Whitney, DVM, 1971, Howell Book House Inc., New York, N.Y.

Why Does Your Dog Do That? by Goran Bergman, 1971, Popular Dogs Publishing Co. Ltd. (England), published by Howell Book House Inc., New York, N.Y.

Dog Training for Kids by Carol Lea Benjamin, 1976, Howell Book House Inc., New York, N.Y.

Collins Guide to Dog Nutrition by Donald R. Collins, DVM, 1972, Howell Book House Inc., New York, N.Y.

Ch. Nan Tando of Pandan CD ROM (left), Pandan's foundation bitch. She is a daughter of Ch. Karma Lobsang and Donna Cardella's Tsng. On the right is Ch. Zijuh Seng Tru ROM.

Ch. Kyi Chu Shufi, by Ch. Kyi Chu Kum Nuk out of Ch. Kyi Chu Kira, CD, bred and owned by Ruth Smith. Kyi Chu Lhasas.

Am. Can. Ch. Balrene's Chia Pao hams as he poses for a dog biscuit ad.

11

Character of the Lhasa Apso

THE LHASA APSO attracts attention by its appearance, and its character retains it. The breed appeals to both men and women because it was bred to be a household companion.

Upon first observation, persons unfamiliar with the breed are struck by the unique qualities of a typical Lhasa Apso, but not until they get to know one personally are they able to appreciate the charm of its character.

Typical Temperament

The words in the Standard are of utmost significance in understanding the breed.

The three key words are *gay, assertive* and *chary*. *Gay* is used in the traditional sense of merry or bright. *Assertive* means positive but neither aggressive nor vicious. *Chary* is the word which has caused the most confusion. It means cautious, circumspect, wary, but not shy or timid.

That word describes a confident dog which is not immediately friendly to strangers rather than a timid animal. Lhasas are unselfconscious with and courteous to strangers but do not immediately make up to them. If the Lhasa Apso was originally used as an inside guard and companion by monks and wealthy nobles, it is easily understood why the breed would react to strangers in this way.

After you are no longer a stranger to a particular Lhasa you will be impressed by its quiet self-assurance. The Lhasa is a basically friendly dog once it has decided that the initial stranger is not a threat to it or its master. It has a good, even temperament characteristic of many larger dogs.

The Lhasa's *chary* trait is not the cause of reticence or timidity in the show ring. That stems from the owner's failure to school the dog and accustom it to sounds and practices of the show ring and the day-to-day bustle outside the home. No dog of any breed, without adequate training, can be expected to perform properly, especially in the unfamiliar surroundings of a dog show. Once Lhasas have become accustomed to life outside the house and are properly trained for the show ring, many of them lie quietly in the midst of a dog show's turmoil until required to perform.

The unknown can upset a Lhasa Apso. If he never rides in automobiles, goes to stores, meets strangers outside of, or in the home, or sees children of all ages, he cannot be expected to be an extrovert.

With their masters Lhasas are loving and lovable. With their family and friends they are warm, open and affectionate.

If a particular Lhasa Apso is morose or seemingly a "loner" it is not typical of the breed and possibly the unfortunate result of some bad experience or improper training and handling. Books on dog behavior such as *The New Knowledge of Dog Behavior* by Clarence Pfaffenberger, 1963, Howell Book House Inc., will help you to better understand your dog.

Untypical Temperament

Lhasa Apsos should not be yappy, high strung or vicious. The Lhasa is not cowardly, shy or retiring even when it is most recalcitrant in accepting a new situation. Lhasas possess the calmness and gracious aplomb of one who has a keen sense of personal dignity. In the show ring that dignity is manifest, although often leavened with a touch of the "ham."

Lhasas are not generally snappy dogs. If molested they try to avoid the molester; but, if hurt, they bite as any dog will under similar circumstances. Only if a Lhasa has been improperly treated or poorly trained will it exhibit undesirable traits.

The Ideal Companion

Just as the Tibetans are physically strong, emotionally courageous and independent so is the Lhasa Apso. That is what the word *assertive* connotes. Tibetans are also merry and fun-loving with their friends. So is the *gay* Lhasa Apso.

Lhasa Apsos are good with children which is obvious at bedtime at the Tompkins home with Karey, Amy and their Lhasa puppies.

Ch. Tabu's Raquel demonstrates that Lhasa Apsos have a sense of humor and are usually willing to go along with theatrics.

The Lhasa Apso likes to consider his home his castle and if allowed may even consider the dining table his throne. It is obvious that Tabu's On The Rocks, owned by Pat Spencer, rules at his house.

197

Ch. Zijuh Seng Tru ROM (right) and Ch. Kyi Chu Kara Nor ROM after their wedding. Keep the people laughing seems to be Kara Nor's message.

Ch. Zijuh Seng Tru ROM in a holiday mood.

Lhasas enjoy romping not only outdoors but also in the house, and love to play with their masters. When your Lhasa has your attention, he may race around like an exhibitionist just for your amusement. Some even reveal a sense of humor. Sensitivity to the master's feelings will quiet a dog when he has had enough play or when the master is not in the mood for games.

When attention time is over the Lhasa is happy to lie near or in the vicinity where it can see its master. In hot weather it enjoys the floor in a cool breeze, but in cooler weather it picks a spot as close to its master as permitted. Given the right climate Lhasas can be cuddled. They are at the same time sufficiently large so they are not so fragile as some of the Toy breeds.

Generally, individual Lhasas get along well with each other and with other household animals. Occasionally, however, one that has been the sole pet resents a newcomer with which it must share attention. This condition is particularly aggravated if, because of the newcomer, the original pet's lifestyle is changed or its access to the household is curtailed.

Lhasas are intelligent dogs. Precisely how their degree of intelligence rates with other dog breeds is a matter not only of the individual dog but also of opinion. Like all opinions, each individual's views depend upon the observer's background, dogs of comparable breeds and the circumstances of that observation.

Lhasa Apso puppies exhibit the typical characteristics of the breed at a comparatively early age.

Everyone living with one or more Lhasas has a number of anecdotes waiting to be told, making clear that everyone owned by a Lhasa Apso loves his dog because it responds in kind.

This brief summary is intended to give you an understanding of how the Lhasa Apso's character melded with that of its originators, and how that makes it such an excellent companion for you today.

America's Sandur, UD is believed to be the first Lhasa Apso to achieve the Utility Dog title.

The late Edward T. Jones with Ching Ching Choti, UD receiving first place in Utility at Salisbury, Maryland, November 13, 1971. The judge is Doris H. Miller. Ching continued in competition until 1973, the year Mr. Jones died.

12

The Lhasa Apso
in Obedience

THE RULES of the American Kennel Club provide for the awarding of CD, CDX, UD and UDT certificates to be gained in obedience trials and tracking tests conducted under AKC sanction.

The titles of Companion Dog (CD), Companion Dog Excellent (CDX) and Utility Dog (UD) are awarded to each dog certified by three different judges to have made 50% of the available scores in a specified number of exercises and final scores of 170 or more in Novice, Open and Utility classes, respectively, at three trials in each class where at least six dogs competed.

The title of Tracking Dog (TD) is awarded after a dog is certified by two judges to have passed a licensed or member club tracking test in which at least three dogs competed.

A dog holding both UD and TD title may use the letters UDT signifying Utility Dog Tracking.

Facts and Figures

The Lhasa Apso's performance in obedience trials appears to have fallen behind the breed's showing in the conformation ring. From the records for the most recently available year, Lhasas have won seven Best in Show awards at all-breed shows, 104 Group firsts and 148 championship titles. In obedience competition only 36 Lhasas earned a

CD degree. Three of the breed went a step further to obtain the CDX degree and only one Lhasa was awarded the UD degree.

Contrasting the figures for such show ring and obedience activities, we find Lhasa Apsos won four times as many championships as CD degrees, 34 times as many Group firsts as CDX degrees and seven times as many Best in Shows as UD degrees.

Deficiency in obedience performance by Lhasa Apsos actually does not exist. The assumption that there is any such deficiency is based on a disregard of the difference in numbers being shown in the conformation ring in contrast to obedience competitors. Once it is recognized that there are fewer Lhasas participating in obedience than in conformation, the assumed deficiency of the breed in obedience vanishes.

This is confirmed by a statement in a letter dated August 26, 1977 from Mr. William F. Stifel, then Executive Vice-President of the American Kennel Club, to Mrs. Keke Blumberg, Chairman of the American Lhasa Apso Club Standards Committee. The letter states that the ratio of CDX certificates obtained by Lhasa Apsos to CD certificates obtained by the breed in 1976, while only 10 per cent, reflects "very favorably compared with the ratios for all breeds taken together." That letter also calls attention to the fact that "the total number of dogs earning a CDX title was only 29, with three going on to the Utility degree."

Three of the 29 dogs earning the CDX title were Lhasa Apsos and one of the three going on to the Utility degree was a Lhasa. Thus 10 percent of those dogs earning CDX certificates and 33$^1/_3$ per cent of those earning UD certificates were Lhasa Apsos. Reflecting on the total number of dogs of all breeds registered with the AKC, that is not a bad record.

Obedience Lhasas and AKC Rules

From time to time, however, those concerned by what appears to be a deficiency in Lhasa Apso performance in obedience, overlook the aforementioned facts of numerical difference of participants in each activity. Seeking for an explanation of such difference, they attribute it to the penultimate paragraph of Section 19 of the AKC *Obedience Regulations,* which reads as follows:

No dog shall be eligible to compete . . . if the dog has anything attached to it whether for medical or corrective purposes, for protection, for adornment or for any other reason except for Maltese, Poodles, Shih Tzus and Yorkshire Terriers which may be shown with the hair over the eyes tied back as they are normally shown in the breed ring.

In 1971 and again in 1976 and 1977 ALAC has submitted a request to

Sheng-La's Tashi Tamina, CDX was not started in obedience training until she was past seven years old and had her CDX title by the time she was eight. "Tami", owned and trained by Florence Dickerson, proves that training success is never limited by a dog's age.

Mee-Tu of Charmel, UD clearing the bar jump for Utility obedience work.

Princess Shana, Am., Can. CD performs a long down exercise at an obedience demonstration. Shana is owned, trained and handled by Susan Gehr, Gar San Lhasas.

203

Ch. Pon Go, CD on the left and Sheng Thun Sachs On, CD when they were in training for their CDs in 1970. Pon Go is a son of BIS Ch. Kham of Norbulingka ROM and Ch-Ha-Ya-Chi and Sachs On is a daughter of Ch. Larrmar De-Tsen ROM and Ch. Kinderland's Sang-Po ROM. They are the foundation of Pon Go Lhasa Apsos owned by Edmund R. and Carolyn G. Sledzik.

Rgyal Bo-Jangles, CD qualified in three consecutive shows to win his companion dog degree. He is owned, bred, trained and handled by Barbara Wood, Anbara.

the AKC to permit the hair of Lhasa Apsos to be tied back in obedience. That request was not granted either time.

The current AKC letter refusing to grant such an application, after calling attention to the fact that Lhasa Apso performance in obedience has been at least comparable to that of other breeds, concluded that if the percentages of the various breeds suggest anything it is that "dogs *and handlers* have more difficulty in training for advanced titles, rather than there being an inability on the part of dogs to perform."

It is thus evident that participation in conformation or obedience or both is a matter of personal taste or choice. If you want to learn more about obedience, beside observing actual performance in obedience rings and talking with those who enjoy it, you should read one or more of the training books listed on the last page of this book to help you choose what you want to do.

Notable Obedience Lhasas

With this background you are now ready to appreciate the performance of Lhasa Apsos in the obedience ring.

From our research we believe that only four Lhasa Apsos have earned UD certificates. They are:

1. American's Sandur, UD, owned and trained by Mrs. Dorothy Wood, was the first of the breed to earn that degree which he did in three successive shows.

2. Ching Ching Choti, UD, owned and trained by Edward T. Jones, was the second of the breed to earn a UD certificate which he did in 1972.

3. Mee-Tu of Charmel, UD, owned and trained by Mrs. Melodye Haverly, was the third of the breed and the first bitch to earn the UD certificate. She was also the top Lhasa Apso in Canadian obedience in 1976 and is a Canadian CDX.

4. Haywood's Alana Pansette Tu, UD, owned and trained by John and Ann Haywood, was the fourth of the breed and the second bitch to earn the UD certificate which she did in 1977.

A number of the breed who have also been a success in the show ring, as producers or both, have earned obedience titles. Dual title holders that we are aware of are: Ch. Dandi Jin Rik'i, CDX, Ch. Crest O Lake Marshi of Robtell, CDX, Ch. Shangri La Tibetan Butterfly, CD, Ch. Miradel's No Kato, CD, Ch. Colarlie's Dokki, CD, Ch. Clyzette's Himsang Lo, CD, Ch. Pon Go, CD, Ch. Reiniet Tashi Kylin, CD, Ch. Crest O Lake King Jorge, CD, Ch. Kyi Chu Shufi, CD, Ch. American's Sing Song, CD, Ch. Kyi Chu Sharif, CD, Ch. Tiffany's O Bin An of Green Pond, CD, Ch. Kyi Chu Inshalla, CD, Ch. Khayham

From left to right are Mee-Tu of Charmel, UD, Canadian CDX; Charmel's Ming-Tu, CDX, Canadian CD and Charmel's Ding A Ling who is working on her CD. These three generations are owned by Melodye Haverly.

Ki Ki Ling of K Wannisky, CD with her pals Kristen Wannisky and Tabu's No No Nanette.

Tabu's Digger O'Dell, CD is owned by Peggy Sampson of Levittown, Pennsylvania. "Dell" has a CD title in both the United States and Canada.

Li Ching, CD, Ch. Ming Tali II, CD, Ch. Pandan Lhamo, CD, Ch. Kyi Chu Kira, CD and Ch. Nan Tando of Pandan, CD, ROM.

Two bitches on the ALAC 1976 Top 20 Dams Register of Merit list also have the Companion Dog degree. They are Ch. Nan Tando of Pandan, CD, ROM (mentioned earlier) owned by Lynn Martin and Shing Thun Sachs On, CD, ROM owned by Edmund and Carolyn Sledzik.

ALAC offers an award to its members who have obtained at least three obedience certificates for their Lhasa Apsos. Melodye Haverly was the first member to earn this award for training Lhasa Apsos in obedience.

An Obedience Lhasa's Success Story

The pride in a goal obtained was reflected by each obedience certificate winner we corresponded with. As a testimonial to the joy of accomplishment to be gained from training a Lhasa Apso for obedience we share with you the following letter from Caroline D. Jones:

It was a tragic, avoidable accident to a previous Lhasa that propelled us into obedience training as soon as we acquired Ching Ching from Mrs. E. J. Bartness of Stafford, Virginia. The Fairfax County Dog Training Class was strictly for amateurs—canine and human—and we were the worst of the lot.

Mee-Tu of Charmel, UD with her owner-trainer-handler, Melodye Haverly. Mee-Tu and Melodye are working toward tracking.

Haywood's Alana Pansette Tu, UD won her CD title at four shows in 1975; her CDX title in five shows in 1976 and she won the often elusive UD title in six shows during two months in 1977. "Pansy" is owned by John and Ann Haywood of St. Louis, Missouri.

Diploma in hand at the end of the brief training, we innocently entered Ching Ching in his first show, in Georgetown. It was, predictably, a fiasco—but it opened up to us a new and wonderful world. We resolved to train him properly, however long it took, and try again when we were ready. Lhasas are bright and eager to please; ultimately Ching realized his exercises were serious business and he reveled in his work. Still, shows were crushing disasters, for the crowds delighted him. He licked judges, courted children and had a merry, feckless time.

Suddenly, it all fell into place. In December, 1969, he earned his CD degree and his mistress was ready to retire, triumphant. Our mutual master decreed otherwise and forthwith started training for CDX. Ching found jumping a lark, but the five-minute down was his nemesis. When he was finally ready, he merrily batted it off in three straight shows in eight days (October 3, 4, and 10, 1970). By that time we were all totally committed and confident. Preparing for the final degree, we went to class almost weekly, let Ching work out his own break-throughs on the difficult hand signal and scenting exercises.

When he achieved the coveted UD at Atlantic City, New Jersey on December 5, 1971, it was especially gratifying that he hadn't just squeaked through his degrees; he had been in the money on numerous occasions, including first place at least three times. He was still a ham and a crowd-pleaser, but he finally made the connection; when he gave it his all he could prance into the winners' circle and eat up the applause.

Throughout the effort we felt that Ching Ching was achieving something unique for the breed. But his greatest accomplishment remains this: the joy and pride and companionship he brought to his devoted master's last few years of life.

13

The Modern Lhasa Apso in Canada

THE DOMINION OF CANADA and the United States have enjoyed a very close relationship in connection with Lhasa Apsos from the outset.

The first Lhasa Apsos imported into this country came from Canada. They were Taikoo of Kokonor and Dinkie. Similarly, the first two of the breed to be registered with the AKC after the Standard became effective also came from Canada. They were Tarzan of Kokonor and Empress of Kokonor.

Leading Canadian Lhasas

Canadian Lhasas have frequently competed here with great success. Am., Can. Ch. Teako of Abbotsford, bred and owned by Mrs. James Roberts of British Columbia, Canada, won the first American Lhasa Apso Club Western Specialty held in 1969 in California and also was second in the Non-Sporting Group at the Beverly Hills all-breed show with which the Specialty was held. He had an enviable record in Canada and for several years was the top Lhasa Apso in that country. During that time he won seven Bests in Show at all-breed shows there, as well as 36 Group firsts and many other Group placements.

Teako was born October 28, 1962, the son of Brackenbury Kandron (a son of Eng. Ch. Brackenbury Gunga Din of Verles) and Kalula of Abbotsford.

Am., Can. Ch. Balrene Chia Pao, bred, owned and handled by Dr. Ellen Brown of Ontario won the 1971 ALAC Eastern Specialty held in conjunction with the Trenton Kennel Club all-breed show at which he also placed in the Group. Chia Pao's sire is Can. Ch. Carroll Panda and his dam is Can. Ch. Licos Yarto La. He, like Teako, had an outstanding record in Canada being the Dominion's top Lhasa Apso for several years.

In 1976 the three top Canadian Lhasa Apsos were Ch. Te Di B'ar of Zaralinga, owned by Nancy E. Bruce and bred by Sheila Pike, Zaralinga Lhasa Apsos of Ontario. His sire is Ch. Potala Ching Tu of Zaralinga and his dam is Taglha Rana. Number two was Am., Can. Ch. Sa Mar of Abbotsford, owned and bred by Mr. and Mrs. James Roberts of British Columbia. Sa Mar is the grandson of Am., Can. Ch. Teako of Abbotsford. Third in the Canadian Kennel Club standing was Am., Can. Ch. Kyma of Abbotsford, owned by Mr. and Mrs. Robert

Canadian BIS Am., Can. Ch. Teako of Abbotsford, a son of Brackenbury Kandron and Kalula of Abbotsford, is owned, bred and handled by Mrs. James Roberts of Canada. Teako's Canadian record is seven Bests in Show and 36 Group firsts, but according to Mrs. Roberts her biggest thrill was winning Best of Breed at the first Western ALAC Specialty in 1969.

Can. Ch. Zaralinga Just By Chance, bred by Sheila Pike and shown with his owner-handler Margaret Northey.

Can., Am. Ch. Balrene Chia Pao, pictured with his owner, breeder and handler, Dr. Ellen Brown.

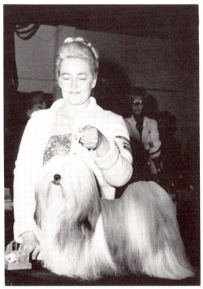

Canadian BIS Can., Am. Ch. Kyma of Abbotsford, bred by Mr. and Mrs. James Roberts and owned by Robert and Nancy Damberg. Pictured with Nancy Damberg, Kyma is a son of Sinbad of Abbotsford and Can., Am. Ch. Chuli of Abbotsford.

Can., Am. Ch. Lady W's Limehouse Blues shown with his breeder-owner, Barbara Chevalier. He is a son of Can. Am. Ch. Potala Keke's Golden Gatsby and Lady W's Miss Sadie Woo.

Can., Am. Ch. Potala Keke's Golden Gatsby shown winning a Group first under Peter Knoop, handled by Garrett Lambert, for owner Barbara Chevalier, Lady W Lhasa Apsos.

Damberg, Pawprints Lhasa Apsos, Boring, Oregon and bred by the Roberts of Abbotsford. Kyma's sire is Sinbad of Abbotsford ROM (a son of Teako) and his dam is Ch. Chuli of Abbotsford.

For the first six months of 1977 the top contenders in Canada were Ch. Te Di B'ar of Zaralinga; Can., Am. Ch. Sa Mar of Abbotsford; Ch. Zaralinga Just By Chance, owned by Margaret Northey and bred by Sheila Pike. He is a son of BIS Am. Ch. Windsong's Gusto of Innsbrook and Can. Ch. Zaralinga's How Sweet She Is (a full sister to Te Di B'ar) and American-bred Am., Can. Ch. Potala Keke's Golden Gatsby, owned by Mrs. Barbara Chevalier of Quebec and Dr. Leon Blumberg of Pennsylvania.

Gatsby also won the Lhasa Apso Club of Quebec Specialty. Incidentally, since that Specialty the club has changed its name to the Canadian Lhasa Apso Club. On June 26, 1977, Gatsby also won the Club VI (i.e. Non Sporting Group Club) Specialty over 134 dogs.

Canadian Shows

Canadian shows usually are smaller in size than in the United States but they have a friendly atmosphere, often fostered by having two or three shows on successive days at the same location.

The reciprocal visits to compete across the border have benefited both sides. Since the number of Canadian breeders and good Canadian dogs has increased so much, it is impossible to refer to as many of them as we would have liked. The best way to enjoy our neighboring breeders, dogs and shows is to attend some Canadian events.

Brackenbury Lhotse owned by Miss Beryl Harding.

Eng. Ch. Brackenbury Chigi-Gyemo, bred and owned by Miss Beryl Harding.

From left to right: "Satru" (gold), "Chora" (silver), "Sonam" (gold) and "Targum" (red), circa 1934. These Apsos come directly from the dogs Mrs. Bailey brought back from Tibet. They were owned by the late Miss Marjorie Wild, Cotsvale. *Photo Courtesy of André Cuny*

14

The Modern Lhasa Apso in England

THE LHASA APSO was known as early as 1901 in England although then called the Lhasa Terrier and divided into 10 inch and 14 inch classes. Miss Marjorie Wild, Cotsvale, was the first to bring Lhasas to England from India and she remained devoted to the breed for 70 years. Challenge Certificates were offered from 1908 for these Lhasa Terriers; however, by the end of World War I they were so few in number that they lost their right to be issued Challenge Certificates.

In 1928, Lieutenant Colonel and Mrs. Eric Bailey returned from service in Tibet with six of the breed. Once again this Tibetan breed was almost extinct in England after World War II.

Lhasas After World War II

Although the breed number was severely reduced, the interest of fanciers such as Miss Wild, Cotsvale; The Honorable Mrs. Eric Bailey; Miss Beryl Harding, Brackenbury; Mrs. Florence Dudman, Ramblersholt; Miss Hervey-Cecil, Furzyhurst and Mrs. Daphne Hesketh-Williams, Verles, was so enthusiastic that by 1957 a separate Lhasa Apso Club was formed. Because of the concerted efforts of these fanciers the reduced number of Lhasa Apsos was built up from the remaining stock and supplemented by imports.

215

One such import was Jigmey Tharkay of Rungit who was imported by Mrs. Jill Henderson. Mrs. Henderson was Secretary to the Himalayan Climbing Club at the time of the British Everest Expedition and brought Jigmey and a bitch back to England from Tibet in 1958. Jigmey was a very good, bright golden dog, very upstanding and fearless. He was imported for the express purpose of improving the breed which he did. Unfortunately, the Hendersons left England after three years and Jigmey left with them.

Leading Breeders and Dogs

Miss Beryl Harding, who obtained her first Apso, Brackenbury Lhotse, in 1953, worked closely with Miss Marjorie Wild. Miss Harding reared and handled to championship status two Cotsvale Apsos when the late Miss Wild was too old to do this for herself. Upon seeing Jigmey Tharkay of Rungit, Miss Harding immediately bred her two best brood bitches, Lhotse and her daughter, Brackenbury Min-nee, to him. Lhotse produced Ch. Brackenbury Chigi-Gyemo. Min-nee produced the famous Ch. Brackenbury Gunga Din of Verles, born in December of 1958 and died in May of 1974.

Mrs. Daphne Hesketh-Williams of Verles chose her first Apso, a present from her husband, at six weeks of age. This Apso was Gunga Din. His owner describes him as being golden and white, very gay and fearless and full of fun and character. He was the first British post-war champion, gaining the first five Challenge Certificates (C.C.s) offered in 1965, after the breed had once again increased its numbers in order to have C.C.s issued. Mrs. Hesketh-Williams states that after retirement she brought him back for Cruft's in 1967 where he again went Best of Breed, winning his sixth C.C. after which she retired him for good. Thereafter he only appeared to lead the Champions Parade at the English Lhasa Apso Club Championship show each year until his death.

Gunga Din sired Ch. Pontac Adham Tarhib, Ch. Verles Yangdup of Cheska, Ch. Cotsvale Brackenbury Kan-Ri, Ch. Verles Nying-Chem-Po, Ch. Verles Keepa, Ch. Sauchrie Mingmatsering and Ch. Willowcroft Kala from Hardacre.

Ch. Verles Tom-Tru, a son of Mrs. Florence Dudman's Rambler-sholt Rham and Verles Dhomtuk (a Gunga Din daughter) was the first English-bred Lhasa Apso to win Best in Show at a really large open show. That was the Sutton Open Show in 1967. Tom-Tru was born in December, 1963 and was still living while this book was being written. He is owned by Mrs. Hesketh-Williams and was retired after winning 10 C.C.s. He is the sire of the famous winning dog, Eng. Ch. Hardacre Hitchcock of Belazieth, and Eng. Ch. Hardacre Hedda.

Eng. Ch. Verles Tom-Tru bred and owned by Mr. and Mrs. F. J. Hesketh-Williams.

Eng. Ch. Brackenbury Gunga Din of Verles (left) was bred by Miss Beryl Harding and owned by Mr. and Mrs. F. J. Hesketh-Williams. His daughter Eng. Ch. Verles Keepa bred by the Hesketh-Williams, Verles Lhasas.

Saraya of Brackenbury owned by Miss Beryl Harding.

217

Growing Popularity

The rising popularity of the Lhasa Apso in England is evidenced by Miss Harding's statement that, "In 1953 it was a record to get five Apsos . . . as against 165 at our Apso Show in March, 1977."

In March, 1969 the Lhasa Apso Club had 91 entries for its first Open show. The judge was Monsieur André Clement-Cuny from France. The next September it held its first Championship show. These two shows are now annual events in early spring and fall, respectively.

With the Lhasa's increase in popularity, a number of new kennels have become prominent. These include such presently well-known names as Belazieth, of Mr. and Mrs. R. G. Richardson; Cheska, of Mrs. Frances Sefton (now residing in Australia); Hardacre, of Anne Matthews; Tintavon, of Paul Stanton; Camvale, of Desmonde Goode and Coburg, of Mr. and Mrs. J. Mason (now residing in Australia).

Some English champions carrying these kennel prefixes are: Ch. Hardacre Hitchcock of Belazieth, Ch. Belazieth's Honey Amber, Ch. Hardacre Hedda, Ch. Wicherty Thea of Tintavon, Ch. Tayung of Coburg, Ch. Cheska Bobette, Ch. Cheska Endymion, Ch. Tungwei of Coburg, Ch. Hardacre Tharkay and Ch. Cheska Gregor.

The greatest triumph for the Lhasa Apso in intervariety competition came in October, 1973 at the Ladies Kennel Association all-breeds Show. There Ch. Cheska Alexander of Sternroc was the first Lhasa Apso ever to win Best in Show at an English all-breeds Championship show. He was bred by his owner Mrs. Frances Sefton and co-owned and handled by Mrs. Pamela Cross-Stern of Sternroc. Alexander was born May 2, 1969 and sired by Ch. Tayung of Coburg out of Ch. Cheska Bobette. He is also the first Lhasa Apso to win Best in Group at an English Championship show (Southern Counties 1973) and to date the only Lhasa Apso ever to win Best in Group at Crufts as well as having won Best of Breed three times there. He won a total of 36 C.C.s as of July 1975.

As proof of his ability to produce, Alexander is the sire of the second Lhasa Apso to win Best in Show at an all-breeds Championship show. She is Ch. Piplaurie Isa Silvergilt of Hardacre who won this title in 1976. He is also the sire of Ch. Clarween Rosella, the 1977 Crufts Best of Breed winner who won her 10th C.C. in a breed entry of 79.

About Crufts

Mention of Crufts calls for an explanation of that annual attraction for dog enthusiasts. The show dates from a meeting in the 1870s between James Spratt, who was about to enter the dog biscuit business

218

Eng. Ch. Cheska Bobette, bred by Frances Sefton, the dam of Eng. Ch. Cheska Alexander of Sternroc.

The winners of the 1973 English Lhasa Apso Club Specialty judged by Monsieur André Cuny (center) are Tintavon Basieren (right), a son of Eng. Ch. Cheska Gregor and Tintavon Nyima of Showa, owned by Mrs. J. S. Luck, the Best in Show Winner and (left) Eng. Ch. Belazieth's Honey Amber, a daughter of Eng. Ch. Hardacre Hitchcock of Belazieth and Verles Jogmaya of Belazieth owned by Mr. and Mrs. R. G. Richardson, the Best of Opposite Sex winner.

Eng. Ch. Cheska Alexander of Sternroc bred and owned by Frances Sefton and co-owned and handled by Pamela Cross-Stern.

and Charles Cruft, who became his traveling salesman. After promoting the dog section at the 1878 Paris Exhibition and managing a number of shows for others, Cruft hired the Royal Agricultural Hall in London in 1891 and staged his own dog show. Under Cruft's management the show snowballed in size and popularity and when he died in 1938 the English Kennel Club took it over and has continued to run it.

That annual institution attracts thousands of spectators from all parts of the world and a handpicked entry of over 8000 entries. A dog must qualify for entry by winning in specified classes at Championship shows held during the previous year.

Names of all Crufts winners become familiar to all English Lhasa Apso fanciers. In 1977, Eng. Ch. Clarween Rosella won Best of Breed for her owner Police Constable Ted Powell and Camvale the Moonshiner won Best of Opposite Sex for his owner, Desmonde Goode.

English Championships

Making an English Champion requires the winning of three Challenge Certificates under three different judges. To win a C.C. a dog must be chosen best of its sex (equivalent of Winners at an American show) at a show where C.C.s are awarded. The number of C.C.s awarded per year are determined by the number of the breed being registered with the English Kennel Club per year.

After surmounting tremendous hardships of having to re-establish the breed twice, it appears that the Lhasa Apso is on solid ground in England. This is due to the perseverance of the pioneer breeders and the more recent fanciers who are continuing to build on this now well-established foundation.

Aust. Ch. Cheska Archee, bred by Frances Sefton and owned and handled by Miss Helen Jardine. Archee is a son of Eng. Ch. Cheska Gregor and Eng., Aust. Ch. Cheska Jesta.

15

The Modern Lhasa Apso in Other Countries

THE QUANTITY and quality of information available in the United States about Lhasa Apsos in foreign countries is not a fair measure of the breed activity. Unfortunately, availability of information limits complete coverage of all countries where Lhasa Apso breeding is being conducted. This is merely a brief view to demonstrate that Lhasa Apsos are known world-wide.

Australia

Lhasa Apsos are comparatively recent arrivals in Australia. Three Lhasa Apsos were imported in 1961 from Mrs. Florence Dudman's Ramblersholt Kennel in England. That year Mrs. Joan Beard (author of *Lhasas and Lamas*, 1976, Stockwell & Co., England) imported Ramblersholt Trag Pon, a dog, Ramblersholt Dzom Tru, a puppy bitch, and Ramblersholt Da Norbu, a proven matron only two generations from Tibet. Ramblersholt Sing Gi came the following year. All four became Australian champions.

One of the first litters born in Australia came in 1962 when Trag Pon sired a litter from Dzom Tru of three males and one female. The bitch, later Aust., New Zealand Ch. Soemiral Pon Dzara, was the outstanding animal in the litter. Bred to Ch. Soemi Rah Dzong of Queensland, a son of Ramblersholt Sing Gi, she was sold in whelp to be foundation bitch for the New Zealand kennel of Miss Marlow.

Shown in center is Eng., Aust. Ch. Cheska Jesta (9½ years) with her owner and breeder, Frances Sefton, and flanked by her two sons—on the left Aust. Ch. Cheska Archee and on the right is his younger brother Group winner Aust. Ch. Cheska Mister Ed.

Eng., Aust. Ch. Cheska Jesta, bred and owned by Frances Sefton is a daughter of Eng. Ch. Verles Yangdup of Cheska and Little Star of Cheska. She is pictured at 10½ years of age.

224

The Asian Breeds Club was formed in 1967 and through lectures and educational exchanges much progress was made.

In 1968 Mrs. Yvonne Mason moved to Australia and took with her the Eng. Ch. Tsangpo of Coburg, a dog, and Nganlpano of Coburg, a puppy bitch sired by Eng. Ch. Verles Tom Tru.

A number of other top-flight dogs were imported into Australia in the 1960s. The group included Ch. Ramblersholt Sonam, Ch. Ramblersholt Ral Loo and Cotsvale Yuam, unfortunately killed before he had an opportunity to prove his quality.

Tsangpo of Coburg sired some excellent dogs including Mangalen Tensing and his sisters. Mangalen Tensing sired Ch. Tasam Ten Tru Tao who was three times Best in Show at the Asian Breeds Club show. Tao, owned by Mrs. A. R. Day, was the top winning Australian Lhasa Apso in 1971. By that time Lhasas were shown in Group six, Non Sporting, with 26 other breeds, which included some large dogs such as Boxers and Dobermans, instead of in the Toy Group where it was shown in 1961.

Gradually Australian Lhasa Apso fanciers have acquired representatives from leading English, French and American Kennels.

In 1970 Mrs. Frances Sefton moved to Australia from England. She wrote *The Lhasa Apso,* first published in 1970, which has had a tremendous impact upon the breed in every country where her book has become available.

The output of her Cheska Kennel showed she could put her theories into successful practice. She bred Eng. Ch. Cheska Alexander of Sternroc, the first Lhasa Apso to win Best in Show at an English all-breed Championship show, as well as his dam, Eng. Ch. Cheska Bobette, and Eng. Ch. Cheska Gregor.

Eng., Aust. Ch. Cheska Jesta, winner of 10 C.C.s in England and Runner-up in Show at the first English Lhasa Apso Club Specialty show in 1969 was exported in whelp (to Eng. Ch. Cheska Gregor) to Australia in December 1971 to join her owner. Jesta had spent the intervening two years in boarding kennels awaiting the lifting of the ban on the import of dogs into Australia. She whelped and raised a litter to eight weeks of age in the Sydney Quarantine.

Jesta went into the show ring in Australia late in 1972 and won her Australian title in six shows. She followed this debut with the following first for a Lhasa Apso in Australia. She won the first Best Exhibit in Show all-breeds Championship show as well as Runner-up in Show all breeds. She was Best Exhibit in Group four times and Best Opposite Sex in Show at the Sydney Royal in 1973 with a total entry all breeds of 4283 dogs.

225

Jesta is the dam of four Australian champions; Ch. Cheska Archee, Australia's top winning Lhasa Apso of all time at this writing with four times Best Exhibit in Show all breeds Championship shows and approximately 1,500 challenge points as well as "Royal" show challenges in four states; Ch. Cheska Mister Ed a Best in Group Winner; Ch. Cheska Anthea and Ch. Cheska Annabelle.

This combination of able breeders should enable Australia to produce many fine Lhasa Apsos in the future.

Belgium

Belgium was one of the first countries in Continental Europe to have Lhasa Apsos.

Shaggy Wonder Ven Ming, one of the first four Lhasas to arrive in Sweden in the 1960s, came from Belgium.

Mrs. Mewis Van Der Ryck, a leading breeder in that country, imported Am. Ch. Orlane's Golden Puppet from Mrs. Dorothy Kendall Lohmann's Orlane Kennel, then located in Iowa. Puppet became an Austrian, French, Netherland and Federal Republic of Germany champion and West German *Bundessieger*. He has many successful progeny in Europe.

Mrs. Der Ryck has exported Lhasa Apsos to many other countries.

Brazil

The South American country of Brazil is very swiftly generating interest in the Lhasa Apso. The top ranking dog, all breeds, for 1977 was the Canadian-bred Int., Can., Braz. Ch. Zaralinga's Lord Raffles, owned by Susy and Joao Maximiliano and bred by Sheila Pike, Ontario, Canada.

The highlight of the Brazilian show year is the Brazil Lhasa Apso Club Specialty held in conjunction with the Rio de Janeiro Kennel Club show in February. The 1977 Specialty featured judge Dr. Adolfo Spector of Argentina. His choice for Best in Show was Ch. Zaralinga's Lord Raffles and Best of Opposite Sex went to Lady Chod Chin Do Daxteri.

Denmark

Interest in the Lhasa Apso in Denmark began about 1970. The foundation stock was imported from the Shaggy Wonder Kennel of Mrs. Mewis Der Ryck in Belgium and mixed with Dutch and Swiss imports.

Int. Ch. Pe-Don van de Warwinckel owned by Britta Andersen.

German Bundessieger Ting La von
Boliba, owned by Dr. Mary Tauber,
Vom Potala, and bred by F. Al-
lefheuser, Germany.

Dshomo vom Potala bred and
owned by Dr. Mary Tauber.

Nal Du vom Potala bred and owned by Dr. Mary Tauber and pictured in Germany at 11 months of age.

Some of the Trashi Deleg Lhasa Apsos of Mrs. Gerti Bracksieck. Upper left is Khamo vom Potala whose sire came from a Tibetan refugee in Nepal. Upper right is Pag Mo von de Warwinckel at seven months of age who is now a champion. Lower left is Soramo and lower right is Tschi Ri vom Potala.

Some kennels now winning to Nordic countries are: Lizette of Mrs. Lizzi Petersen, El Gunga Din of Lis Davidsen, Banzai of Asta and Jorgen Hindlev and Nordhoj of Ann Dilso.

Federal Republic of Germany

The Federal Republic of Germany or West Germany has an International Club for Tibetan Breeds. Professor Heinrich Harrer (author of *My Seven Years in Tibet* and co-author with Norbu of *Tibet*) is Honorary President.

The first Lhasa Apso imported into West Germany was Verles Norbu who came from England in 1966. Ting Ambrosia of Cheska, a daughter of Licos Ting La (from Mrs. Grace Licos of California), also was imported from England.

Norbu and Ting Ambrosia were mated and produced Ting La von Boliba, the first German-bred Lhasa Apso to gain the title of German *Bundessieger*.

Ting La and a bitch, Krysants Lendzema, imported from Sweden became the foundation stock of Docteur Mary Tauber's Vom Potala Kennel. These two when bred produced Dshomo Vom Potala.

Docteur Tauber bred Dshomo to Ch. Dolsa Marlo Matador, bred by Mrs. Jean Kausch of California and owned by Mrs. Schneider-Louter of the Netherlands, and produced Nal Du Vom Potala.

Mrs. Gerti Bracksieck of Trashi Deleg Kennel acquired a Ch. Dolsa Marlo Matador son from Mrs. Schneider-Louter who is the big winning German *Bundessieger* Int. Ch. Pag-Mo van de Warwinckel. Mrs. Bracksieck also has a very strong competitor in Dolsa Red Alert, bred by Mrs. Jean Kausch, California.

As the Lhasa Apso became more popular in West Germany, other kennels became established and Lhasas such as Brackenbury Nanttle, Lucy of Torrens and Ramblersholt Tsake La, as well as imports from Belgium and Holland provided foundation stock.

Currently the base of the breeding stock is narrow. However, with the excellent results the German breeders are having by combining the English and American bloodlines, there will be much future success for the Lhasa Apso in West Germany.

France

Monsieur André Cuny, well known European breeder and judge, has supplied us with this very interesting story of the origin of Lhasa Apsos in France:

"In 1949, Mademoiselle Dupont was traveling in Flanders. Quite by

Foundation bitch of Dr. F. P. Clement's de Gandamak Kennel is
Jo Wa de l'Annapurna bred by Miss V. Dupont.

The new star of Mrs. Bracsieck's Kennel is Europasieger (European champion) Dolsa Red
Alert bred by Mrs. Jean Kausch, Dolsa Lhasa Apsos in California.

Ch. Annapurna Veda bred and owned by Mademoiselle Dupont, Annapurna Kennel, France. *Courtesy of André Cuny*

Int. Ch. Annapurna U'Hyoko bred by Miss Dupont and owned by Mrs. Quemard. *Courtesy of André Cuny*

Am., Fr., Lux. Ch. Dolsa Tamika, bred by Jean Kausch in the United States and owned by Dr. Clement, France.

Fr., Int. Ch. Sinbad de la Nanda Devi bred by Mrs. Lajaunie and owned by Mrs. Chauvin-Daroux, de la Nerto Lhasa Apsos.

Int. Ch. Kyang van de Warwinckel owned and bred by Mrs. Annie Schneider-Louter, De Warwinckel Kennels, the Netherlands.

accident while strolling through the town square in Lille she was taken aback, quite literally, by a rare specimen of dog with long hair, a Lhasa Apso. Following a hasty inquiry as to the origin of this sparky little dog she learned that he was there 'thanks to the English' . . .

"In effect, she learned that two English subjects succeeded in bringing from India, by boat, two Lhasa Apsos. Faced with the impossibility of paying, themselves, the 'quarantine charges' (every dog entering England must be placed in quarantine in specially designated establishments or kennels at the expense of the owner or importer) the Englishmen were forced to relinquish the dogs to some people living in Antwerp, Belgium. So it was then, in Antwerp, that a young lady from Lille, France was to marry the captain of a boat and receive as a wedding gift one of the Lhasa Apsos. The young lady, not recognizing nor appreciating the value of her gift, promptly handed him over to a pet shop owner in Lille for resale. And Mademoiselle Dupont made her way to that shop.

"From 1949 to 1977, over 27 years went by; a long period of determined, hard work, of rigorous selection marked by periods of violent optimism and sometimes fatigue, as well, as things did not always go well for the Lhasa Apsos. But, as we were to see, nothing pays off more, in the end, than work well done as, in itself, it regenerates the courage to continue, even in the face of difficulties and setbacks.

"So that the breed might continue and, more importantly *multiply,* Mademoiselle Dupont was pressed to find a 'foundation bitch' who could carry on her shoulders the entire future of the Lhasa Apso in France. After a tremendous volume of correspondence with the United States, Mademoiselle Dupont succeeded in obtaining a female from Mrs. Cutting.

"This female carried the registration number 'one' in the *Livre des Origines Francaises* (the official French Kennel Club registration book of purebred dogs and bitches) for Lhasa Apso. This bitch was named Hamilton Kangmar, her origins were prestigious—a daughter of Ch. Hamilton Tatsienlu. She was the queen of the ring at dog shows and soon became champion of both France and Switzerland and International champion. Her greatest glory rested on her many descendants, notably the marvelous champion Fo de l'Annapurna, who was a fantastic and prolific stud for the Annapurna Kennel and others.

"Full of enthusiasm, Mademoiselle Dupont, now surrounded by a great number of like enthusiasts of the breed, created a special club officially recognized and registered by the French Kennel Club.

"The first breeder to have produced champions, after Mademoiselle

Am., Fr., Int. Ch. Sharbo Tsan Chu bred by Sharon Rouse, Sharbo, and owned by Dr. Clement. Tsan Chu resides with Rosemarie Crandahl in the United States.

Int. Ch. Troubadour de Gandamak, on a 17th Century prayer table. On the right and left of his head are Apsos carved in the wood over 300 years ago.

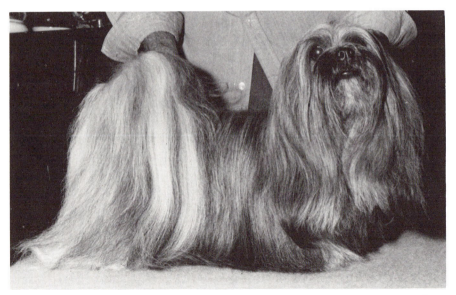

Ch. Mani de Gandamak, Europe's top-winning Lhasa Apso of all times, pictured at 12 years of age, is owned and bred by Dr. Clement.

Dupont, was Dr. F. P. Clement. Dr. Clement uses the kennel name de Gandamak. It must be noted that Docteur Clement had the fortunate opportunity to secure from Miss Dupont a female of remarkable quality, Jo Wa de l'Annapurna (a Fo daughter). Jo Wa produced two litters rendering a total of four females and one of these bitches died very young. The remaining three are International Ch. Mumtaz de Gandamak, French Ch. Noctuelle de Gandamak, both belonged to Mrs. Tikhobrazoff; the third was the unrivalled International champion, Mani de Gandamak, top-winning European Lhasa Apso of all times.

"Madam Tikhobrazoff, who had been interested in the breed for a long time, subsequently became the owner of Noctuelle, litter sister of International Ch. Mumtaz de Gandamak. Mumtaz was the foundation bitch of her now famous kennel, de Bodh Gaya. In the meantime Dr. Clement imported from the United States a superb stud, International Ch. Licos Djesi La. The breeding of this dog with Mumtaz produced French and International Ch. Padme de Bodh Gaya, International and World Ch. Po Yang de Bodh Gaya and all the de Bodh Gaya Lhasa Apsos come from this line.

"Another very active breeder is Mrs. Chauvin-Daroux who uses the kennel name de la Nerto. Mrs. Chauvin is priviledged to own a quality stud in French and International Ch. Sinbad de la Nanda Devi. Her kennel is producing considerable quality and typical Lhasa Apsos."

The French International Championship Show held in March 1977 in Paris was a real international contest. Eng. Ch. Hardacre Sinful Skinful, bred and owned by Mrs. Anne Matthews of the Hardacre Kennel in England won the open dog class; Fr. and Int. Ch. Sinbad de la Nanda Devi, bred by Mr. Lajunie and owned by Mrs. Chauvin-Daroux of de la Nerto Kennel won Best Dog; Int. Ch. Jhora de Bodh Gaya, bred and owned by Mrs. Tikhobrazoff of de Bodh Gaya Kennel won the open bitch class and Am., Fr. and Luxembourg Ch. Dolsa Tamika, bred by Mrs. Jean Kausch and owned by Dr. Clement, won both Best Bitch and Best of Breed. The entry at this Paris show demonstrates the high quality and keen competition of Lhasa Apsos in France.

A dog or bitch needs four National Certificates (CAC) under three different judges to become a French champion, but since the Paris show is a Championship show one French Champion is made in each breed and sex each year. Similarly, a dog or bitch requires four International Certificates (CACIB) under three different judges with a full year between the first and last certificate in order to become an International champion.

We have not mentioned, in this short space alloted to French Lhasa

Apsos, other breeders who have also worked hard for the breed. Those breeders are equally serious and noteworthy but it is impossible to name them all.

India

Present day Tibetans-in-exile in India, Nepal, Sikkim, Bhutan and other countries of the world continue to raise and treasure their dogs. Lhasa Apsos are found in all Tibetan communities, in monasteries, and even in the Dalai Lama's Palace in Dharmsala, India. The Dalai Lama makes special efforts to protect and shelter dogs in the Buddhist tradition of respect for all life.

As the economic picture of the exiled Tibetans improves, the care and attention to their dogs improves accordingly. Each year it is evident that more attention is being paid to the grooming, health and care of Lhasa Apsos owned by exiled Tibetans though in most areas little canine veterinarian help is available.

Breeding is not considered important; however, those who own good dogs generally raise future generations from them. Modern genetics does not enter into breeding among breeders in India. The hardships of maintaining a healthy kennel are great, but kennels do exist. At one time Tenzing Norgay Sherpa, the famous Sherpa guide who climbed Mount Everest with Sir Edmund Hillary, raised Lhasa Apsos. Now he concentrates on his kennel of Tibetan Mastiffs. Others in Delhi, and the Simla area hill stations have produced good Lhasa Apsos. Even in Ladakh, in Northwest India near the Western Tibetan borders there is a small breeding program under the sponsorship of the government agriculture department.

The Indian Kennel Club includes the exhibition of Lhasa Apsos. Also, the Tibetans sponsor their own dog show in Delhi. The Lhasa Apso is still much a part of the exiled Tibetan household. As for the dogs in Tibet today, there are no reports of Lhasa Apsos being seen by recent visitors to Tibet. Recent refugees indicate that a few dogs probably have been hidden in villages and outlying areas but all dogs, except working and herding dogs, have disappeared from the cities. Very few dogs were brought out by refugee groups because the journey was too difficult so little stock remains of dogs that actually came from Tibet. Most dogs in India and neighboring Himalayan countries would be descended from dogs brought out of Tibet prior to 1959.

The Sherpa Tenzing and family with one of their favorites, a little bitch "Blanche Neige" as photographed many years ago. *Courtesy of André Cuny*

The 1971 Western ALAC Specialty Parade of Champions awards were presented by Tenzing Norgay Sherpa. Shown receiving theirs is Mrs. Grace Licos and Am. Ch. Licos Omorfo La.

Mexico

The Lhasa Apso became a resident of Mexico very recently, although the breed has been shown in that country successfully for many years, with a fair number of Lhasa Apsos from the United States becoming Mexican champions.

The Lhasa's establishment in Mexico dates from the arrival in 1975 of Mr. and Mrs. Howard (Mary) Croninger to live at the Club de Golf, Santa Anita, Guadalajara.

Mary Croninger, whose kennel name is Takster, was a breeder in the United States for a number of years and active in the American Lhasa Apso Club, Inc. and the local Specialty club where she lived.

Currently she is active in the all-breed *Club Canofilo de Jalisco A.C.* located in Guadalajara. That club is affililiated with the National *Asociacion Canofila Mexicana, A. C.* (ACM) which belongs to the *Federation Cynologique Internationale* (FCI), the world organization with headquarters in Thuin, Belgium.

Both the Mexican National and the Guadalajara Clubs give shows during the year. Each year, in late November and early December, there is an International circuit held at Mexico City. There both Mexican National and International points and championships can be won.

There are presently so few Lhasa Apsos in Mexico that there is no separate formal organization for the breed. With the interest of Mrs. Croninger in the breed and her activity in the regional Jalisco Club the best interests of the breed will be best fostered within that all-breed organization until the Lhasa's numbers become larger.

Mrs. Croninger's foundation stud, Mex. Ch. Chen Ti Mar Lo Nor, is sired by Ch. Chen Nyun Ti ROM and her foundation bitch is Chen Katrin of Takster, sired by BIS Am., Bda., Col. Ch. Chen Korum Ti ROM.

Tia Deputy has acquired a bitch, Tali-Fu, from Mrs. Croninger. Mrs. Deputy lives in the Guadalajara area.

With these two Lhasa Apso enthusiasts we can look forward to the breed increasing in number and gaining status in Mexico.

The Netherlands

Lhasa Apsos arrived in the Netherlands around 1965 when Mrs. Annie Schneider-Louter imported several from England, one of which was Verles Nang Wa, a daughter of Eng. Ch. Brackenbury Gunga Din of Verles. Nang-Wa became a champion as well as the *Bundessieger,* Winter 1969 and was the first Lhasa Apso to win Best of all Tibetan breeds in Frankfurt Germany in June of 1969.

Int. Ch. Pag-Mo van de War-winckel, bred by Annie Schneider-Louter and owned by Gerti Bracksieck in Germany.

Int. Ch. Cinderella van de Lancelot with her Bearded Collie friend.

Int. Ch., World Ch. Pan-di-tha van de Warwinckel owned by Annie Schneider-Louter.

Some of Mrs. Schneider-Louter's other winners are National, International, Austrian and Swiss Ch. Kyang van de Warwinckel, *Hungaria Prima Junior, Bundessieger* 1971, winner 1971, 1973, *Sieger* Dornbirn, Innsbruck, Linz. Kyang is the first Lhasa who was Best Dog, bred by exhibitor, of an International dog show. Kyang is sired by Shaggy Wonder Pitan ex Ch. Verles Nag-Wa.

International and National Ch. Midon v. d. Warwinckel, World Youth Ch. 1973, Junior Brabo, Europa Ch. 1974, *Sieger* Bern, Linz won the Reserve Best in Show at the International dog show in Bellagio, Italy in 1974.

In 1975 Mrs. Schneider-Louter's International, National Ch. Dolsa Marlo Matador, Youth Winner 1974, Winner 1974, 1975, *Bundesseiger* 1977, Saarland *Sieger* 1976 also won Reserve Best in Show at the International Dog Show in Bellagio, Italy. Matador is the first Lhasa to win Best in Show in the Netherlands. He won this honor at the Haag in December of 1975.

Matador's influence as a sire is demonstrated by his get from Ch. Cinderella van de Lancelot. The three champions from this litter are Danish, CSSR, International Ch. Pe-Don van de Warwinckel, owned by Britta Andersen in Denmark; Best in Show winner, German, International Ch. Pag-Mo van de Warwinckel, *Bundessieger,* owned by Gerti Bracksieck in Germany and International World Champion Pan-di-tha van de Warwinckel, Youth Winner 1975, Europa Youth Ch. 1975, Luxembourg Youth Ch., Brabo Ch., owned by Annie Schneider-Louter of the Netherlands.

It is apparent that as the breed has become known on the Continent of Europe, dogs from the Netherlands as well as other countries may be campaigned in many different countries (i.e. Austria, Belgium, France, Italy, Luxembourg, the Netherlands and Switzerland) besides Denmark and the Nordic countries. In a sense, such campaigning is similar to the same kind of activity in this country but with two differences. In Europe, competition is not only under the *Federation Cynologique International* (FCI), comparable to AKC, but also under national organizations. Although travel may take a European dog into different countries, the distance he travels may well be far less than leading American show dogs cover, in going to Maine, the New England circuit, the Florida circuit, East Coast, Midwest and West Coast shows, not of course necessarily in that order, with possible side trips to Bermuda, Canada and Mexico.

Mrs. Schneider-Louter has supplied us with the many titles that a winning European dog is privileged to list with his name. As is demonstrated by using all the titles it is much less complicated to use

Int. Ch. Dolsa Marlo Matador owned by Annie Schneider-Louter and bred by Mrs. Jean Kausch and Marc Lowy in the United States.

Petite Mouche (left) and Neo van de Warwinckel both owned by Asta and Jorgen Hindlev, Banzai Lhasa Apsos, Denmark.

241

only the title, Champion or International Champion, as has been done in the rest of this chapter.

Netherland Antilles

Am., Can., Bda. Ch. Potala H. B. Big John owned by Mae White of Connecticut went Best in Show at the first Curacao Kennel Club International dog show held May 30, 1976 at Netherland Antilles.

Sweden

Sweden is another of the countries where Lhasa Apsos are a new breed. The first ones to be imported were Swedish Ch. Cheska Yang Tru, a dog, and Swedish Ch. Dryhill Tansi, a bitch, who arrived in 1965 and Nordic Ch. Brackenbury Lhamo, a bitch, came in 1966. These Lhasa Apsos from leading English kennels were imported by Mrs. Marianne Baurne, Krysants Kennel. She later imported Shaggy Wonder Pin Ming from Belgium and Montsweag Chumulary Chumbi, a bitch, from America. Chumbi whelped a litter by Rondelay Chuk Tuk.

Scan., Int. Ch. Dolsa Tsamten Tu was the first Lhasa Apso to win Best in Show in Sweden.

Other imports to Sweden were Ch. Brackenbury Yama, Nordic Ch. Namista Yu-Lin, Nordic Ch. Cheska Ting Anthony, Eng., Nordic Ch. Namista Yarsi and Nordic Ch. Camvale Jason, all arriving in 1968 and 1969. These imports became the foundation of the breed in Sweden.

Swedish dogs have National, Nordic and International championships available to them. A National championship requires three C.C.s won after a dog becomes eight months old. A Nordic championship requires a C.C. after that age from each of the countries, Finland, Norway and Sweden. Requirements for an International Championship are given in the section on Lhasa Apsos in France.

The Swedish Standard is similar to the original English and current American Standards. Lhasa Apsos compete in the Toy Group, which consists of 26 breeds and is essentially a combination of the American Non-Sporting and Toy Groups.

Even though Lhasa Apsos were a comparatively new breed, three had won the Toy Group by 1972. Mrs. Gunilla Anderson's Nordic Ch. Namista Yu-Lin and Mrs. Greta Lindenwall's Ting E Ling's Geisha and Ting E Ling's Bagatelle were Toy Group winners.

In 1976 Scan., Int. Ch. Dolsa Tsamten Tu was the first Lhasa Apso to win Best in Show in Sweden, which he did twice in that one year.

This brief story of the breed in Sweden should make it clear that Lhasa Apsos are well on their way to becoming popular in that country.

Switzerland

Lhasa Apsos are being bred in Switzerland by Mrs. Stoeklin-Pobe under the kennel name of Rohilla.

BIS Ch. Hamilton Torma with Mrs. Randolph Scott (Mrs. Stillman's daughter), a study in glamour.

16

The Lhasa Apso in Literature, Art, and as Pets of Celebrities

IT IS NOT SURPRISING that the Lhasa Apso has not been mentioned very often in literature of the Western World until very recently.

In modern times Tibet as a country was not,even partially open to the West until after the 1904 Younghusband Expedition.

Lhasa Apsos and Tibetan Terriers, were imported as a single breed, called Lhasa Terriers into England about 1901. They increased in number so that by 1908 the breed could issue Challenge Certificates. World War I caused their virtual extinction. Their initial resurgence in England dates from the 1928 return of Lieutenant Colonel Eric and The Honorable Mrs. Bailey from Tibet bringing their six Lhasa Apsos with them.

The first Lhasa Apsos imported into the United States arrived in the 1930s, but it was not until after the mid 1960s that there was any substantial number spread out in this country.

References in Literature

"In Chinese literature" wrote Annie Coath Dixey in 1931 (in *The Lion Dog of Peking,* 1967 republished 1969, Cox & Wyman Ltd. England, page 73) "surprisingly enough, any mention of dogs, especially of pet dogs, is extremely rare."

The situation in Tibetan literature is similar. Tibetan writing has been primarily devoted to religion and mysticism.

Unlike the Chinese, the Tibetans also have an alphabet (different of course from our Aryan alphabets) as well as an ideographic written language. Tibetan words using the alphabet are as incomprehensible to the Westerner as the oriental picture languages. Spelling became standardized in the eighth century and has since lapsed into phonetic decay so that to the uninitiated the spelling of a word is no indication of how it is pronounced. The difficulty is compounded by the fact that there are at least two, and in most cases three, words for each object due to the honorific system of use of different words depending upon the addressee.

For that reason little Tibetan writing has become available in the Western World. That little does not tell us about the Apso.

Norbu, brother of the 14th Dalai Lama, in his two books, and his friend, Heinrich Harrer, in his book, do not mention the Apso.

Although Tibet was partially open to the Western World after 1904 the access to the country was not available to everyone and permission to enter was not easy to obtain even for an Englishman. Dr. McGovern's story makes that difficulty clear in his book, *To Lhasa in Disguise,* 1924.

Most of the few hardy souls who were permitted to travel in Tibet were British. The bulk of their writing does not refer to the Apso. This may be due to the fact, as Dr. Robert Berndt suggests in his book (*Your Lhasa Apso,* 1974, William W. Denlinger, Fairfax, Virginia) that the breed was "kept hidden and well protected from strangers." The British, reputedly being heartily disliked by the Tibetans and the Chinese because of forced concessions of trade rights and financial tribute, were treated as strangers. Concealment of Apsos would match the alleged Chinese concealment of the preferred smaller Shih Tzus from the British. (*This Is The Shih Tzu* by Rev. D. Allan Easton and Joan McDonald Brearley, 1969, TFH Publications, Jersey City, N.J., pages 31–6).

Other nationalities were accorded different treatment by the Chinese and Tibetans. Louise Pulari in 1974 mentions that the 13th Dalai Lama had "pet horses and the Tibetan breed called Lhasa

Ch. Ba Ba Tarin of Garten, litter sister of Kash Gar of Garten, finished her championship in only two months. Ba Ba is bred and owned by Isabelle Loyd.

Ch. Marlo's Tom Tru of Garten.

Ch. Licos Karo La, a full sister of BIS Ch. Licos Kulu La and Ch. Licos Nyapso La.

Apsos'' but she did not say that she saw them. (*Tibet: Heart of Asia*, 1974, The Bobbs-Merrill Company Inc. Indianapolis and New York City, page 92).

C. Suydam Cutting's *Fire Ox and Other Years*, 1940, Scribners, New York City, is one of the few books specifically referring to Lhasa Apsos. The following excerpts give a snapshot of the breed in Tibet:

p. 178. In sending me a pair of Apsos (special breed of Tibetan dogs), the Dalai Lama wrote, "I am sending you two dogs by way of Kalimpong. Please take great care of them when you receive them. Dated 7th of the 1st Tibetan month of the Water Bird Year." (1933).

p. 189. In the throng (at a nomad camp somewhere in Central Tibet) my wife picked out (noticed) a very good black and white Apso dog.

p. 196. Rai Sahib Wangdi, charming and entertaining, received us in his office, where we saw three beautiful jet-black Apso dogs.

p. 221. At parting, the ruler (the Regent) told my wife he would send her a pair of Apso dogs, which greatly delighted her. I had received five of these dogs from the late Dalai Lama and started to breed them successfully in New Jersey. They are a pure Tibetan breed, usually golden, blue-gray, or black; to describe them, I can only say that if a Pekingese were mated with a Yorkshire Terrier, the offspring would look like a first cousin of the Apso. The name, by the way, was first registered outside Tibet by Lieutenant-Colonel and Mrs. Bailey, who introduced them to England.

p. 241. The Regent kept his promise, and the last day we received two golden Apsos, the dogs so much admired by the Tibetans.

p. 242. (en route back to India) . . . there was a great deal of milk for the male and female Apso.

p. 243. The dogs rode well, especially Tsing Tu, the female, who bounced miraculously on my wife's saddle mile after mile. A mile and a half from every stop they would race ahead chasing marmots, which would squeal at the edge of their holes, waiting till the dogs were on them before ducking in.

facing p. 245 is a photograph of American origin with the legend: Apso (Lhasa Terrier). One of those presented to the author by the late Dalai Lama.

Since the Lhasa is a household pet and not a working dog like a Collie, or a guard dog like a Mastiff and is not used for hunting or racing, the number of possible areas for stories of the breed as a principal character is severely limited. Even as a subsidiary character its use tends, at least in the past, to be restricted to stories in which it could be used as a status symbol. The movie *Race With the Devil*, starring Peter Fonda, showed a departure from such use.

248

Ch. Kash Gar's Chen Chen of Garten is a son of Ch. Kash Gar of Garten and is out of Hello Dolly of Garten.

Ch. Licos Nyapso La is the paternal Grand-dam of BIS Ch. Kham of Norbulingka ROM and maternal Grand-dam of BIS Ch. Tibet of Cornwallis ROM. Handled by George Payton.

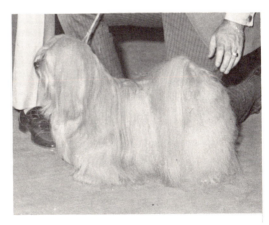

Ch. Karma Rus Tigu is the son of Ch. Karma Rus Ti and Karma Mantra.

A modern Tibetan rug with the figure of
the symbolic snow lion woven into it.

Renderings in Art

We have not seen or are we aware of beautiful paintings or statues of Lhasa Apsos comparable to those depicting early dogs of some other breeds. That, however, does not prove that there are none. We have seen figurines of the breed made of pottery and different kinds of metal.

Companions of the Famous

Lhasa Apsos were so rare in this country until well past the mid-1950s that to some extent they became status symbols and many celebrities owned them.

Famous women like the Duchess of Windsor; Lily Pons, the opera singer; Peggy Lee, the pop singer; Elizabeth Taylor, who gave a couple as gifts and kept four aboard a yacht in the London harbor during a six-month quarantine period; Mrs. Randolph Scott, wife of the movie actor and daughter of Mrs. Marie Stillman of Americal Kennels; Shirley MacLaine, movie actress and Peggy Guggenheim, wealthy art connoisseur, had Lhasa Apsos during the time when they were comparatively few in number.

Well-known male figures such as the Shah of Iran; the stage and movie director, Mike Nichols; the actor, Errol Flynn; actor George

Hamilton and singer Glen Campbell also have or have had Lhasa Apsos.

Lhasas have appeared from time to time on television. In the 1962–1963 period, for example, they appeared on Captain Kangaroo's educational program originating on CBS-TV, from New York City. Currently they are more apt to appear with celebrities on talk shows, such as Phyllis Diller and her Lhasa on the *Dinah Shore Show*.

BIS Ch. Tibet of Cornwallis ROM appeared on the *Mike Douglas Show* along with several dogs of other breeds.

A Tale of Heroism

From time to time there are stories of alertness in times of stress and heroism on the part of Lhasa Apsos. The American Lhasa Apso Club at its 1975 Awards Dinner presented a special award for herosim during 1974 to Zim Zim Ray and Tabu's Bric A Brac. They had alerted their owners to a fire.

With the tremendous increase in Lhasa Apso population in the United States since the 1960s it is probable that Lhasas, in the next decade, will appear more frequently in American literature and plays, in the movies and on television and become subjects of works of art; but, more importantly, they will become, as they are becoming, the pets and companions they were bred to be.

The figure in this photo is the young Dalai Lama and the cute gal guarding him is America's Cookie a special favorite of Mrs. Marie Stillman when this photo was taken. The statue was part of the Ripley Estate.

The first ALAC match show held in 1959 on the grounds of Hamilton Farms.

252

17

The American Lhasa Apso Club and Regional Clubs

THE FOUNDING of the American Lhasa Apso Club (ALAC) was official on February 9, 1959, at Madison Square Garden during the Westminster Kennel Club Show. Fourteen members answered the roll call at that first organizational meeting and the Secretary reported 61 members enrolled.

Charter Officers

That Secretary was Dorothy Benitez and she was never absent from the list of officers in the following eighteen years having served as Secretary, Secretary-Treasurer and Treasurer. Mrs. Benitez has also been the true keeper of records for it is Dorothy who answered all our questions for this book about early Club information.

Another charter member who did not move from her position as First Vice-President for fifteen years is the great lady and foundation breeder of Lhasas, Grace Licos. Mrs. Licos coordinated many of the Western ALAC Specialties including the first, held in 1969.

Dorothy Cohen, who acquired many of the Hamilton Lhasas after the death of Mrs. Cutting, was in the first founding group as a member of the Board of Directors.

Marie Stillman, Americal, Frank T. Lloyd, Ming, and Paul Williams, Cornwallis, were also founding members and members of the first Board of Directors.

Mr. C. Suydam Cutting was made Honorary President, a position he held until the time of his death in 1972. Fred Huyler was the first President and Treasurer for the $590.92 that ALAC started with. Marilyn Sorci, Shangri La, was the first Corresponding Secretary, and James Anderson, who first dreamed of starting a club, was the Second Vice President.

Early Goals

The members at this first meeting discussed the financial report and plans, along with plans for a first Specialty show and also their membership in the American Kennel Club. They declared the ALAC colors to be Tibetan turquoise and silver. The Constitution and By-Laws were drawn up in that first year and were not changed until the time of ALAC's incorporation in the State of Virginia in 1972.

The second meeting of ALAC, held again in conjunction with the Westminster Kennel Club Show in February, 1960, found twelve members present. Among them, in addition to the officers, were Dorothy de Gray, Las Sa Gre; Ann Griffing, Chig; Frank T. Lloyd, Ming; John Partanen, Rinpoche and Paul Williams, Cornwallis.

This team is composed of (left to right) Licos Gingti La, Licos Shargun La, Licos Gen La and Licos Angden La. They are from one to three years, are all golden and weigh 14 pounds each. They each have different sires and dams and are living proof of the line breeding at Licos. They are shown winning a Non-Sporting Group Team first, handled by Walt Phaler for owner Grace Licos at the 1973 Beverly Hills show. The judge is Isidore Schoenberg.

254

The 1972 Eastern ALAC Specialty winners. Frank Landgraf chose Ch. Kasha's Nyima Zu Nam Che (left) Best of Opposite Sex, owned by Marlene Annunziata and handled by Ann Hoffman. Best of Breed was Ch. Chen Korum Ti (right) owned by Patricia Chenoweth and handled by Robert Sharp. Korum Ti followed this record entry BB win by winning BIS over 4000 dogs at the Trenton KC show with which the Specialty was held.

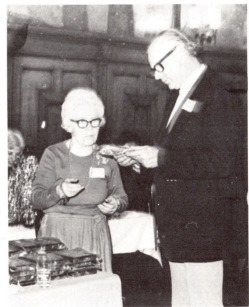

The late Anna Griffing presenting an ALAC award to Robert Sharp at the 1973 Annual Awards dinner in New York City.

The Secretary reported a membership of 81. The election of officers made no change from the previous year.

In May of 1960 the President appointed Robert and Anna Griffing, Frank Lloyd and Dorothy Benitez to serve on a committee to decide upon a match show.

First Sanctioned Match

The first ALAC sanctioned B match was held on September 16, 1962 on the grounds of Hamilton Farms and judged by Mr. Edward H. Goodwin, with Robert Griffing presiding as Match Chairman. The entry fee was fifty cents per dog. An entry of 38 was on hand for the historic event.

Best in Match was Kham of Norbulingka and Best Adult Bitch was his dam, Karma Kosala, both owned by Phyllis Fulton (Marcy) of Washington D.C. Best Puppy in Match was Chig Seng, owned by Robert Griffing, Mountainside, New Jersey.

The Parade of Champions included:

Ch. Linga-Drog-Po (3 yrs.), owner Robert Griffing
Ch. Hamilton Namsa (3 yrs.), owner Dorothy Benitez
Ch. Ming Thudi (4 yrs.), owner Estate of Frank T. Lloyd, Jr.
Ch. Ming Teri (5 yrs.), owner Estate of Frank T. Lloyd, Jr.
Ch. Ming Siming (6 yrs.), owner Estate of Frank T. Lloyd, Jr.
Ch. Hamilton Sandupa (7 yrs.), owner C. S. Cutting
Ch. Hamilton Kung (7 yrs.), owner C. S. Cutting
Ch. Ming Toy Nola (8 yrs.), owner Anna M. Griffing
Ch. Hamilton Tatsienlu (13 yrs.), owner C. S. Cutting
Ch. Le (14 yrs.), owner Dorothy Benitez

ALAC Moves Ahead

The 1963 election of officers saw a change with Robert Griffing becoming ALAC's new President and Alfred Stillman, Marie Stillman's son, the new Second Vice-President. Secretary and Treasurer became one job and Dorothy Benitez was elected to that office. The new Corresponding Secretary was Anna Griffing.

The second ALAC match show was held on June 2, 1963 at the Griffing residence in Mountainside New Jersey with Dorothy Benitez the judge. The entry of 37 included Lhasas from Georgia, Florida, Maine, Pennsylvania, New York and New Jersey. Best in Match went to Chig Seng owned by Robert Griffing.

The 1964 election saw all officers the same as the previous year. The Club approved the publication of a Club pamphlet describing the

Multiple Group winner Am., Mex. Ch. Tsan's Drima is a son of Ch. Shangri La Sho George and Ch. Tsan's Datso. He is pictured winning the Non-Sporting Group at the 1967 Kennel Club of Beverly Hills show with his owner, La Verne Payton under Alva Rosenberg.

Ch. Karma Kan-Sa ROM is the dam of three champions; one is BIS Am., Can., Bda. Ch. Ku Ka Boh of Pickwick. She is pictured winning under the late Robert Kerns, handler Dot Primm.

history, Standard and requirements for membership. By now the Club had a *Bulletin* that was to be sent to the membership four times a year.

On July 12, 1964 the Club conducted a Plan A sanctioned match, again held at the Griffing home. There were 36 entries judged by Mrs. Elbertine Campbell. Best in Match was won by Lama of Norbulingka, owned by Phyllis Taylor (Marcy) and Best of Opposite Sex was Licos Cheti La, owned by Paul Williams.

The slate of officers for 1965 did not change and by April, 1965 the *Bulletin* reported plans for the second Plan A match at the home of the Griffings, but the focus of this *Bulletin* was the hope for a Specialty show in 1966.

The 1965 Plan A match had a total of 47 entries with some coming from as far away as Arizona, Nevada, Michigan and Florida. Frank Landgraf, who had judged at Westminster the previous year, officiated and Mrs. Landgraf worked, as she often did, as his ring steward. Best in Match was Merda Cai owned by Aleta D. Styers of Niles, Michigan and Best of Opposite Sex was Rondelay's Dorje Gyalpo, owned by George H. Montgomery of New York City.

The October 1965 *Bulletin* included the following memorandum to the members: " . . . Your Club, The American Lhasa Apso Club, has decided to hold it's first Specialty Show in conjunction with the Trenton Kennel Club Show in Trenton, New Jersey, on May 8, 1966 . . ."

The 1966 annual election was held as usual at the time of the Westminster show and the officers again remained the same. A motion was made and passed that a committee be appointed to see if the Standard of the breed could be revised to make it more understandable not only to the members but also to the public and dog show judges.

The First Specialty

Plans were made for the important first annual Specialty show and in a membership *Bulletin* President Griffing announced that the AKC approved the application for holding the Specialty in conjunction with the Trenton Kennel Club Show. As part of this announcement Griffing wrote: "At last we have arrived! Yes, after three years of match shows, a Plan B in 1962 and 1963, a Plan A in 1964 and 1965, we have finally arrived."

President Griffing's enthusiasm continued as he reported the results of the first Specialty. The successful entry of 52 Lhasa Apsos was, he believed, a record. Mr. James Trullinger was the judge and his choice for Best of Breed was Ch. Kham of Norbulingka, owned by Mrs. Phyllis Taylor (Marcy) and Winners bitch was Ebbtides Sing Kye Koko, owned by Alfred Likewise.

258

The panel participating in the Forum held in conjunction with the 1974 ALAC Annual meeting. Sitting left to right; David Goldfarb, Stephen Campbell, Phyllis Marcy, David Marshall, Paula Lieberman, Dorothy Lohmann, Grace Licos. Standing Edmund Sledzik, Robert Sharp and Carolyn Herbel.

Ch. Licos Namni La and handler Robert Sharp in the Veterans class at the 1973 Eastern ALAC Specialty.

259

The Pace Increases

Bulletins were being sent out more frequently by President Griffing as the pace of Club activity also was increasing under his leadership. One reported a successful 1966 fun match and a new record entry of 62 Lhasas. The match was judged by Cyril Bernfeld and Americal's Lhasa, owned by Dorothy Benitez, won Best in Match.

This same *Bulletin* announced that ALAC's second annual Specialty was approved. The *Bulletin* added that, "we are still hoping to run a Specialty with the Beverly Hills Kennel Club. We are working on it and if successful will let you know at once."

By now the registrations of Lhasa Apsos with the AKC had increased from 245 in 1960 to 859 for 1965 and jumped over the thousand mark in 1966.

The annual election in 1967 provided a new President, Alfred Likewise, and the office of Secretary-Treasurer again was split with Dorothy Benitez remaining as the Treasurer and Patricia Gleeson was the new Secretary. All other officers remained the same.

There was much discussion at this meeting concerning the responsibility of ALAC to have involved members, nationwide. There was also concern about the revision of the Standard but attending members were informed by their new President that such a change could not be attempted until ALAC had been accepted by the AKC as a member club.

In a May issue, Alfred Likewise apologized for the lateness of the *Bulletin* and gave a report on the second Specialty show held on May 5, 1967 at Trenton. He wrote that, "the weather made this one of the cruelest shows I have ever attended. A buffet, planned by the committee, was soon forgotten because of the rain and high winds." The judge, Keith Browne, chose Ch. Kyi Chu Shara, owned by Mrs. Leon Blumberg for Best of Breed and Best of Opposite Sex was her litter brother, Ch. Kyi Chu Whimsi of Sharbet, owned by Dr. Monroe Kornfeld.

The July *Bulletin* gave notice of the planned September match and also reported a suggestion by Robert Sharp that ALAC consider Achievement Awards for its members.

The September 1967 match was a success with 47 entries judged by Mrs. Alan Braunstein.

There was no change in officers resulting from the 1968 annual election. The club voted to sponsor a Futurity in conjunction with the 1969 Specialty show and Robert Griffing was appointed Futurity Chairman.

The highlight of this annual meeting was the presentation of the first annual Achievement Awards. The winners of Achievement Awards

Stephen Campbell, ALAC Awards Chairman, presenting an award to Barry Tompkins at the 1974 Annual Awards Dinner in New York.

Some of the champions competing for Best of Breed at the 1975 Eastern ALAC Specialty show.

The open bitch class at the 1975 Western ALAC Specialty held in conjunction with the Beverly Hills KC.

Ch. Crest-O-Lake Pretti Plez winning a Group first under Winifred Heckmann in 1971, shown by junior handler Karen Haas. Bred by Crest-O-Lake Kennels, she is a daughter of Maraja Dolpho Karmo and Ch. Crest O Lake Mandy Lee.

that first year were: Ch. Tyba Le of Ebbtide, Ch. Tn Hi Di-Ly-Hri, Ch. Tibet of Cornwallis, Ch. Kinderland's Sang-Po, Ch. Chig Chig, Ch. Sharpa Chenga Eastcroft, Ch. Agra's Imprecious and Ch. Kyi Chu Kum Nuk.

Harry H. Brunt judged the 59 Lhasa Apsos entered in the third ALAC Specialty held in 1968, at Trenton. His choice for Best of Breed was Ch. Kyi Chu Friar Tuck and Best of Opposite Sex was Ch. Kinderland's Shu Jin. The 1968 ALAC match was a success with Phyllis Marcy judging an entry of 59 and an attendance of about 200 people.

The 1969 annual election provided only one change in the slate of officers. Mary Likewise became the new Secretary. Grace Licos announced that the Western Specialty was approved to be held in conjunction with the Kennel Club of Beverly Hills and that all the preparations were made.

May 4, 1969 was the date of the fourth Eastern ALAC Specialty and the first ALAC Futurity. The judge for both events was Henry Stoecker. He chose Kinderland's Tonka as Best Puppy in Futurity and Potala Keke's Luckee was Best Adult in Futurity. His Best of Breed winner was Ch. Ku Ka Boh of Pickwick and Best of Opposite Sex was Kinderland's Gay La.

The first Western ALAC Specialty was held in conjunction with the Kennel Club of Beverly Hills on June 21–22, 1969. The judge was Forrest Hall who chose Ch.Teako of Abbotsford for Best of Breed and Ch. Karma Skar-Cen Best of Opposite Sex. The inception of the Western Specialty insured the national complexion of the Club.

ALAC into the Seventies

The 1970 annual election found competition from additional write-in nominations because of the enthusiasm of the increasing membership. Counting of the 77 ballots resulted in a new President, Ruth Deck, Rondelay, and a new Secretary, Cheryl Hueneke. All other officers remained the same.

On May 3, 1970 the fifth Eastern ALAC Specialty and the second ALAC Futurity was held at Trenton once more, with Grace Licos choosing Chen Tompar Nor as Best Puppy in Futurity and Ch. Kinderland's Nichola as Best Adult in Futurity. Cyril Bernfeld chose Ch. Kyi Chu Friar Tuck as Best of Breed and Ch. Pon Go's Chi Kha was Best of Opposite Sex.

The second Western ALAC Specialty was a great success, again under the guidance of Grace Licos. It was held in June, again in conjunction with the Kennel Club of Beverly Hills and Heywood Hartley chose Ch. Everglo Zijuh Tomba as Best of Breed. Chamdos Serena was Mr. Hartley's Choice for Best of Opposite Sex.

The only change in officers after the 1971 annual election was the position of Secretary, now filled by Jean Stang.

The sixth Eastern ALAC Specialty and the third ALAC Futurity, both held at Trenton, were beginning to have a more national flavor with Jay Shaeffer drawing an entry of 112 and selecting the Canadian winner, Am., Can. Ch. Balrene's Chia Pao, as his Best of Breed and Best of Opposite Sex was Ch. Kinderland's Tonka. The Futurity judging procedure had changed so the judge, Phyllis Marcy, was able to choose the Grand Futurity Winner which was Potala Keke's Kal-E-Ko.

On the West Coast the 1971 Specialty winner was Ch. Chen Korum Ti who was chosen by O. C. Harriman for Best of Breed. The Best of Opposite Sex choice was Ch. America1's Moma. The Western Specialty still being held in conjunction with the Kennel Club of Beverly Hills was organized again by Grace Licos. This show was highlighted by the presence of Tenzing Norgay Sherpa, of Mount Everest fame, who presented the trophies.

President Ruth Deck wrote in the August, 1971 Bulletin, "It is felt that serious consideration should be given by all of our members to the proposal by Norman Herbel regarding a new *Bulletin*. As perhaps most members do not realize, the *Bulletin* at present is pretty much the result of the President's effort . . . ."

The Club had continued to sponsor fun matches and reported that there were regional clubs springing up all over the country.

The 1972 annual election results showed Robert Sharp as the new President and Ruth Smith, Second Vice-President, with all other officers unchanged.

Under the leadership of Robert Sharp, ALAC accepted the proposal of Norman Herbel for a new format for the *Bulletin*. It was now a magazine, printed professionally. It was subsidized by the Club but paid advertising made it possible. For the first time the *Bulletin* printed photographs of the dogs.

Keke Blumberg was appointed to head the Breed Standard Committee, and the Annual Awards program was revitalized with the establishment of the Annual Awards dinner, held in New York City in conjunction with the Westminster show.

President Sharp, working closely with Edmund Sledzik and David Goldfarb, succeeded in the incorporation of ALAC.

The President's Message in the September 1972 *Lhasa Bulletin*

BIS Ch. Chen Korum Ti ROM shown winning the Stud Dog class at the 1975 ALAC Western Specialty under judge Robert Berndt. Shown left to right is Kori with Carol Smith; Am., Can., Mex. Ch. Krisna Kaitu with Al Lynch and Ch. Krisna Kam-Tora of Sunji with Wendy Harper. Presenting the trophy is Norman Herbel, the ALAC President. Kori was also Best of Breed at 8½ years from the Veterans class at this Specialty.

contained the plea for all members to return questionaires with the necessary information needed to request approval from the AKC to be a member club.

The 1972 Eastern Specialty, judged by Frank Landgraf, had a record entry of 172. The Best of Breed winner was Ch. Chen Korum Ti. Best of Opposite Sex went to Ch. Kasha's Nyima Zu Nam Che. The 1972 Grand Futurity Winner chosen by Sharon Binkowski, Arborhill, was Kinderland's L'oo-Ky.

The Western ALAC Specialty, held in Beverly Hills again, was judged by William Bergum and he chose as his Best of Breed winner, Ch. Chen Korum Ti over an entry of 124. The Best of Opposite Sex winner was Ch. Kinderland's Tonka.

Robert Sharp was re-elected at the 1973 annual election and Carolyn Herbel was elected the new Secretary. The other officers remained unchanged.

Futurity Chairman Norman Herbel presented a new Futurity program to be implemented in 1974. This program called for three regional Futurities (Eastern, Midwestern and Western) thereby allowing more participation in this event throughout the country.

President Sharp appointed Stephen Campbell as the new Awards Chairman and under his guidance 1973 was the first year that ALAC offered Register of Merit (ROM) recognition to outstanding producers, both individual dogs and breeders, as well as top twenty listings for these categories.

Because of the large entry of the previous year the eighth Eastern ALAC Specialty provided for two judges. Kenneth Stine judged bitches and Dr. David Doane judged dogs and intersex classes. Mr. Stine chose Taglha Pokara of Nottoway as his Winners Bitch. Dr. Doane chose Ch. Barcon's The Avenger as Best of Breed, Ch. Kinderland's Tonka as Best of Opposite Sex, and Tabu's Double or Nuthin was Winners Dog.

The 1973 Futurity, judged by Patricia Chenoweth, was also at Trenton. Shyr Lyz De Ly Lah of Ritos was the Grand Futurity winner.

The fifth Western ALAC Specialty was judged by breeder-judge Alfred Likewise at Beverly Hills. He chose Ch. Sharpette's Gaylord as Best of Breed and Best of Opposite Sex went to Everglo Flair.

The most rewarding announcement President Sharp made in 1973 was that ALAC would be first published in the March issue of *Pure-bred Dogs—American Kennel Gazette,* and if all went as expected ALAC should be accepted as an AKC member club in June of 1974. Another goal had been reached.

To meet requirements for acceptance as an AKC member club the

266

Ch. Shyr Lyz Fabalous Flirt, Grand Futurity winner at the 1975 Eastern region ALAC Futurity, is handled by her breeder and owner Shirley Scott (Shyr Lyz). The judge is Georgia Palmer.

Ch. Dandi Fanci Dandi is a full brother of Ch. Dandi's Wahoo and is owned and bred by Diane Dansereau. He is shown winning a Best of Breed under Dr. Malcolm Phelps, handled by Mrs. Dansereau.

267

original Constitution and By-Laws had been changed and the annual election was next held in May, 1974. This election provided the Club with a new President, Edmund R. Sledzik. The new constitution eliminated the offices of Second Vice-President and Corresponding Secretary, but all other officers remained unchanged.

President Sledzik was very active in office and worked to stimulate a completely national Club by traveling extensively. He also put much emphasis on increasing the number of regional clubs as well as stressing the need for revising the Standard.

David Goldfarb suggested having nationwide forums to be held in conjunction with other ALAC events around the country. Appointed chairman of the Forum Committee, Goldfarb conducted many forums and the Club was truly a parent club; performing service to its members and other Lhasa enthusiasts.

The 1974 Eastern Specialty held at Trenton once again provided for two judges. Joseph Faigel judged bitches and chose Potala Keke's Andromeda as Winners Bitch. Alfred Likewise judged dogs and intersex classes and chose Ch. Barcon's The Avenger for Best of Breed, Ch. Potala Keke's Yum Yum ROM for Best of Opposite Sex and Oliver Twist of Cedar Lake for Winners Dog.

The 1974 Western Specialty was held at Beverly Hills with breeder-judge Keke Blumberg officiating. Ch. Blackbay Georgana of Yin Hi I. Q. was her choice for Best of Breed and Ch. Goodway's Chuho Lama was Best of Opposite Sex.

Futurity activity for 1974 was now in three locations with Onnie Martin, Pandan, judging the Western region and choosing San Jo's Looki Mei as Western Grand Futurity winner. Ellen Lonigro, Kinderland, chose Chok's Coffey as Eastern Grand Futurity winner and Dr. Ellen Brown, of Canadian fame, chose Taglha Sinsa of Kinderland for Midwestern Grand Futurity winner.

The 1974 third Annual Awards Dinner announced many more Lhasa Apsos and breeders entitled to display ROM behind their names. This gala event was, as usual, organized by Raena Wilks, Hospitality Chairman.

In compliance with President Sledzik's desire to make ALAC a truly national club the membership voted to change the locations of the Specialties.

The 1975 Annual election provided the Club with still another new President, Norman Herbel. Carol Kuendel was the new Secretary and for the first time ALAC had the privilege to elect an AKC Delegate, namely Stephen Campbell. There was no change in the other officers.

The agenda for the officers this year seemed to be travel for now there were many events being held in various parts of the country.

The Open Dog class at the 1976 Western ALAC Specialty judged by Onnie Martin.

Winner of the Stud Dog class at the 1976 Western ALAC Specialty is (left to right) BIS Ch. Tibet of Cornwallis ROM, handled by Carolyn Herbel, and his progeny BIS Ch. Tulku's Yeti of Milarepa with Ruth Barker and Ch. Tabu's Dresden Doll with Norman Herbel.

269

The 1975 tenth Eastern ALAC Specialty was held in Trenton with Keke Blumberg, the only judge, choosing Ch. Daktazl Tsung as Best of Breed and Ch. Chick Chick's Shen Lee as Best of Opposite Sex.

The 1975 seventh Western ALAC Specialty was held again at Beverly Hills, with breeder-judge Robert Berndt officiating. He chose from the veteran's class Ch. Chen Korum Ti ROM as Best of Breed and Ch. Potala Keke's Yum Yum ROM as Best of Opposite Sex.

With the annual election now in May, the 1976 Eastern Specialty, held in February in conjunction with the Louisville Specialties, was also during the term of the same officers. Robert Berndt judged this show and chose Ch. Potala Keke's Yum Yum ROM as Best of Breed and Ch. La Ta's Dus Ten Wun as Best of Opposite Sex.

The 1976 Western ALAC Specialty was held in conjunction with the Texas Kennel Club in Dallas. This March event was judged by breeder-judge Onnie Martin who chose Ch. Potala Keke's Yum Yum ROM as Best of Breed. Ch. Little Fir's Shel Ari of Chiz was Best of Opposite Sex.

The 1975 ALAC Western Futurity was judged by Carol Kuendel, Chok, who chose San Jo's Orain as Grand Futurity winner. The Midwestern Futurity was judged by Stephen Campbell, Rimar, and his choice for Grand Futurity winner was Windsong Madoro's Mai Li Chin. Georgia Palmer, Ruffway, chose Shyr Lyz Fabalous Flirt as the Eastern Grand Futurity winner.

The 1976 and 1977 election of officers found Edmund R. Sledzik again in the President's chair. During these terms of office President Sledzik developed the format for an annual Championship-Obedience handbook to be published by ALAC.

Much work was also done on the revision of the Standard which was approved by AKC on July 11, 1978.

The 1976 Western Grand Futurity winner was chosen by Ruth Smith, Kyi Chu, and was San Jo's Shenanigan. Alfred Likewise, Ebbtide, chose Chok's Summa Puma as the Eastern Grand Futurity winner and Marianne Nixon, San Jo, chose Anbara's Abra Ka Dabra as the Midwestern Grand Futurity winner.

The 1977 Western Grand Futurity winner was Ch. San Jo's Hussel Bussel, chosen by Stephen Campbell, and Ellen Lonigro chose Mor Knoll Rgyal Arisa Volents as the Eastern Grand Futurity winner. Joan Kendall Lohmann, Orlane, chose Ch. Luty Diamond Lil as the Midwestern Grand Futurity winner.

The 1977 Eastern ALAC Specialty, held in Syracuse, New York, was judged by Edmund R. Sledzik who chose Ch. Rimar's Rumpelstiltskin as Best of Breed and Ch. Anbara's Abra Ka Dabra as Best of Opposite Sex.

Ch. Kyi Chu Kara Nor ROM is the dam of eight champions. Bred by Ruth Smith and owned by Patricia and Tom Chenoweth she is a litter sister to Ch. Kyi Chu Kaliph Nor. She is shown here with Onnie Martin.

BIS Am., Bda., Col. Ch. Chen Korum Ti ROM won the 1971, 1972 and 1975 Western ALAC Specialties and the 1972 Eastern ALAC Specialty. He is shown with handler Robert Sharp.

The 1977 Western Specialty was held in Houston, Texas and was judged by Jay Shaeffer who chose as Best of Breed, Ch. Yojimbo Orion and Best of Opposite Sex, Ch. Taglha Kusu.

ALAC, as of the last roster, has in excess of 500 members, a direct result of the leadership of the Club and the skyrocketing popularity of the breed. More than 22,000 Lhasa Apsos were registered with the American Kennel Club in 1977 making it the 13th most popular of all breeds in the United States and second only to Poodles in the Non-Sporting Group.

Regional Lhasa Apso Clubs

The many activities of ALAC throughout the United States has been possible because of the hosting of these events by the many hard working members of the regional clubs. The following is a list of these clubs as supplied to us by ALAC:

Baltimore Area Lhasa Apso Club
Cascade Lhasa Apso Fanciers of Greater Seattle
Central New York Lhasa Apso Club
Greater Albuquerque Lhasa Apso Club
Greater Columbus Lhasa Apso Club
Greater Dallas Lhasa Apso Club
Greater Detroit Lhasa Apso Club
Greater Memphis Area Lhasa Apso Club
Greater Milwaukee Lhasa Apso Club
Heart of America Lhasa Apso Club
Kentuckiana Lhasa Apso Club
Lhasa Apso Club of Greater Houston
Lhasa Apso Club of Greater New York
Lhasa Apso Club of Greater St. Louis
Lhasa Apso Club of the Greater Twin Cities Area
Lhasa Apso Club of Hawaii
Lhasa Apso Club of Northern California
Lhasa Apso Club of Southern California
Lhasa Apso Club of Westchester, Inc.
Lhasa Apso Society of Atlanta
Long Island Lhasa Apso Club
Merrimack Lhasa Apso Club
Miami Valley Lhasa Apso Club
National Capital Area Lhasa Apso Club
North East Lhasa Apso Specialty Club
North Texas Lhasa Apso Club
Northern Illinois Lhasa Apso Association
Worcester Lhasa Apso Club

American Lhasa Apso Club Futurities

Year	Place	Judge	Entry	Puppy Class Winner	Adult Class Winner
1969	Trenton, NJ	Henry H. Stoecker	22	Kinderland's Tonka	Potala Keke's Luckee
1970	Trenton, NJ	Grace Licos	10	Chen Tompar Nor	Ch. Kinderland's Nicola
1971	Trenton, NJ	Phyllis Marcy	33	Potala Keke's Kal E Ko*	Chok Ke Tu
1972	Trenton, NJ	Sharon Binkowski	39	Tabu's Gold Galaxy	Kinderland's L'oo-Ky*
1973	Trenton, NJ	Patricia Chenoweth	41	Potala Keke's Fraser	Shyr Lyz D Ly Lah of Ritos*
1974	Western Region				
	Seattle, WA	Onnie Martin	27	San Jo's Raaga Looki Mei*	Chen Krisna Tob Zan
	Eastern Region				
	Trenton, NJ	Ellen Lonigro	63	Chok's Joker	Chok's Coffey*
	Midwest Region				
	Detroit, MI	Ellen Brown	27	Taglha Sinsa of Kinderland*	Ming's Lord Cognac
1975	Western Region				
	Seattle, WA	Carol Kuendel	13	San Jo's Orain*	Mingtree Raaga Marauder
	Eastern Region				
	Oxon Hill, MD	Georgia Palmer	51	Shyr Lyz Fabalous Flirt*	Potala Keke's Golden Gatsby
	Midwest Region				
	New Orleans, LA	Stephen Campbell	21	Blahapolo Topaz Ghemston	Windsong Madoro's Mai Li Chin*
1976	Western Region				
	Pebble Beach, CA	Ruth Smith		Alabastrine Girl of Clyde	San Jo's Shenanigan*
	Eastern Region				
	Boxford, MA	Alfred Likewise	30	Kymba Yeti Copper Knight	Chok's Summa Puma*
	Midwest Region				
	Cincinnati, OH	Marianne Nixon	53	Anbara's Abra Ka Dabra*	Bet R's Shangrelu Tuff Stuff
1977	Western Region				
	Beverly Hills, CA	Stephen Campbell	31	San Jo's Kian Kandi Kan	Ch. San Jo's Hussel Bussel*
	Eastern Region				
	Queens, NY	Ellen Lonigro	30	Misti's I've Got Da Spirit	Mor Knoll Rgyal Arisa Volents*
	Midwest Region				
	Appleton, WI	Dorothy K. Lohmann	44	Ch. Luty Diamond Lil*	Ch. Mor Knoll Enchantress

*Indicates Grand Futurity Winner

273

Eastern American Lhasa Apso Club Specialties

Year	Place	Judge	Entry	Dogs	Bitches	Champions	Best of Breed
1966	Trenton, NJ	James Trullinger	52	21	16	11	Ch. Kham of Norbulingka ROM
1967	Trenton, NJ	Keith Browne	50	20	22	8	Ch. Kyi Chu Shara ROM
1968	Trenton, NJ	Harry H. Brunt	59	21	23	15	Ch. Kyi Chu Friar Tuck ROM
1969	Trenton, NJ	Henry H. Stoecker	83	23	44	14	Ch. Ku Ka Boh of Pickwick
1970	Trenton, NJ	Cyril Bernfeld	112	39	52	21	Ch. Kyi Chu Friar Tuck ROM
1971	Trenton, NJ	Jay C. Shaeffer	116	45	50	21	Ch. Balrene Chia Pao
1972	Trenton, NJ	Frank Landgraf	172	60	75	34	Ch. Chen Korum Ti ROM
1973	Trenton, NJ	David Doane (Dogs & Intersex) Kenneth Stine (Bitches)	167	62	75	29	Ch. Barcon's The Avenger
1974	Trenton, NJ	Alfred Likewise (Dogs & Intersex) Joseph Faigel (Bitches)	155	67	76	24	Ch. Barcon's The Avenger
1975	Trenton, NJ	Keke Blumberg	105	45	42	17	Ch. Daktazl Tsung
1976	Louisville, KY	Robert Berndt	101	36	46	17	Ch. Potala Keke's Yum Yum ROM
1977	Syracuse, NY	Edmund R. Sledzik	113	34	54	21	Ch. Rimar's Rumpelstiltskin

Western American Lhasa Apso Club Specialties

Year	Place	Judge	Entry	Dogs	Bitches	Champions	Best of Breed
1969	Beverly Hills, CA	Forrest N. Hall	62	28	20	14	Ch. Teako of Abbotsford
1970	Beverly Hills, CA	Heywood Hartley	85	40	27	18	Ch. Everglo Zijuh Tomba
1971	Beverly Hills, CA	O. C. Harriman	100	43	34	23	Ch. Chen Korum Ti ROM
1972	Beverly Hills, CA	William Bergum	124	49	46	29	Ch. Chen Korum Ti ROM
1973	Beverly Hills, CA	Alfred Likewise	103	44	37	15	Ch. Sharpette's Gaylord
1974	Beverly Hills, CA	Keke Blumberg	92	40	34	15	Ch. Blackbay Georgana of Yin Hi I. Q.
1975	Beverly Hills, CA	Robert Berndt	111	44	43	19	Ch. Chen Korum Ti ROM
1976	Dallas, TX	Onnie Martin	73	30	29	14	Ch. Potala Keke's Yum Yum ROM
1977	Houston, TX	Jay C. Shaeffer	95	52	34	9	Ch. Yojimbo Orion

Pedigrees

A PEDIGREE is much more than a decorative piece of paper with the names of a dog's ancestors on it. Properly used, a pedigree is a vital, indispensable tool with which the breeder works to constantly improve and upgrade his dogs.

The Lhasa Apso has only been a part of the American purebred family since the 1930s, but the breed's strides forward since that time have been dramatic. The credit for this tremendous accomplishment must go entirely to those who have spent years in study and experimentation. The Lhasa breeders of the United States and Canada have worked hard and long and today can look upon the results of their work with justifiable pride. A Lhasa won a BIS in the United States in 1957 and since then many have followed that first one into the charmed spotlight.

The pedigrees on the following pages tell the story, in their own way, of the breed's steady climb to the heights of acclaim. From the pinnacles of the Himalayas to the summit of fame in the show ring is a long journey, but the endearing Lhasa has truly arrived. This last statement is no empty superlative. It has substance in the large numbers of fine specimens to be seen at shows in every part of the land. The breeders have developed the Lhasa Apso into a being of unusual beauty, and by careful, meticulous work will continue to do so for the future generations of the breed.

```
                          Ch. Hamilton Chang Tang
              America's Sandar of Pamu
                          Lady Pamu
        Ch. Kyi Chu Kaliph Nor
                          Hamilton Shi-Pon
              Ch. Karma Ami Chiri
                          Ch. Hamilton Karma
   Ch. Cherryshores Bah Bieh Boi
                          Kay Dan's Simba Conda
              Ch. Chu-La's Mieh T'u
                          Ch. Cameo's Ta-Lei Ta Shan
        Ch. Cherryshores Mah Dahm
                          Hamilton Kesang
              Green Diamond Decidedly
                          Clyzett's Butterlamp
CH. ARBORHILL'S LEE-SAH ROM
                          Ch. Hamilton Kalon
              Ch. Hamilton Jimpa
                          Ch. Hamilton Samada
        Ch. Jima's Kana Rinpoche
                          Ch. Colarlie's Shan Bangalor ROM
              Ch. Shar Ming of Bangalor
                          Kathy's Miradel of Copi
   Ch. Arborhill's Karoling Karolyn ROM
                          Ch. Shangri of Glen Pines
              Joli Grumpa of Glen Pines
                          Joli Ja Kali of Glen Pines
        Gser Jo-Mo of La-Sari
                          Ch. Shenji Sing of Kyi Chu
              Shenji's Moppsie
                          Ch. Shar Ming of Bangalor


                                   Las-Sa-Gre's Hijo D'Al Tiro
                       Glen Pines Chagpo-Ri
                                   Ch. Miradel's Nima
                 Ch. Kai Sang's Clown of Everglo
                                   Ch. Las-Sa-Gre's Manchado Dorado
                       Kai Sang's Tzi-Ren of Miradel
                                   Chika Rinpoche
           BIS Ch. Everglo's Spark of Gold ROM
                                   Glen Pines chagpo-Ri
                       Ch. Kai Sang's Clown of Everglo
                                   Kai Sang's Tzi-Ren of Miradel
                 Tibetian Cookie of Everglo
                                   Ch. Miradel's Ming Fu-Tzu
                       Ruffway Hun-Nee-Bun
                                   Ch. Glenflo's Girja
           CH. ARBORHILL's BHRAN DIEH ROM
                                   America's Sander of Pamu
                       Ch. Kyi Chu Kaliph Nor
                                   Ch. Karma Ami Chiri
                 Ch. Cherryshores Bah Bieh Boi
                                   Ch. Chu-La's Mieh T'u
                       Ch. Cherryshores Mah Dahm
                                   Green Diamond Decidedly
           Ch. Arborhill's Lee Sah ROM
                                   Ch. Hamilton Jimpa
                       Ch. Jimpa's Kana Rinpoche
                                   Ch. Shar Ming of Bangalor
                 Ch. Arborhill's Karoling Karolyn ROM
                                   Gser Joli Grumpa of Glen Pines
                       Gser Jo-Mo of La-Sari
                                   Shenji's Moppsie
```
276

```
                                        Ch. Licos Kulu La
                        Ch. Licos Omorfo La
                                        Ch. Hamilton Pluti
                Ch. Chen Makalu Nor of Dzungar
                                        America's Sandar of Pamu
                        Ch. Kyi Chu Kara Nor ROM
                                        Ch. Karma Ami Chiri
        Ch. Chen Nyun Ti ROM
                                        Ch. Hamilton Achok
                        Ch. Licos Chulung La
                                        Ch. Licos Nyapso La
                Licos Gia La
                                        Ch. Hamilton Sandupa
                        Ch. Hamilton Pluti
                                        Ch. Hamilton Den Sa
AM. BDA. COL. CH. CHEN KORUM TI ROM (Best in Show)
                                        Rincan of Kelea
                        Ch. Colarlie's Shan Bangalor ROM
                                        Ai Wu Ting Ling
                Ch. Panda Bear Sing of Kyi Chu
                                        Ch. Taylor's Ming of Miradel
                        Colarlie's Pitti Sing
                                        Miradel's Ming Fu Chia
        Ch. Chen Karakorum
                                        Ch. Hamilton Chang Tang
                        America's Sandar of Pamu
                        Lady Pamu
                Ch. Kyi Chu Kara Nor ROM
                                        Hamilton Shi-Pon
                        Ch. Karma Ami Chiri
                                        Ch. Hamilton Karma


                        Ch. America's Leng Kong
                BIS Ch. Licos Kulu La
                        Ch. America's Rika
        Ch. Licos Omorfo La
                        Ch. Hamilton Sandupa
                Ch. Hamilton Pluti
                        Ch. Hamilton Den Sa
    Ch. Chen Maka Lu Nor of Dzungar
                        Ch. Hamilton Chang Tang
                America's Sandar of Pamu
                Lady Pamu
        Ch. Kyi Chu Kara Nor ROM
                        Hamilton Shi-Pon
                Ch. Karma Ami Chiri
                        Ch. Hamilton Karma
CH. CHEN NYUN TI ROM
                        Ch. Hamilton Tatsienlu
                Ch. Hamilton Achok
                        Hamilton Dobra
        Ch. Licos Chulung La
                        Ch. America's Leng Kong
                Ch. Licos Nyapso La
                        Ch. America's Rika
    Licos Gia La
                        Ch. Hamilton Tatsienlu
                Ch. Hamilton Sandupa
                        Hamilton Docheno
        Ch. Hamilton Pluti
                        Ch. Hamilton Tatsienlu       277
                Ch. Hamilton Den Sa
                        Hamilton Dobra
```

Hamilton Maroh

Ch. Hamilton Chang Tang

Ch. Hamilton Samada

America's Sandar of Pamu

Lin Li Poo

Lady Pamu

Lo Tsien

Ch. Kyi Chu Kaliph Nor

Ch. Hamilton Sandupa

Hamilton Shi-Pon

Ch. Hamilton Den Sa

Ch. Karma Ami Chiri

Hamilton Maroh

Ch. Hamilton Karma

Hamilton Docheno

CH. CHERRYSHORES BAH BIEH BOI

Kham Drukke

Kay Dan's Simba Conda

Kay Dan's Ne Ne Mo

Ch. Chu-La's Mieh T'u

Clyzetts Bonpo

Ch. Cameo's Ta-Lei Ta Shan

Kay Dan's Ne Ne Mo

Ch. Cherryshores Mah Dahm

Hamilton Maroh

Hamilton Kesang

Hamilton Amdo

Green Diamond Decidedly

Stittigs Tao'Tzu'Cee

Clyzett's Butterlamp

Stittigs Moka Kara Dei Mar

Ch. Fu Al Tirito

Ch. Las-Sa-Gre's Manchado Dorado

Ch. Fu La Diablita

Rincan of Kelea

Ch. Ming Changnopa

Karma Rinpoche

Chika Rinpoche

Ch. Colarlie's Shan Bangalor ROM

Kham Drukke

Hsiao-Ti Sambo of Teri Tot

Karma Rinpoche

Ai Wu Ting Ling

Chiang Foo

Ch. Fu La Simpatica

Ch. Fardale Fu Ssi

CH. COLARLIE'S MISS SHANDA ROM

Hamilton Dakmar

Ch. Wu Tai

Ch. Ming Lu

Ch. Ming Tali II C.D.

Pedro

Ch. Ming Kyi

Ch. Ming Lu

Miradel's Ming Fu Chia C.D.

Ming Foo

Chiang Foo

Ch. Las-Sa-Gre

Ch. Fu La Simpatica

Pu of Oulton

Ch. Fardale Fu Ssi

Mu Chi of Lhakang

278

                                    Chiang Foo
                          Ch. Fu Al Tirito
                                    Ch. Fardale Fu Ssi
                Ch. Las-Sa-Gre's Manchado Dorado
                                    Chiang Foo
                          Ch. Fu La Diablita
                                    Ch. Fardale Fu Ssi
          Rincan of Kelea
                                    Pedro
                          Ch. Ming Changnopa
                                    Ming Lu
                Karma Rinpoche
                                    Hamilton Sandur
                          Chika Rinpoche
                                    Ch. Yay Sih of Shebo
CH. COLARLIE'S SHAN BANGALOR ROM
                                    Ch. Ming Changnopa
                          Kham Drukke
                                    Chika Rinpoche
                Hsiao-Ti Sambo of Teri Tul
                                    Ch. Ming Changnopa
                          Karma Rinpoche
                                    Chika Rinpoche
          Ai Wu Ting Ling
                                    Ming Foo
                          Chiang Foo
                                    Ch. Las-Sa-Gre
                Ch. Fu La Simpatica
                                    Pu of Oulton
                          Ch. Fardale Fu Ssi
                                    Mu Chi of Lhakang

                                    Ch. Hamilton Chang Tang
                          America's Sandar of Pamu
                                    Lady Pamu
                Ch. Karma Dmar-Po
                                    Ch. Hamilton Kung
                          Mex. Am. Ch. Karma Sangpo
                                    Ch. Hamilton Karma
          Karma Kacho
                                    Ch. Hamilton Tatsienlu
                          Ch. Hamilton Sandupa
                                    Hamilton Docheno
                Hamilton Druk Tru
                                    Ch. Hamilton Tatsienlu
                          Hamilton Phema II
                                    Hamilton Tista
CORDOVA SIN-SA ROM
                                    Ch. Hamilton Sandupa
                          Hamilton Shi-Pon
                                    Ch. Hamilton Den Sa
                Ch. Karma Kushog
                                    Hamilton Maroh
                          Ch. Hamilton Karma
                                    Hamilton Docheno
          Ch. Karma Sakyi
                                    America's Sandar of Pamu
                          Ch. Karma Dmar-Pro
                                    Mex. Am. Ch. Karma Sangpo
                Ch. Karma Sanga II
                                    Ch. Hamilton Sandupa   279
                          Hamilton Lhamo
                                    Hamilton Yogi

```
                              Ch. Ming Changnopa
                    Kham Drukke
                              Chika Rinpoche
          Kay Dan's Simba Conda
                              Kham Drukke
                    Kay Dan's Ne Ne Mo
                              Karma Rinpoche
    Ch. Chu-La's Mieh T'u
                              Stittigs Tao'Tzu'Cee
                    Clyzett's Bonpo
                              Stittigs Moka Kara Dei Mar
          Ch. Cameo's Ta-Lei Ta Shan
                              Kham Drukke
                    Kay Dan's Ne Ne Mo
                              Karma Rinpoche
CREST O LAKE TRU SO
                              Ch. Hamilton Tatsienlu
                    Hamilton Maroh
                              Hamilton Tigu
          Hamilton Kesang
                              Ch. Hamilton Kalon
                    Hamilton Amdo
                              Hamilton Yogi
    Green Diamond Decidedly
                              Pu Yao Cheng of Masque
                    Stittigs Tao'Tzu'Cee
                              Si'San of Masque
          Clyzett's Butterlamp
                              Ch. Hamilton Peking
                    Stittigs Moka Kara Dei Mar
                              Hamilton Durga


                                        Ch. Le
                              Ch. Hamilton Tsang
                                        Hamilton Gindi
                    Ch. America's Leng Kong
                                        Ch. Le
                              Hamilton Suchau
                                        Hamilton Muni
          BIS Licos Kulu La
                                        Ch. Le.
                              Ch. Hamilton Tsang
                                        Hamilton Gindi
                    Ch. America's Rika
                                        Ch. Hamilton Tatsienlu
                              BIS Ch. Hamilton Torma
                                        Hamilton Lachen
    DAMA'S LU COUNTRY FAIR
                                        Hamilton Yangchen
                              Ch. Hamilton Tatsienlu
                                        Hamilton Novo
                    Ch. Hamilton Achok
                                        Ch. Hamilton Tatsienlu
                              Hamilton Dobra
                                        Hamilton Tughar
          Licos Dama La
                                        Ch. Hamilton Tsang
                              Ch. America's Leng Kong
                                        Hamilton Suchau
                    Ch. Licos Nyapso La
                                        Ch. Hamilton Tsang
                              Ch. America's Rika
                                        BIS Ch. Hamilton Torma
```

280

```
                                              Ch. Fu Al Tirito
                              Las-Sa-Gre's Hijo D'Al Tiro
                                              Ch. Fu La Diablita
                      Glen Pines Chagpo-Ri
                                              Ch. Ming Tali II
                              Ch. Miradel's Nima
                                              Miradel's Fa Li
              Ch. Kai Sang's Clown Of Everglo
                                              Ch. Fu Al Tirito
                              Ch. Las-Sa-Gre's Manchado Dorado
                                              Ch. Fu La Diabilta
                      Kai Sang's Tzi-Ren of Miradel
                                              Ch. Hamilton Sandar
                              Chika Rinpoche
                                              Ch. Yay Sih of Shebo
CH. EVERGLO'S SPARK OF GOLD ROM (Best in Show)
                                              Las-Sa-Gre's Hijo D'Al Tiro
                              Glen Pines Chagpo-Ri
                                              Ch. Miradel's Nima
              Ch. Kai Sang's Clown Of Everglo
                                              Ch. Las-Sa-Gre's Manchado Dorado
                              Kai Sang's Tzi-Ren of Miradel
                                              Chika Rinpoche
              Tibetian Cookie of Everglo
                                              Ch. Ming Tali II
                              Ch. Miradel's Ming Fu-Tzu
                                              Miradel's Kahn Dee C.D.
                      Ruffway Hun-Nee-Bun
                                              Las-Sa-Gre's Hijo D'Al Tiro
                              Ch. Glenflo's Girja
                                              Ch. Miradel's Nima


                                      Ch. Hamilton Sandupa
                      Hamilton Shi-Pon
                                      Ch. Hamilton Den Sa
              Ch. Karma Kushog
                                      Hamilton Maroh
                      Ch. Hamilton Karma
                                      Hamilton Docheno
BIS Ch. Karma Frosty Knight O Everglo Rom
                                      Ch. Hamilton Tatsienlu
                      Ch. Hamilton Sandupa
                                      Hamilton Docheno
              Ch. Hamilton Sha Tru
                                      Hamilton Maroh
                      Hamilton Ghar Pon
                                      Hamilton Saung
CH. EVERGLO ZIJUH TOMBA
                                      Ch. Hamilton Achok
                      Ch. Licos Chulung La
                                      Ch. Licos Nyapso La
              Cubbi Kyeri of Everglo
                                      Ch. Hamilton Sandupa
                      Hamilton Norden
                                      Ch. Hamilton Den Sa
              Khambu of Everglo
                                      Ch. Hamilton Sandupa
                      Hamilton Yi Tru
                                      Ch. Hamilton Den Sa
              Ch. Kyima of Everglo ROM
                                      Ch. Hamilton Peking
                      Stittigs Moka Kara Dei Mar
                                      Hamilton Durga
```

281

```
                              Ch. Hamilton Tatsienlu
                Ch. Hamilton Achok
                              Hamilton Dobra
          Licos Khung La
                              Ch. American's Leng Kong
                Ch. Licos Nyapso La
                              Ch. American's Rika
    BIS Ch. Kham of Norbulingka ROM
                              Ch. Hamilton Tatsienlu
                Ch. Hamilton Sandupa
                              Hamilton Docheno
          Karma Kosala
                              Ch. Hamilton Kung
                Mex. Am. Ch. Karma Sangpo
                              Ch. Hamilton Karma
CH. GINDY OF NORBULINGKA ROM
                              Ch. Hamilton Chang Tang
                American's Sandar of Pamu
                              Lady Pamu
          Ch. Karma Dmar-Po
                              Ch. Hamilton Kung
                Mex. Am. Ch. Karma Sang Po
                              Ch. Hamilton Karma
    Ch. Karma Muffin of Norbulingka
                              Hamilton Yanchen
                Ch. Hamilton Tatsienlu
                              Hamilton Novo
          Hamilton Chang Tru
                              Ch. Hamilton Sandupa
                Hamilton Nirvana
                              Hamilton Amdo


                                                Hamilton Chusul
                                  Hamilton Kusog
                                                Hamilton Nakkin
                            Hamilton Yanchen
                                                Hamilton Sigmi
                                  Hamilton Kyi Chu
                                                Shanghai
                      Ch. Hamilton Tatsienlu
                                                Hamilton Tien Shan
                                  Hamilton Dakmar
                                                Hamilton Nakkin
                            Hamilton Novo
                                                Hamilton Kusog
                                  Hamilton Maru
                                                Hamilton Kyi Chu
          HAMILTON CHANG TRU
                                                Hamilton Yangchen
                                  Ch. Hamilton Tatsienlu
                                                Hamilton Novo
                      Ch. Hamilton Sandupa
                                                Hamilton Urga
                                  Hamilton Docheno
                                                Hamilton Dobra
                            Hamilton Nirvana
                                                Ch. Hamilton Tatsienlu
                                  Ch. Hamilton Kalon
                                                Hamilton Tughar
                            Hamilton Amdo
                                                Hamilton Maroh
                                  Hamilton Yogi
                                                Hamilton Dong
```

282

```
                              Ch. Hamilton Tatsienlu
                    Hamilton Maroh
                              Hamilton Tigu
          Ch. Hamilton Chang Tang
                              Ch. Hamilton Tatsienlu
                    Ch. Hamilton Samada
                              Hamilton Lachen
     America's Sandar of Pamu
                              Shan Sun
                    Lin Li Poo
                              Hamilton Cafra
          Lady Pamu
                              Sin
                    Lo Tsien
                              Hamilton Cafra


CH. KARMA DMAR-PO
                              Hamilton Yanchen
                    Ch. Hamilton Tatsienlu
                              Hamilton Novo
          Ch. Hamilton Kung
                              Ch. Hamilton Tatsienlu
                    Hamilton Dobra
                              Hamilton Tughar
     Mex. Am. Ch. Karma Sangpo
                              Ch. Hamilton Tatsienlu
                    Hamilton Maroh
                              Hamilton Tigu
          Ch. Hamilton Karma
                              Hamilton Urga
                    Hamilton Docheno
                              Hamilton Dobra


                              Ch. Hamilton Tatsienlu
                    Ch. Hamilton Sandupa
                              Hamilton Docheno
          Hamilton Shi-Pon
                              Ch. Hamilton Tatsienlu
                    Ch. Hamilton Den Sa
                              Hamilton Dobra
     Ch. Karma Kushog
                              Ch. Hamilton Tatsienlu
                    Hamilton Maroh
                              Hamilton Tigu
          Ch. Hamilton Karma
                              Hamilton Urga
                    Hamilton Docheno
                              Hamilton Dobra
CH. KARMA FROSTY KNIGHT O' EVERGLOW ROM (Best in Show)
                              Hamilton Yanchen
                    Ch. Hamilton Tatsienlu
                              Hamilton Novo
          Ch. Hamilton Sandupa
                              Hamilton Urga
                    Ch. Hamilton Docheno
                              Hamilton Dobra
     Ch. Hamilton Sha Tru
                              Ch. Hamilton Tatsienlu
                    Hamilton Maroh
                              Hamilton Tigu
          Hamilton Ghar Pon
                              Ch. Hamilton Kalon
                    Hamilton Saung
                              Ch. Hamilton Mardree
```

283

Hamilton Yanchen
Ch. Hamilton Tatsienlu
Hamilton Novo
Ch. Hamilton Sandupa
Hamilton Urga
Hamilton Docheno
Hamilton Dobra
Hamilton Shi-Pon
Hamilton Yangchen
Ch. Hamilton Tatsienlu
Hamilton Novo
Ch. Hamilton Den Sa
Ch. Hamilton Tatsienlu
Hamilton Dobra
Hamilton Tughar
CH. KASHGAR OF GAR-TEN
Ch. Hamilton Tatsienlu
Ch. Hamilton Kung
Hamilton Dobra
Ch. Karma Getson
Hamilton Maroh
Ch. Hamilton Karma
Hamilton Docheno
Tengin of Gar-Ten
Ch. Hamilton Kalon
Hamilton Kala
Hamilton Tista
Lou-Lan of Gar-Ten
Hamilton Maroh
Hamilton Sakya
Hamilton Docheno

Ch. Hamilton Sandupa
Karma on-Ten
Karma Zurwang
Karma Tharpa
America's Sandar of Pamu
Karma Kam-Bu
Hamilton Khib Tru
BIS Ch. Tibet of Cornwallis ROM
Ch. Hamilton Achok
Ch. Licos Chaplia La
Ch. Licos Karo La
Ch. Licos Cheti La
Ch. America's Leng Kong
Ch. Licos Nyapso La
Ch. America's Rika
CH. KEKE'S BAMBOO ROM
Ch. Hamilton Achok
Licos Khung La
Ch. Licos Nyapso La
BIS Ch. Kham of Norbulingka ROM
Ch. Hamilton Sandupa
Karma Kosala
Mex. Am. Ch. Karma Sangpo
Ch. Keke's T'Chin Ting T'Chin ROM
Ch. Hamilton Sandupa
Ch. Hamilton Namsa ROM
Hamilton Dong
Ch. Keke's T'Chin T'Chin
284
Country Fair Mei Chen
Smedley's Seeou Ying
Ro-Jo's Cheng Chin-Koo

```
                                        Hamilton Yangchen
                                Ch. Hamilton Tatsienlu
                                        Hamilton Novo
                        Ch. Hamilton Achok
                                        Ch. Hamilton Tatsienlu
                                Hamilton Dobra
                                        Hamilton Tughar
                Licos Khung La
                                        Ch. Hamilton Tsang
                                Ch. American's Leng Kong
                                        Hamilton Suchau
                        Ch. Licos Nyapso La
                                        Ch. Hamilton Tsang
                                Ch. American's Rika
                                        Ch. Hamilton Torma
        CH. KHAM OF NORBULINGKA ROM (Best in Show)
                                        Hamilton Yangchen
                                Ch. Hamilton Tatsienlu
                                        Hamilton Novo
                        Ch. Hamilton Sandupa
                                        Hamilton Urga
                                Hamilton Docheno
                                        Hamilton Dobra
                Karma Kosala
                                        Ch. Hamilton Tatsienlu
                                Ch. Hamilton Kung
                                        Hamilton Dobra
                        Mex. Am. Ch. Karma Sangpo
                                        Hamilton Maroh
                                Ch. Hamilton Karma
                                        Hamilton Docheno



                                Ch. Hamilton Tatsienlu
                        Ch. Hamilton Achok
                                Hamilton Dobra
                Licos Khung La
                                Ch. American's Leng Kong
                        Ch. Licos Nyapso La
                                Ch. American's Rika
        BIS Ch. Kham of Norbulingka ROM
                                Ch. Hamilton Tatsienlu
                        Ch. Hamilton Sandupa
                                Hamilton Docheno
                Karma Kosala
                                Ch. Hamilton Kung
                        Mex. Am. Ch. Karma Sangpo
                                Ch. Hamilton Karma
CH. KINDERLAND'S SANG-PO ROM
                                Ch. Fu Al Tirito
                        Ch. Las-Sa-Gre Manchado Dorado
                                Ch. Fu La Diablita
                Dzin-Po Rinpoche
                                Hamilton Sandur
                        Chika Rinpoche
                                Ch. Yay Sih of Shebo
        Ch-Ha-Ya-Chi
                                Ch. Las-Sa-Gre's Manchado Dorado
                        Kepa Rinpoche
                                Chiko Rinpoche
                Ron-Si Rinpoche
                                Ch. Las-Sa-Gre's Manchado Dorado
                        Ch. Tashi Rinpoche
                                Karma Rinpoche
```

Ch. Hamilton Tatsienlu

Ch. Hamilton Kalon

Hamilton Tughar

Ch. Hamilton Jimpa

Ch. Hamilton Tatsienlu

Ch. Hamilton Samada

Hamilton Lachen

Ch. Quetzal's Feyla of Kyi Chu

Rincan of Kelea

Ch. Colarlie's Shan Bangalor ROM

Ai Wu Ting Ling

Ch. Colarlie's Miss Shandha ROM

Ch. Ming Tali II C.D.

Miradel's Ming Fu chia C.D.

Ch. Fu La Simpatica

AM. CAN. BDA. MEX. CH. KYI CHU FRIAR TUCK ROM (Best in Show)

Ch. Las-Sa-Gre's Manchado Dorado

Rincan of Kelea

Karma Rinpoche

Ch. Colarlie's Shan Bangalor ROM

Hsiao Ti Sambo of Teri Tot

Ai Wu Ting Ling

Ch. Fu La Simpatica

Ch. Colarlie's Miss Shandha ROM

Ch. Wu Tai

Ch. Ming Tali II C.D.

Ch. Ming Kyi

Miradel's Ming Fu Chia C.D.

Chiang Foo

Ch. Fu La Simpatica

Ch. Fardale Fu Ssi

Hamilton Yangchen

Ch. Hamilton Tatsienlu

Hamilton Novo

Ch. Hamilton Kalon

Hamilton Dakmar

Hamilton Tughar

Hamilton Nanning

Ch. Hamilton Jimpa

Hamilton Yangchen

Ch. Hamilton Tatsienlu

Hamilton Novo

Ch. Hamilton Samada

Hamilton Dakmar

Hamilton Lachen

Takla

CH. KYI CHU KIRA C.D.

Ch. Las-Sa-Gre's Manchado Dorado

Rincan of Kelea

Karma Rinpoche

Ch. Colarlie's Shan Bangalor ROM

Hsiao Ti Sambo of Teri Tot

Ai Wu Ting Ling

Ch. Fu La Simpatica

Ch. Colarlie's Miss Shandha ROM

Ch. Wu Tai

Ch. Ming Tali II C.D.

Ch. Ming Kyi

Miradel's Ming Fu Chia C.D.

Chiang Foo

Ch. Fu La Simpatica

Ch. Fardale Fu Ssi

```
                                              Hamilton Kusog
                                   Hamilton Yangchen
                                              Hamilton Kyichu
                        Ch. Hamilton Tatsienlu
                                              Hamilton Dakmar
                                   Hamilton Novo
                                              Hamilton Maru
             Ch. Hamilton Achok
                                              Hamilton Yangchen
                                   Ch. Hamilton Tatsienlu
                                              Hamilton Novo
                        Hamilton Dobra
                                              Hamilton Dakmar
                                   Hamilton Tughar
                                              Hamilton Nanning
          CH. LICOS CHULUNG LA
                                              Ch. Le
                                   Ch. Hamilton Tsang
                                              Hamilton Gindi
                        Ch. Americal's Leng Kong
                                              Ch. Le
                                   Hamilton Suchau
                                              Hamilton Muni
             Ch. Licos Nyapso La
                                              Ch. Le
                                   Ch. Hamilton Tsang
                                              Hamilton Gindi
                        Ch. Americal's Rika
                                              Ch. Hamilton Tatsienlu
                                   BIS Ch. Hamilton Torma
                                              Hamilton Lachen


                          Nanchen
              Ch. Le
                          Lucknow
        Ch. Hamilton Tsang
                          Hamilton Dakmar
              Hamilton Gindi
                          Hamilton Sonak
        Ch. Americal's Leng Kong
                          Nanchen
              Ch. Le.
                          Lucknow
        Hamilton Suchau
                          Hamilton Yangchen
              Hamilton Muni
                          Hamilton Nanning
   CH. LICOS NYAPSO LA
                          Nanchen
              Ch. Le
                          Lucknow
        Ch. Hamilton Tsang
                          Hamilton Dakmar
              Hamilton Gindi
                          Hamilton Sonak
        Ch. Americal's Rika
                          Hamilton Yangchen
              Ch. Hamilton Tatsienlu
                          Hamilton Novo
        BIS Ch. Hamilton Torma
                          Hamilton Dakmar
              Hamilton Lachen              287
                          Takla
```

```
                                    Hamilton Tien Shan
                        Hamilton Dakmar
                                    Hamilton Nakkin
            Ch. Wu Tai
                                    Ming Tai
                    Ming Lu
                                    Tai Ho
    Ch. Ming Tali II CD
                                    Chang Tso Lin
                    Pedro
                                    Mai Ling of Boyd
            Ch. Ming Kyi
                                    Ming Tai
                    Ming Lu
                                    Tai Ho
MIRADEL'S MING FU CHIA C.D.
                                    Ming Tai
                    Ming Foo
                                    Tai Ho
            Chiang Foo
                                    Sikkim Johnny
                    Ch. Las-Sa-Gre
                                    Chong Fey
    Ch. Fu La Simpatica
                                    Peko of the Mynd
                    Pu of Oulton
                                    Li Hing Chao
            Ch. Fardale Fu Ssi
                                    Eng. Ch. Hoo Long
                    Mu Chi of Lhakang
                                    Mee Nee of Taishan


                                            Rincan of Kelea
                                Ch. Lakeland's Ta Hsing of Miradel
                                            Ai Wu Ting Ling
                        Lakeland's La Hsi Of Lo Coco
                                            Rincan of Kelea
                                Miradel's La Char Ming
                                            Ch. Fu La Simpatica
                El Poco's Hi-Hey Sing
                                            Stittigs Jang Dei Mar
                                Errand De-Mar
                                            Stittigs Gurla Dei Mar
                        El Poco's Shan Teka
                                            Miradel's Ebony-Lad-Chi
                                Kali Shan Dee
                                            Miradel's Kahn Dee C.D.
    CH. NEIKA'S MINKA LEE
                                            Ch. Ming Tali II C.D.
                                Ch. Tai Feng Yu Tien of Miradel
                                            Pu Hao Soosie
                        Hel-Max Sambo
                                            Country Fair's Kushi Kahn
                                Milbryan's Zandra-Mo
                                            Stittigs Lei Cha Dei Mar
                Neika Sing
                                            Stittigs Jang Dei Mar
                                Errand De-Mar
                                            Stittigs Gurla Dei Mar
                        El Poco's Shan Teka
                                            Miradel's Ebony-Lad-Chi
                                Kalli Shan Dee
                                            Miradel's Kahn Dee C.D.
```

288

```
                                        Ch. Hamilton Sandupa
                              Hamilton Shi-Pon
                                        Ch. Hamilton Den Sa
                    Ch. Karma Kushog
                                        Hamilton Maroh
                    Ch. Hamilton Karma
                                        Hamilton Docheno
          BIS Ch. Karma Frosty Knight O' Everglo ROM
                                        Ch. Hamilton Tatsienlu
                    Ch. Hamilton Sandupa
                                        Hamilton Docheno
                    Ch. Hamilton Sha Tru
                                        Hamilton Maroh
                              Hamilton Ghar Pon
                                        Hamilton Saung
          CH. ORLANE'S CHITRA OF RUFFWAY ROM
                                        Ch. Hamiton Achok
                    Ch. Licos Chulung La
                                        Ch. Licos Nyapso La
                    Cubbi Kyeri of Everglo
                                        Ch. Hamilton Sandupa
                              Hamilton Norden
                                        Ch. Hamilton Den Sa
                    Ruffway Khambu
                                        Ch. Le
                    Ch. Hamilton Peking
                                        Hamilton Gindi
                    Stittigs Moka Kara Dei Mar
                                        Ch. Hamilton Tatsienlu
                              Hamilton Durga
                                        Hamilton Tista

          Las-Sa-Gre's Hijo D'Al Tiro
          Glen Pines Chagpo-Ri
                    Ch. Miradel's Nima
          Ch. Kai Sang's Clown of Everglo
                    Ch. Las-Sa-Gre's Manchado Dorado
          Kai Sang's Tzi-Ren of Miradel
                    Chika Rinpoche
BIS Ch. Everglo's Spark of Gold ROM
                    Glen Pines Chagpo-Ri
          Ch. Kai Sang's Clown of Everglo
                    Kai Sang's Tzi-Ren of Miradel
          Tibetian Cookie of Everglo
                    Ch. Miradel's Ming Fu-Tzu
          Ruffway Hun-Nee-Bun
                    Ch. Glenflo's Girja
CH. ORLANE'S DULMO ROM
                    Hamilton Shi-Pon
          Ch. Karma Kushog
                    Ch. Hamilton Karma
          BIS Ch. Karma Frosty Knight O' Everglo ROM
                    Ch. Hamilton Sandupa
          Ch. Hamilton Sha Tru
                    Hamilton Garpon
          Ch. Orlane's Chitra of Ruffway
                    Ch. Licos Chulung La
          Cubbi Kyeri of Everglo
                    Hamilton Norden
          Ruffway Khambu
                    Ch. Hamilton Peking
          Stittigs Moka Kara Dei Mar       289
                    Hamilton Durga
```

Las-Sa-Gre's Hijo D'Al Tiro
Glenn Pines Chagpo-Ri
Ch. Miradel's Nima
Ch. Kai Sang's Clown of Everglo
Ch. Las-Sa-Gre's Manchado Dorado
Kai Sang's Tzi-Ren of Miradel
Chika Rinpoche
BIS Ch. Everglo's Spark of Gold ROM
Glenn Pines Chagpo-Ri
Ch. Kai Sang's Clown of Everglo
Kai Sang's Tzi-Ren of Miradel
Tibetian Cookie of Everglo
Ch. Miradel's Ming Fu-Tzu
Ruffway Hun-Nee-Bun
Ch. Glenflo's Girja

CH. RUFFWAY MARPA ROM

Ch. Karma Kushog
BIS Ch. Karma Frosty Knight O' Everglo ROM
Ch. Hamilton Sha Tru
Ch. Ruffway Chogal
Cubbi Kyeri of Everglo
Ruffway Khambu
Stittig's Moka Kara Dei Mar
Ch. Ruffway Kara Shing ROM
Glenn Pines Chagpo-Ri
Ch. Kai Sang's Clown of Everglo
Kai Sang's Tzi-Ren of Miradel
Ch. Ruffway Lholung
Ch. Hamilton Sandupa
Hamilton Norden
Ch. Hamilton Den Sa

Ch. Hamilton Tatsienlu
Ch. Hamilton Kalon
Hamilton Tughar
Hamilton Toradga
Ch. Hamilton Tatsienlu
Ch. Hamilton Den Sa
Hamilton Dobra
Ch. Zijuh Seng Tru ROM
Ch. Hamilton Tatsienlu
Ch. Hamilton Sandupa
Hamilton Docheno
Ch. Hamilton Shim Tru
Ch. Hamilton Kalon
Hamilton Saung
Hamilton Mardree

CH. TABU'S KING OF HEARTS ROM

Karma Yon-Ten
Karma Tharpa
Karma Kam-Bu
BIS Ch. Tibet of Cornwallis ROM
Ch. Licos Chaplia La
Ch. Licos Cheti La
Ch. Licos Nyapso La
BIS Ch. Kinderland's Tonka ROM
Licos Khung La
BIS Ch. Kham of Norbulingka ROM
Karma Kosala
Ch. Kinderland's Sang-Po ROM
Dzin-Po Rinpoche
Ch-Ha-Ya-Chi
Ron-Si Rinpoche

290

```
                                        Ch. Hamilton Tatsienlu
                            Ch. Hamilton Sandupa
                                        Hamilton Docheno
                Karma Yon-Ten
                                        Hamilton Shi-Pon
                            Karma Zurwang
                                        Karma Tara
        Karma Tharpa
                                        Ch. Hamilton Chang Tang
                            American's Sandar of Pamu
                                        Lady Pamu
                Karma Kam-Bu
                                        Hamilton Toradga
                            Hamilton Khib-Tru
                                        Hamilton Nirvana
            CH. TIBET OF CORNWALLIS ROM Best in Show
                                        Ch. Hamilton Tatsienlu
                            Ch. Hamilton Achok
                                        Hamilton Dobra
                Ch. Licos Chaplia La
                                        Ch. American's Leng Kong
                            Ch. Licos Karo La
                                        Ch. American's Rika
        Ch. Licos Cheti La
                                        Ch. Hamilton Tsang
                            Ch. American's Leng Kong
                                        Hamilton Suchau
                Ch. Licos Nyapso La
                                        Ch. Hamilton Tsang
                            Ch. American's Rika
                                        BIS Ch. Hamilton Torma


                                        Ch. Hamilton Kalong
                            Hamilton Toradga
                                        Ch. Hamilton Den Sa
                Ch. Zijuh Seng Tru ROM
                                        Ch. Hamilton Sandupa
                            Ch. Hamilton Shim Tru
                                        Hamilton Saung
        Ch. Chen Changri Nor
                                        BIS Ch. Licos Kulu La
                            Ch. Licos Omorfo La
                                        Ch. Hamilton Pluti
                Chen Himalayan Hanah Nor ROM
                                        American's Sandar of Pamu
                            Ch. Kyi Chu Kara Nor ROM
                                        Ch. Karma Ami Chiri
    ZIJUH ON-BA ZIM ZIM ROM
                                        BIS Ch. Licos Kulu La
                            Ch. Licos Omorfo La
                                        Ch. Hamilton Pluti
                Ch. Chen Makalu Nor of Dzungar
                                        American's Sandar of Pamu
                            Ch. Kyi Chu Kara Nor ROM
                                        Ch. Karma Ami Chiri
        Tai Foon
                                        Ch. Hamilton Kalon
                            Ch. Hamilton Jimpa
                                        Ch. Hamilton Samada
                Zijuh Ngor
                                        Ch. Karma Lobsang
                            Donna Cardella's Tsng
                                        Karma Dakini
```

291

```
                                          Hamilton Yangchen
                            Ch. Hamilton Tatsienlu
                                          Hamilton Novo
                Ch. Hamilton Kalon
                                          Hamilton Dakmar
                            Hamilton Tughar
                                          Hamilton Nanning
      Hamilton Toradga
                                          Hamilton Yangchen
                            Ch. Hamilton Tatsienlu
                                          Hamilton Novo
                Ch. Hamilton Den Sa
                                          Ch. Hamilton Tatsienlu
                            Hamilton Dobra
                                          Hamilton Tughar
CH. ZIJUH SENG TRU ROM
                                          Hamilton Yangchen
                            Ch. Hamilton Tatsienlu
                                          Hamilton Novo
                Ch. Hamilton Sandupa
                                          Hamilton Urga
                            Hamilton Docheno
                                          Hamilton Dobra
      Ch. Hamilton Shim Tru
                                          Ch. Hamilton Tatsienlu
                            Ch. Hamilton Kalon
                                          Hamilton Tughar
                Hamilton Saung
                                          Ch. Hamilton Tatsienlu
                            Hamilton Mardree
                                          Hamilton Tista
```

Seven-week-old daughters of Tabu's Jazz Man.

"Lhasa-rama"

IT IS ALMOST TIME to bring this story of the Lhasa Apso to a close. But, truly, the story of the Lhasa Apso is an ongoing, unending saga of success. In the 1930s and for a long time thereafter, the Lhasa was often looked upon as a novelty and a curiosity by many dog lovers. Today he is universally admired as an exquisite show dog and a delightful pet. It is quite safe to predict that in the years ahead his star will rise even higher.

To close the pages of THE COMPLETE LHASA APSO we offer you several more glimpses of dogs from yesterday and today, dogs that have won well in competition and have also brought their own special warmth and charm into the lives of their human families. The authors and the publisher hope you enjoy this photo farewell and, in fact, the entire book. We further hope THE COMPLETE LHASA APSO has increased your knowledge and pleasure of this wonderful breed and that this book will be the cornerstone of your canine library for many years to come.

Cordova Sin Sa ROM is a daughter of Karma Kacho and Ch. Karma Sakyi. Sin Sa, owned by Lynette Clooney and Jean Kausch, is the dam of at least nine champions.

Ch. Le, bred by the 13th Dalai Lama, was a foundation stud at Hamilton Farm.

Ch. Pehma, who never had a litter, is shown here with her adopted baby; a little wild rabbit.

294

Group winner Ch. Potala Keke's Gladiator is a son of BIS Ch. Tibet of Cornwallis ROM and Ch. Karma Rus Timala ROM. Gladiator was bred by Keke Blumberg and is owned by Dorothy Schottgen.

Ch. Yeti's Paper Tiger is the son of Am. Can. Ch. Kyi Chu Chaos and Ginger Lee Ruby ROM. He was bred by Clark and Patricia Pritchett.

Ch. Tabu's Naturally Nutmeg was bred by Susan Rayner and Carolyn Herbel and is owned by Anna M. Heinze and Carolyn Herbel.

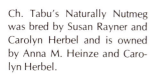

295

Ch. Blackbay Georgana of Yin Hi I. Q., winner of the 1974 Western ALAC Specialty, was bred by I. E. Quistgard and owned and handled by Robert H. Black. She is by Gorgeous George of Yin Sui ex Ch. Chen Bzan-Po.

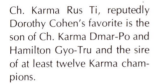

Ch. Karma Rus Ti, reputedly Dorothy Cohen's favorite is the son of Ch. Karma Dmar-Po and Hamilton Gyo-Tru and the sire of at least twelve Karma champions.

Ch. Keke's Bamboo ROM shown at 10 months with her co-breeder and owner Keke Blumberg. Bamboo is the daughter of BIS Ch. Tibet of Cornwallis ROM and Ch. Keke's T'Chin Ting T'Chin ROM and the dam of seven champions.

Group winner Ch. Tabu's Gold Galaxy was bred by Norman and Carolyn Herbel and is owned by Susan Lefferts.

Ch. Tabu's Double or Nuthin, owned by Carolyn Herbel and Connie Tompkins, Barcon.

Ch. Rinchen Dorje is a son of BIS Ch. Chen Korum Ti ROM and Lucy Tashi (a Friar Tuck daughter). He is owned and bred by Lenore Rosselot.

Tabu's Rags to Riches, owned by Milford and Arlene Scheeler and bred by Carolyn Herbel.

Ch. Tabu's Dresden Doll, a litter sister to Ch. Tabu's Double or Nuthin. Dolly is owned by Susan Rayner, and bred and co-owned by Carolyn Herbel.

Ch. Potala Keke's Tibet; litter brother to Gladiator, owned by Bill and Jo Bowman and handled by Jean Lade.

Ch. Potala Keke's Zin Zin ROM; bred and owned by Keke Blumberg.

Tabu's Unsinkable Molly Brown is a daughter of Tabu's Jazz Man and Goldmere Dharma (a Kham grandaughter). She is owned by Sy and Ann Goldberg and Carolyn Herbel and is shown with Gerri Goldberg.

Ch. Potala Keke's Andromeda is a daughter of Ch. Daktazl Tsung and Ch. Potala Keke's Yum Yum ROM. She is owned by Jeanne and John Hope, Hope-Full.

Ch. Potala Keke's Sharabara is a daughter of Ch. Karma San Po and Ch. Karma Rus Timala ROM; owned by her breeder Keke Blumberg and handler Carolyn Herbel.

300

Ch. Astra Traba Ling A Tantras, litter sister to Ahisma, was bred and is owned by Charles and Barbara Steele. She is photographed winning a Best of Breed under Edd Bivin, handler Carolyn Herbel.

Group winner Ch. Tibs Tribulation of Milarepa, by BIS Ch. Tibet of Cornwallis ROM out of Carter's Tara of Everglo ROM, is owned and bred by Mary Carter and handled by Carolyn Herbel.

Ch. Tabu's Indian Summer owned and handled by Bobbie Lee and bred by Valerie Reed, Joval and Carolyn Herbel.

Ch. Mae's Toiling of Cornwallis is the son of Karma Tharpa and Ch. Miss Kim of Cornwallis. He was co-bred by Paul Williams and Mae Sterling.

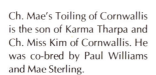

302

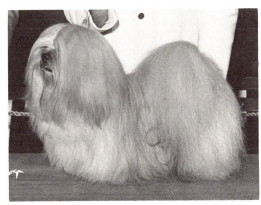

Ch. Karma Lingtam is the son of Ch. Karma Dmar Po and Hamilton Chang Tru. Lingtam, bred by Dorothy Cohen, is still living at this writing and resides with Ann Crawford, Walshana.

Ch. Ruffway Chogal, owned and bred by Georgia Palmer is a son of BIS Ch. Karma Frosty Knight O Evergo ROM and Ruffway Khambu, dam of four champions.

Lady Pamu, the dam of Americal's Sandar of Pamu.

BIBLIOGRAPHY

ALL OWNERS of pure-bred dogs will benefit themselves and their dogs by enriching their knowledge of breeds and of canine care, training, breeding, psychology and other important aspects of dog management. The following list of books covers further reading recommended by judges, veterinarians, breeders, trainers and other authorities. Books may be obtained at the finer book stores and pet shops, or through Howell Book House Inc., publishers, New York.

Breed Books

AFGHAN HOUND, Complete	Miller & Gilbert
AIREDALE, New Complete	Edwards
ALASKAN MALAMUTE, Complete	Riddle & Seeley
BASSET HOUND, Complete	Braun
BEAGLE, Complete	Noted Authorities
BLOODHOUND, Complete	Brey & Reed
BOXER, Complete	Denlinger
BRITTANY SPANIEL, Complete	Riddle
BULLDOG, New Complete	Hanes
BULL TERRIER, New Complete	Eberhard
CAIRN TERRIER, Complete	Marvin
CHESAPEAKE BAY RETRIEVER, Complete	Cherry
CHIHUAHUA, Complete	Noted Authorities
COCKER SPANIEL, New	Kraeuchi
COLLIE, Complete	Official Publication of the Collie Club of America
DACHSHUND, The New	Meistrell
DALMATIAN, The	Treen
DOBERMAN PINSCHER, New	Walker
ENGLISH SETTER, New Complete	Tuck & Howell
ENGLISH SPRINGER SPANIEL, New	Goodall & Gasow
FOX TERRIER, New Complete	Silvernail
GERMAN SHEPHERD DOG, Complete	Bennett
GERMAN SHORTHAIRED POINTER, New	Maxwell
GOLDEN RETRIEVER, Complete	Fischer
GREAT DANE, New Complete	Noted Authorities
GREAT PYRENEES, Complete	Strang & Giffin
IRISH SETTER, New	Thompson
IRISH WOLFHOUND, Complete	Starbuck
KEESHOND, Complete	Peterson
LABRADOR RETRIEVER, Complete	Warwick
LHASA APSO, Complete	Herbel
MINIATURE SCHNAUZER, Complete	Eskrigge
NEWFOUNDLAND, New Complete	Chern
NORWEGIAN ELKHOUND, New Complete	Wallo
OLD ENGLISH SHEEPDOG, Complete	Mandeville
PEKINGESE, Quigley Book of	Quigley
PEMBROKE WELSH CORGI, Complete	Sargent & Harper
POMERANIAN, New Complete	Ricketts
POODLE, New Complete	Hopkins & Irick
POODLE CLIPPING AND GROOMING BOOK, Complete	Kalstone
PUG, Complete	Trullinger
PULI, Complete	Owen
ST. BERNARD, New Complete	Noted Authorities, rev. Raulston
SAMOYED, Complete	Ward
SCHIPPERKE, Official Book of	Root, Martin, Kent
SCOTTISH TERRIER, Complete	Marvin
SHETLAND SHEEPDOG, The New	Riddle
SHIH TZU, The (English)	Dadds
SIBERIAN HUSKY, Complete	Demidoff
TERRIERS, The Book of All	Marvin
WEST HIGHLAND WHITE TERRIER, Complete	Marvin
WHIPPET, Complete	Pegram
YORKSHIRE TERRIER, Complete	Gordon & Bennett

Breeding

ART OF BREEDING BETTER DOGS, New	Onsott
BREEDING YOUR SHOW DOG, Joy of	Seranne
HOW TO BREED DOGS	Whitney
HOW PUPPIES ARE BORN	Prine
INHERITANCE OF COAT COLOR IN DOGS	Little

Care and Training

DOG OBEDIENCE, Complete Book of	Saunders
NOVICE, OPEN AND UTILITY COURSES	Saunders
DOG CARE AND TRAINING FOR BOYS AND GIRLS	Saunders
DOG NUTRITION, Collins Guide to	Collins
DOG TRAINING FOR KIDS	Benjamin
DOG TRAINING, Koehler Method of	Koehler
GO FIND! Training Your Dog to Track	Davis
GUARD DOG TRAINING, Koehler Method of	Koehler
OPEN OBEDIENCE FOR RING, HOME AND FIELD, Koehler Method of	Koehler
SPANIELS FOR SPORT (English)	Radcliffe
SUCCESSFUL DOG TRAINING, The Pearsall Guide to	Pearsall
TOY DOGS, Kalstone Guide to Grooming All	Kalstone
TRAINING THE RETRIEVER	Kersley
TRAINING YOUR DOG TO WIN OBEDIENCE TITLES,	Morsell
TRAIN YOUR OWN GUN DOG, How to	Goodall
UTILITY DOG TRAINING, Koehler Method of	Koehler
VETERINARY HANDBOOK, Dog Owner's Home	Carlson & Giffin

General

COMPLETE DOG BOOK, The	Official Publication of American Kennel Club
DISNEY ANIMALS, World of	Koehler
DOG IN ACTION, The	Lyon
DOG BEHAVIOR, New Knowledge of	Pfaffenberger
DOG JUDGE'S HANDBOOK	Tietjen
DOG JUDGING, Nicholas Guide to	Nicholas
DOG PEOPLE ARE CRAZY	Riddle
DOG PSYCHOLOGY	Whitney
DOG STANDARDS ILLUSTRATED	
DOGSTEPS, Illustrated Gait at a Glance	Elliott
ENCYCLOPEDIA OF DOGS, International	Dangerfield, Howell & Riddle
JUNIOR SHOWMANSHIP HANDBOOK	Brown & Mason
MY TIMES WITH DOGS	Fletcher
OUR PUPPY'S BABY BOOK (blue or pink)	
RICHES TO BITCHES	Shattuck
SUCCESSFUL DOG SHOWING, Forsyth Guide to	Forsyth
TRIM, GROOM AND SHOW YOUR DOG, How to	Saunders
WHY DOES YOUR DOG DO THAT?	Bergman
WILD DOGS in Life and Legend	Riddle
WORLD OF SLED DOGS, From Siberia to Sport Racing	Coppinger